BEATLES FOR SALE

BEATLES FOR SALE
The Beatles Memorabilia Guide

Bill Harry

Virgin

First published in Great Britain in 1985 by
Virgin Books Ltd, 328 Kensal Road, London W10 5XJ

ISBN 0 86369 097 1

Printed and bound in Great Britain by Richard Clay Ltd
(The Chaucer Press), Suffolk

Typeset by Keyline Graphics, London NW6

Cover and design by Sue Walliker and Ursula Shaw

Distributed by Arrow Books

CONTENTS

Introduction	9
The Beatles' Liverpool	13
The Beatles' London	83
Conventions	89
Memorials	95
Courses	97
Entertainments	105
Publications	109
Videos	129
Computer Games	131
Fan Clubs and Fanzines	133
Merchandising	157

Acknowledgements

What a splendid team at Virgin; they help you feel that book production goes like greased lightning. John Brown (a good body), Cat Ledger (a feline with books), Jane Charteris (the Saint), Ursula Shaw (another Saint), Sue Walliker (she has designs) and Cathy O'Brian-Tear (she deserves promotion), all ensconsed near the balmy canal on Kensal Road.

I would like to thank the many Beatle fans throughout the world who have been so co-operative in kindly granting me permission to use illustrative material; Liz and Jim Hughes, who, sadly, have said farewell to Cavern Mecca, but provided me with early shots of the Beatles on stage at the Cavern; Spencer Leigh for the Swinging Blue Jeans pic; Ron Jones for the Mersey Tourist Office merchandise and Art of the Beatles photos; Ian Wallace for the Beatles Shop material; Ken Townsend, Kathy Varley and Paul Bates for the shots of the Cavern fans from their 'Cavern Beat' video and the Abbey Road Studios photos; EMI Records for their Cavern album cover and Beatles publicity photo; Hilary Kay of Sotheby's and Eldon E Worrall of Liverpool for the auction samples; the Liverpool Echo for the Lennon book cover; Picture Music International for the Beatles video picture; Les Chadwick for the Liverpool location shots; the Beatles Bazaar for the T-shirt cut-outs; Danny Friedman for the V&A Theatre Museum photo; Mark and Carol Lapidos for the Beatlefest shots; the *Mersey Beat* archives; Roger White (who has moved to pastures new), Terry and Ron Smith, Helen Simpson and Phil Taylor of Beatle City for the photo selection; James Sauceda, Joseph Gallian, Joel Glazier, Tom Schulltheis, John Squire, Anthony White, Tetsu Hamada, Peter Schuster, Ramsey Lawrence, Barb Fenick, Marsha Ewing, Beatles Unlimited, John Chambers, Tom McDonald, Vicki Woods-Lovett, Charles Rosenay III, Sally Smallwood, Johnny te Lintelo, Eddie Porter, Roger Akehurst, William King, Brian Roylance and Jeremy Stockwell, for various covers, posters and merchandise photographs.

Hello to Johnny 'Guitar' Byrne, Virginia and Sean Harry, Yoko Ono, Paul McCartney, Ringo Starr, George Harrison, Arthur Ballard, Tony Barrow, Ray Coleman, Iris Davenport, Kevin Conneely, Steve Phillips, Mark Lewisohn, Sean O'Mahoney, Pete Doggett, Ginny Cerrella, Hunter Davies, Clive Epstein, Jonathan Hague, Doylene Kindsvater, Cynthia and Julian Lennon, Sam Leach, Mike McGear (he's very famous) Charles Lennon, Rod Murray, Gerry Marsden, Brian and Freda Norris, Dick Matthews, Mike Read, Pat Simmons, David J Smith, Mimi Smith, Jimmy Tarbuck, Jacques Volcouve, Fenno Werkmann, Lu Walters, Tony Millikan, Ken Howard and Peter Trollope.

TO THE MEMORY OF SUSAN HARRY

INTRODUCTION

1984 was a high point in the history of Liverpool. It saw the opening of the International Garden Festival, the biggest event in the world that year. During the 166 days it was open, 3.3 million visitors poured into the Festival. "The Year Of The Scouser!" proclaimed the *Liverpool Echo* as the city played host to a vast range of visitors. Her Majesty the Queen opened the Festival; Yoko and Sean Ono visited the city for the first time; and Paul McCartney collected his Freedom of the City award and gave his regards to Lime Street.

There were 125 acres of exotic gardens, theme gardens and fun gardens, a flower-filled Festival Hall and soothing water displays, with picturesque lake, waterfalls and rapids. There was a miniature narrow-gauge steam railway to take visitors on a 2½-mile trip around the site. Naturally, the Beatles were not forgotten in this 'Scouseland' celebration. There was a special Beatles Maze, a Yellow Submarine and a statue of John Lennon. The Merseyside Development Corporation sent me some information on the Maze:

"No Liverpool phenomenon has brought greater global fame to the city than the music of the Beatles, so it is fitting that the feature which commemorates that success is as enticing as their songs.

"Any labyrinth is intriguing but the style with which the Beatles Maze is tailored to its theme makes it additionally attractive and exciting. For one thing, the route leads entirely through water. Don't fall in – it's 30cm deep.

"The Maze recreates an apple sliced in half like the motif used by the Beatles' record company, Apple. The 'core' is a Yellow Submarine, preparing to submerge into the rippling waters. Clustered round the core are black apple-pips, which also represent musical notes and serve, in fact, as stepping-stones linking one of the pathways with the submarine. Then, in the truly tantalising manner of a well-planned maze, the stepping-stones lead the visitor away from the submarine and into the second part of the one-way route. Only at the end of that path can the Yellow Submarine be boarded.

"The paths curve in the form of two ears to depict the ears of the world listening to Beatles music. They incorporate a central design using a three-brick pattern to denote the surviving Beatles."

With the Festival, the opening of Beatle City, Cavern Walks, the Cavern Club, the Art of the Beatles exhibition and other events, the city had a summer of celebration. The winter, however, brought gloom.

The saddest event was the closing of Cavern Mecca by dedicated Beatle fans, Liz and Jim Hughes. Liz and Jim championed the Fab Four in Liverpool in the seventies when the local authorities refused to believe the group could be a tourist attraction in their home town. For almost ten years they worked against the odds, establishing first a Beatles shop, then a Beatles information centre, a Beatles museum and an annual convention. However, because of ill health and the weight of their financial difficulties, they closed their operation in October 1984. Their unique collection of Beatles memorabilia, built up over the years, was sold to an American collector, thus depriving Liverpool of a valuable part of its heritage. The premises of Cavern Mecca within the Cavern Walks complex have suffered the ignominous fate of becoming a fast food joint. The Merseyside County Council now runs the Mersey Beatles Conventions.

The County Council did in fact ask Royal Life if they could take over the responsibility of running Cavern Mecca, but the insurance company turned down the request. The Conservative Government intends to dispense with the County Councils in 1986 – this will be an even bigger blow to Beatles enthusiasts in Liverpool since it is the Council who has given so much support to Beatle ventures in the city.

Even more bad news reared its ugly head at the beginning of 1985. The *Liverpool Echo* ran a story hinting that Beatle City was in financial trouble, less than twelve months after its official opening. There will in fact be some changes made at Beatle City, but the situation is certainly not as drastic as the *Echo* suggested. The centre is likely to concentrate on the promotion of special events, taking particular advantage of the summer months; during the winter it will send the exhibition on the road to countries such as Japan and America.

The most successful section of the reopened Cavern Club seems to be the Abbey Road pub. The club did not renew their licence for their Cavern Beat film when it lapsed at the end of 1984 and it now resides on the shelves at the Abbey Road Studios in London, waiting to be revived in some form in the future. The Cavern itself has been fitted out, quite inappropriately, with plush carpeting. Why spend millions recreating the Cavern exactly as it was and then start altering it? Johnny 'Guitar' Byrne – formerly with Rory Storm and the Hurricanes – phoned me to express his horror: "What'll they be doing next? Putting pebble-dash on the walls?!"

But Jim and Liz are not the only Beatle fans who found that financial problems strangled their dreams. David Dunn wrote to tell me that he's officially closing down the Paul McCartney Club of Scotland, and enclosed a brief history:

October '82: Club started.
May 1983: Successful Beatles Gala Disco held in Glasgow for Samaritans.
December 1983: Beatles Gala Night in Glasgow held by the club not a success. Lost the club over £150. Poor turn-out in spite of good TV coverage.
March '84: Two-day Beatles convention on the same scale as the Liverpool conventions. Not a very good turn-out and the club lost £2,000.
March-November '84: The club struggles along, membership still going up and down, depending on Paul's popularity and chart success. On 10-11 November the first club trip to Liverpool is a great success. But the club magazine gets worse as finances dry up. The club lives on borrowed time and money. Members complain about the

Their first-ever award: the Mersey Beat Shield, presented by the author in 1962

drop in standards. My disillusionment is complete when folk write saying they are not rejoining. Only my most loyal members rejoin, but that's not enough.
February '85: I decide to close the club after the October '85 trip to Liverpool.
March '85: On the anniversary of the club's convention, a club trip to Liverpool is sold out.
July '85: Trip to Paris.
October '85: Trip to Liverpool and the end of the Paul McCartney Fan Club of Scotland.

It is sad that the situation in Liverpool is not more encouraging. Merseyside is Britain's major unemployment black spot, and tourism and the leisure industry seem the most likely course for future development in an area which has seen rapid industrial decline. Nevertheless, the future looks bright for Beatles enthusiasts and collectors. Hunter Davies' authorised biography is being reprinted and numerous other Beatles books have found a ready market. There is great demand for Beatles videos. Cable Communications will be making a special Beatles cassette, as will Picture Music International. Several other Beatles-related ventures for cassette, TV and cinema are being planned by various British and American companies, including Brian Epstein and John and Yoko biopics. Beatles conventions continue to attract the fans.

In 1964 a flood of Beatles merchandise swept the market: cans of Beatle Breath were being sold in New York, and record executives were wearing horrendous Beatle wigs. Twenty years later this memorabilia is still turning up at prestigious auction houses.

During the course of writing this book, I discovered that the area I wished to report on was far more extensive than I'd first envisaged. It is also constantly changing, and I would like to hear from anyone who thinks they would be eligible for inclusion when I update the material. They can contact me via the publishers of this book.

Bill Harry
London
March 1985

THE BEATLES' LIVERPOOL

BEATLE CITY
Seel Street, Liverpool L69 1RA

I first became aware of Terry Smith in 1963. He was running a press agency in Liverpool called Mercury Press and was the press agent for a number of local groups such as the Undertakers. Naturally, one of his main promotional outlets was my *Mersey Beat* newspaper. Terry later became involved in the birth of Radio City, Liverpool's commercial station, which grew into the most successful commercial station in Britain during his years as Managing Director.

He attracted a great deal of attention when he attended the Sotheby's auctions in 1981 and 1982, spending a five-figure sum each time on Beatles memorabilia. He then revealed that he was purchasing material for a major Beatles museum. He was concerned that Liverpool had virtually ignored its most famous sons over the years. Liverpool boasted no references to the Fab Four, unlike Memphis with its many Elvis museums and shrines. Even the world-famous Cavern Club had been knocked down to make way for a vent for an underground railway. As Terry commented in his introduction to Beatle City's catalogue: "It never ceased to amaze me that Liverpool, the Beatles' own city, never chose to acknowledge the fame they had brought. Indeed, the vandalism of demolishing the Cavern Club, where it all started, remains to this day an act of unequalled civic stupidity."

Terry developed the idea of a Beatles museum with financial support from Radio City, as well as grants from the Merseyside County Council and, later, the English Tourist Board and the Department of the Environment. Altogether, £2 million were raised to create a unique multi-media museum.

Premises were found in Seel Street, within a two-minute walk of the city's main shopping centre. The buildings cover 14,000 square feet, with a main hall of approximately 10,000 square feet, an office of 2,000 square feet, as well as administration space, a yard and a workshop. There is service access at the rear and a

coach park; eating facilities for either full meals or snacks, such as toasted Beatle jam-butties; and a well-stocked Beatles souvenir shop (which, like the cafe, you can enter from Seel Street, without having to pay for admission to the main exhibition area).

Colin Milnes was commissioned to design the museum. Educated at Beverly Grammar School, near Hull, he later studied at the Hull College of Art. During his National Service he headed a small art section of the RAOC in Cyprus. Over the years he became specifically involved with exhibition design and for a time worked as assistant to John Hardner, an internationally respected designer whose achievements included the exterior of the QEII liner and the British Pavilion at the Montreal Expo.

Colin established his own practice in Coventry in 1975 and his personal successes include the designs for the City of Stoke museum – which won a Museum of the Year Award – and the Chatterley Whitfield Mine Exhibition – which won an Industrial Museum of the Year Award.

When approached to work on Beatle City, he greeted the project as his most exciting and prestigious challenge to date. He was shown the £150,000 collection of Beatles memorabilia and was asked to avoid the glass-case approach of more traditional museums. The rest was left to him.

A working sketch by designer, Colin Milnes, of the main exhibition fascia.

In addition to Colin's, other firms which worked on the project were: the Colin Stananought Partnership, of Liverpool (architects); Kevin Gaskell Associates, of Birkenhead (consultant services engineers); the Dennis Eaton Partnership, of Liverpool (consultant structural engineers); Triangle Builders, of Bootle (building contractors); Foster and Done, of Birkenhead (electrical contractors); and the How Group Northern Ltd, of Liverpool (mechanical services).

In 1982, Roger White was the Sales and Marketing Director of Leeds Castle, a stately home and tourist attraction in Kent, when he heard that Radio City were looking for someone to run their new exhibition. Although he was perfectly content with his position at Leeds Castle, he felt that the Beatle City venture was too challenging to be overlooked. He applied for the job and was appointed General Manager of Beatle City. Roger then set about organising the team who carried out the project and he has been running the day-to-day affairs of the museum ever since. He commented: "I can honestly say that I do not know of any other exhibition quite like Beatle City, because the single idea of a permanent Beatles museum in Liverpool has developed into nothing less than a totally engrossing experience in which a constantly flowing audience will be surrounded by the sights and sounds of the Mersey Beat era."

Beatle City's curator, Helen Simpson, was 27 when the museum opened. Reared at Bowling in Bradford, she graduated in History and Classical Studies at Aberystwyth College and received a post-graduate diploma in Archives Administration from Liverpool University. She was not, however, among the 100 applicants who applied for the job when it was advertised. Roger White remembers: "We suddenly realized that we already had the perfect person working right on our doorstep in Liverpool City Centre at the Merseyside County Museums." It was Helen. Roger continues: "She's a specialist in English and medieval history, an enthusiast for both the Renaissance and modern, popular music, organizes living-history shows in stately homes based on real-life Civil War incidents, advises on genealogical studies, knows everything worth knowing about Liverpool's history as a seaport, taught medieval scripts and, on top of all that, is an expert in putting together computer package deals for commercial companies."

Press and publicity are handled by Ronald Smith of Trans-Press Public Relations Consultants. His information sheet on the museum reads, in part:

". . .Beatle City is very much more than an imaginative, magnificent museum. Its General Manager, Roger White, says: 'We have created here a living, moving, total experience which will enchant and delight visitors of all ages. They will appreciate the intensely human story of how four youngsters who knew next to nothing of music made their own indelible mark on twentieth-century pop music—and in fact on the whole British social history scene from the late fifties right through to the seventies.

'That's the tale to be told at Beatle City in a wonderful walkabout lasting around an hour. And this is no glass-case museum. Beatle City has been created and crafted so that our visitors will feel that they're living in Beatleland through the sixties, making records or going to America with the fabled four, putting together the Beatles television shows, and finally feeling the painful void left by the lost Lennon. When we talk about a living, total experience here at Beatle City, well, that's exactly what we're offering.'

"In all, there are more than 1,000 absolutely original, authentic exhibits within the Beatle City collection, with new items arriving literally every day from Beatle enthusiasts who wish to see their treasures housed in total warmth and security.

"And then there is the eternally appealing dimension of the Beatles music, tastefully and splendidly blended into the exhibition design-theme to maintain a meaningful, enjoyable link between the fifties, sixties, seventies and into the eighties. . .Colin Milnes has worked closely with Roger White on Beatle City's story-line and the selection of the exhibition's musical themes. These include: 'Twist And Shout'; 'Please, Please Me'; 'This Boy'; 'I Want To Hold Your Hand'; 'Eleanor Rigby'; 'Sergeant Pepper'; All You Need Is Love'; 'Strawberry Fields'; 'Penny Lane'; 'Yellow Submarine'; 'Imagine' (John Lennon); 'In My Life'; 'Within You, Without You' (George Harrison), and 'Roll Over Beethoven' (Chuck Berry).

"The rich variety of Beatle memorabilia within the museum's stocks will enable significant changes to be made from time to time in the items displayed. And there will also be featured a mini-theatre where productions with a Beatles, contemporary music or Liverpool social history background will be staged occasionally."

The centre is open every day from 10 to 6, with the exception of Christmas Day and Boxing Day. The entrance charge is £2, and £1 for children, senior citizens, students and the unemployed. All raised areas are accessible to the disabled.

Beatle City officially opened on 8 April 1984 with a champagne reception in the foyer. Brian Epstein's mother Queenie – making her first public appearance since the sixties – was the Guest of Honour. Other guests included Gerry and Pauline Marsden, Allan and Beryl Williams, Alistair Taylor, Tony Barrow, Alan Bleasdale, Brian O'Hara of the Fourmost, Mike McCartney, Peter Shotton, Bill Turner, Brian and Freda Norris, Pat and Margaret Delaney, Joyce Sutcliffe, Liz and Jim Hughes, Joe Flannery and his mother Agnes, Steve Phillips and Ron Jones.

Queenie, who was accompanied by her son Clive, his wife Barbara and their three children, had had a bad fall a fortnight before and was looking rather frail. She had also suffered great depression over the Peter Brown book, *The Love You Make,* which had savagely attacked Brian's personal lifestyle. So it was good to see her obviously pleased at the tribute to her late son; his office had been recreated, using the original furniture and personal items, donated by the Epstein family. Queenie gave a moving and dignified speech in which she voiced her pleasure in the venture. Several other speeches from civic dignatories followed, after which the guests were free to explore the museum.

Roger White, the author, and Terry Smith

The entrance itself is very impressive. The bold façade has been designed in the style of a yellow submarine, and outside is parked the very bus in which the Beatles and their friends set off on their Magical Mystery Tour in the eponymous film. The coach, repainted exactly as it was in the film, is now used for tours of the city.

You enter a passageway and are initially confronted by an area complete with recorded sounds of Liverpool's docklands and a large visual representation of the waterfront. This small section, called 'In My Liverpool Home', contains views of Liverpool and the Mersey in the early sixties, including the *Brittanic* Isle of Man ferry, the *Empress of Canada* liner and the Liverpool landing-stage, provided by Merseyside County Museums. I have often wondered why Liverpool's maritime heritage should be linked with the Mersey Beat scene, since I can see no real connection between them. The docks, for instance, had nothing to do with the groups and were already in decline before the Beat scene started to emerge. The large liners had long since stopped using Liverpool as a stopping-off place, and anyway such history had more to do with folk singers and sea-shanties than with the

Liverpool: a panoramic landscape

rock bands. The old myth that groups were brought their records by merchant seamen has been exaggerated out of all proportion. Apart from John McNally of the Searchers and some of the country music bands on Merseyside, none of the groups received records from merchant seamen (who mainly brought back C&W records). Records by Chuck Berry, Little Richard, Buddy Holly and other rock artists were freely available in Britain. The small Oriole white-label company was issuing Tamla Motown records, which were eagerly bought by local bands, and the groups scoured the record shops for interesting American releases.

The next exhibit area is headed 'Rock 'n' Roll Music'. It features a model of Liverpool circa 1959, made by Simon Dray. There is a life-size replica of a front-room of a house from that period, containing John Lennon's actual radiogram, and a display of early contracts and letters. Allan Williams has lent a handbill relating to the engagement of groups, including the Silver Beatles and Gene Vincent, and he has also provided the sign which hung above the Jacaranda coffee-bar.

Of particular interest is the photograph of Joe Flannery's mother, Agnes, supplied by Joe. Background information reveals why:

SECRET OF BEATLES 'BOB' HAIR-STYLE REVEALED – BY 60-YEAR-OLD PHOTOGRAPH.

"Detective work by archivists at Liverpool's Beatle City museum has solved the mystery of how the Beatles came by their famous 'bobbed' hair-style. John Lennon, discovered the archivists, fell in love with the girl in the photograph on the mantelpiece of Beatles booking manager Joe Flannery – and admired the girl's across-the-forehead 'bob' cut so much that he took his chums Paul, George and Ringo along to their local barber's shop with the photo to have their own hair styled in what was to become the famous Beatle 'bob'.

Joe Flannery with his Mum, Agnes: what is the secret of the Beatle bob?

"Beatle City General Manager Roger White explained: 'While researching the early sixties period in the Beatles story for eventual inclusion in our exhibition, our archivists interviewed Joe Flannery, who in the sixties was the member of Brian Epstein's organisation responsible for the Beatles' bookings out on the road. Our people spotted a photograph of an attractive teenage girl on Joe's fireplace with a picture of John Lennon in the same frame. The Beatles and the girl wore identical hair-styles – yet Joe revealed that the girl's photograph was more than 60 years old. The archivists were fascinated by this remarkable story, and checked out every detail for authenticity. It turned out that the four Beatles used to rehearse at Joe Flannery's flat long before they became famous. The lads were often penniless; they welcomed the warmth of Joe's flat and the toasted jam-butties he often served up as they rehearsed. And it was there, early in 1962, that John Lennon fell for the mystery girl in Joe's photograph'.

Agnes Flannery, mother of six, recalls the Beatles 'bob' incident well. Now 76 and living at Aintree, she said: "It was a great joke between Joe, the Beatles and myself at the time, and I still smile now when I think about John falling for my photo.

'Even at my age, I'm still a great Beatles fan. The picture that intrigued John was taken at a studio in Bold Street, Liverpool, when I was just sixteen, two years before I married. And now I'm delighted to hear that the photograph is going on exhibition at Beatle City museum. I'm sure many folk will be thrilled to learn the true story of how the Beatles came by their distinctive hair-style which, incidentally, I'd created for myself by washing and trimming my own hair in that particular fashion.' "

Although this makes a good story, it should be taken with a pinch of salt. I remember being told in 1961 that Stuart Sutcliffe's girlfriend Astrid Kirchherr had given the Beatles a new hair-style when they were in Germany. Mrs Millie Sutcliffe later described to me how the Beatles got the hair-style: "As for the haircut, it started when Stuart's hair was falling down and sticking out. One night Astrid had been moaning about his hair and then took him into the bathroom and cut it."

Hunter Davies, in his authorised biography of the Beatles, corroborates this version: "It was at this time [1960-61] that Astrid got round to telling Stu that she didn't like his greasy, Teddy boy hair-style. She said he would suit the sort of style that Klaus and Jurgen had. After a lot of persuading, Stu let her do a special style for him. She brushed it all down, snipped bits off and tidied it up.

"Stu turned up at the Top Ten that evening with his hair in the new style, and the others collapsed on the floor with hysterics. Half-way through he gave up and combed his hair high. But thanks to Astrid, he tried it again the next night. He was ridiculed again, but the night after George turned up with the same style. Then Paul had a go, though for a long time he was always changing it back to the old style as John hadn't yet made up his mind. Pete Best ignored the whole craze. But the Beatle hair-style had been born."

Philip Norman, in his book *Shout!*, has this to say: "She [Astrid] did away with his Teddy boy hair-style, cutting it short like hers, then shaping it to lie across the forehead in what was called the French cut, although high-class German boys had worn a similar style since the days of Bismarck."

Ray Coleman, in his book *John Winston Lennon,* covers the incident in detail: "Tired of the fast-scissored, traditional formula of Hamburg hairdressers and looking for something that would emulate her own sense of the eccentric, Astrid had cut Klaus's hair for years. She *never* combed his hair backwards, always out from the side, and it was always longer than the accepted length. . .Stuart, the first to have his hair cut and styled by Astrid, faced John's scorn when, one night, he arrived at the club for work with what later became known as the Beatle haircut. . . Paul, always more conscious than the others about his appearance, was the next to ask Astrid to style his hair. . . John was the last Beatle to succumb to the Beatle cut. Only Pete Best declined, retaining his quiff and Teddy boy aura that attracted the girls."

Jurgen Vollmer, one of the students in Hamburg who befriended the Beatles, puts forward his own claim in his book *Rock 'n' Roll Times:* "When I moved to Paris in late 1961, John and Paul visited me and decided to have their hair like mine. A lot of French youth wore it that way. I gave both of them their first 'Beatles' haircut in my hotel room on the Left Bank."

So, although it is reasonable to assume that John did see the photograph of Joe's mother, the Beatles had already adopted their own 'bobs' during a trip to Hamburg.

The Jacaranda sign is an evocative memento. The coffee-bar was originally opened in Slater Street by Allan Williams in the late fifties. Virginia – now my wife – and I used to sit around there in the company of John, Stuart, Pete Best, Adrian Barber and one or two other members of the local music scene. Few groups, however, got to play in its tiny cellar. Music was invariably provided by the resident steel band, and only when they were away did the Silver Beatles perform a couple of gigs. Stuart Sutcliffe also painted some murals in the Jacaranda, with the help of fellow art student Rod Murray. Allan went on to concentrate on his new venture, the Blue Angel club which he had opened in 1962 and the Jacaranda changed hands and names several times over the years. It was known for a while as the Maxi Sans Suzie and it wasn't until late in 1983 – to take advantage of the forthcoming Beatles-related events in the 'Pool – that the club reverted to its original name. During the refurbishing of the Jacaranda the original murals were uncovered – or, at least, parts of them were. Allan claimed, quite mistakenly, that the murals were done by John Lennon and Stu, and the headlines in the press read: "Legacy Of Lennon". The murals have been preserved and can be viewed at the club.

The Beatle City display 'Early Beatle Days' contains early photographs, including a shot of John Lennon with the Quarrymen. This photograph, taken by Charles Roberts in 1959, shows the skiffle group on the back of a lorry at the Rosebury Street festival.

A Colin Milnes sketch for the interior of Beatle City

The picture has appeared in several publications over the years without Charles' permission and Beatle City is now his agent for this particular shot. There are three early posters advertising the Beatles and other Liverpool groups. These were originally offered as Lot 123 in the December 1982 Sotheby's auction and were purchased by Terry Smith for the museum. They came from the collection of Johnny Byrne (former member of Rory Storm and the Hurricanes, known as Johnny Guitar), who collected every poster, leaflet and hand-out referring to a Hurricane gig. As they appeared often with the Beatles, both in Liverpool and in Hamburg, invaluable posters have been preserved for posterity, and Johnny is to be congratulated for having kept the material over the years. The posters were designed and executed by a small Liverpool firm called MPA which used fluorescent colours to get its distinctively bold style. I shall describe two of the posters, both advertising local promotions by Sam Leach, in detail.

The first reads:

Leach Promotions invite you to
A Night To Remember
Tower Ballroom New Brighton
Friday 6th April 7.30 – 1.0 am
Back again by public demand. . .the fabulous
Emile Ford and the Checkmates
with
The Beetles [*sic*]
(Their farewell performance prior to a two month season in Germany)
Also
Merseyside's top 4 groups
Gerry and the Pacemakers
Howie Casey and the Seniors
Rory Storm and the Hurricanes
and the Original Kingtwisters
Licensed Bars
Late transport all areas Liverpool and Wirral
Excursions leaving St. John's Lane Lime Street 7.30 – 8.30
Tickets 6/-
From Rushworth's. Nems. Lewis's. Strothers and Tower Ballroom

The other reads:

Leach Entertainments present
The Beatles Show
Rialto Ballroom Stanhope Street Liverpool 8
Thur Sept 6th
7.30 – midnight
Starring the north's top rock combo
The Beatles
and
The Big 3
The Mersey Beats
and the first Merseyside appearance following
his season at Butlin's Skegness
Rory Storm with the all-star Hurricanes
Buffet licensed bar applied for
5/- tickets from Rushworth's. Nems. Lewis's
Top Hat Record Bar. Strothers. Rialto Ballroom

The next main display section is entitled 'Hamburg'. Here is a letter from Stuart Sutcliffe to his sister Pauline in which he describes and sketches ideas for their stage suits designed by Astrid. There are also two photographs taken by Astrid Kirchherr, one a double-image photo of Stu, the other a picture of Stu and John

One of the many silk-screen posters of Mersey Beat attractions by MPA, a Liverpool design firm

Beatle City's Cavern mock-up

fooling about on the beach. Two Stuart Sutcliffe paintings are on show – an abstract from the collection of George and Brenda Moore, and a nude, the property of Allan Williams. The nude painting is of June Furlong, a model at Liverpool College of Art in the days when John, Stu and ! were enrolled there. When she attended a press reception at Beatle City, for Ray Coleman's book *John Winston Lennon,* she identified herself as the model.

The 'Cavern' display includes an attempt at a replica of the club itself. In an arched, bricked room, a series of cardboard cut-outs peer at two television screens on which the Beatles' performance of 'Some Other Guy' – filmed on stage at the Cavern by Granada Television in 1962 – is endlessly repeated. This particular item has been criticised for failing to capture the atmosphere of the Cavern. A section on Cavern memorabilia includes photographs (lent by Liz and Jim Hughes) of the Beatles at the Cavern, with Pete Best on drums; early photographs of the Beatles, particularly of George, circa 1961; a display of Cavern microphones, circa 1962; a Cavern Club membership card (courtesy of Charles Roberts); and a Cavern magazine written by Tony Barrow.

Another display includes Christmas cards, a publicity photograph of Billy J Kramer, and a handwritten leaflet by Paul McCartney giving his address in Hamburg. There is a photograph of John Lennon and Paul McCartney receiving guitars from J Rushworth of the music store Rushworth & Dreaper in 1962; and there is a visitors' book from the first reopening of the Cavern in 1967.

The 'Getting Better' studio features studio equipment from 1960, bought from a private collector. On the studio floor itself there are various items, including George Harrison's Gretsch guitar which he used between 1962 and 1964, John Lennon's stage jacket from the 1964 period and Paul McCartney's drumkit from 1963. In a display case there is George Harrison's 12-string Harptone guitar, a photograph of the Beatles with Roy Orbison and Gerry and the Pacemakers, a signed copy of *With The Beatles*, the script of *A Hard Day's Night*, Ringo Starr's tie, and signed Royal Variety Performance programmes on loan from the Epstein family. There are three jackets which belonged to John Lennon in 1964 and a jacket reputedly worn by Paul McCartney at Shea Stadium in 1965.

The 'Apple Box' display includes 'Our First Four' from Apple Records, which was a package containing the first four Apple releases in a presentation folder with special explanatory folders for each disc. There are also celluloids from the cartoon film *Yellow Submarine* and six front-of-house stills.

A section entitled 'All Things Must Pass' contains stock transfers from July 1969; placards from London newspapers (one from the *Evening News* announcing "Beatles Split – Paul's Statement" and one from the *Evening Standard* declaring "Paul Not Quitting Beatles – Yet"); George Harrison's Lewis Les Paul Guitar, circa 1974, and amplifier; three photographs of the Harrison family and another of George with fan club secretary Freda Kelly; the signed lid of the *Wedding Album* box; the Cosset Pop

Poll Award of 1970; a Citation of Achievement awarded to John Lennon; Ringo Starr's Austin Cooper that was especially adapted to take his drumkit, on loan from Peter Smith; John Lennon's moped; fan club material including an autograph book; a Beatle wig and blow up models; the second front door from the Apple premises of 3 Savile Row; John Lennon's Steinway piano that he purchased in 1970, and a Cavern Club Hammond organ, circa 1967.

The next display is a Brian Epstein showcase containing several items, all on loan from the Epstein family. They include a conference table and chair from his office and a collection of the gold, silver and other album awards made to Brian Epstein, together with a photograph of the Epstein family shop in Walton Road, Liverpool, and a collection of personal photographs.

The John Lennon display contains some Bag One lithographs from 1969; a mixing console used by John Lennon to record the *Imagine* album in his private studio, circa 1970; a *Walls And Bridges* promotional kit; a letter from John and Yoko and John Lennon's Rickenbacker guitar, owned by him between 1977 and 1979.

New items are being added to the Beatle City collection of memorabilia all the time. In addition to the exhibits on display, the museum has been building up an archive of photographic and printed material. It also acts as an agent for individual copyright holders (as in the case of Charlie Roberts, who took the Quarrymen photo).

. I am frankly disappointed at the lack of recognition for *Mersey Beat. Mersey Beat* was a regular newspaper reporting on the local music scene, the first of its kind in the world; it gave the scene its name and identity and acted as the organ of communication between the groups and the fans. In its own way, it was just as important to the development of the Beatles and the Liverpool scene as the Cavern. It was a major factor in the Beatles becoming the top local band, and led directly to Brian Epstein finding out about the Beatles. Brian awaited the results of the *Mersey Beat* poll in order to promote the group both locally and nationally – and he signed up his subsequent bands on the basis of their positions in it. *Mersey Beat* commissioned 90 per cent of the photographs of the Beatles which now exist from those early days. Brian Epstein, moreover, asked permission to name a tour 'The Mersey Beat Tour', while the Pacifics asked if they could call themselves the 'Mersey Beats'. Mersey Beat was the name used to describe the music being performed by Liverpool groups (many writers these days erroneously write it as one word).

A *Mersey Beat* display could have been devised quite easily. A selection of different issues would have shown the paper's growth from a small six-page fortnightly printed by James E James, via a large-size publication printed by Swales of Widnes, to a full-colour weekly newspaper printed in webb offset by the *Bootle Times'* Marsh Lane plant. There could have been invitations to the *Mersey Beat* Poll awards; a photograph of the Beatles receiving their first-ever award, the *Mersey Beat* shield; the *Mersey Beat* shield itself; and a selection of exclusive *Mersey Beat* photographs, to mention but a few possible items.

The replica of Brian Epstein's office

Beatle City Catalogue

To remind you of your visit to Beatle City, *The Beatles,* a lavishly produced 32-page souvenir booklet is available from the museum (exclusively). After consultations with Peter Matthews of the Northern Design Unit in Liverpool, it was decided to give the book a bold, colourful design and the dimensions of an album cover (12¼" square). Roger White asked me to write a short history of the Beatles' career, divided into ten sections, for it. Terry Smith, Beatle City's founder, outlines the origins of the idea and pays credit to the many people involved in getting it off the ground. There are many illustrations and some humorous advertisements (from Smirnoff and Gillette) which have Beatles themes. *The Beatles,* which also contains a plan of the museum, costs £1.50 and can be obtained by post.

The Collection

Here is a list of the major items in Beatle City's collection of memorabilia, with details of where they were originally purchased.

Those bought at the Rock 'n' Roll and Advertising Art auction at Sotheby's, Belgravia, on Tuesday, 22 December 1981 were as follows:

1. The album *With The Beatles* and its sleeve, autographed on the back by the Beatles.

2. Eight red-vinyl, foreign-issue LPs on Odeon, comprising two copies of *With The Beatles, A Hard Days's Night,* two copies of *Beatles For Sale, Meet The Beatles, Please Please Me* and *Rubber Soul.*

3. A collection of Beatles fan club material comprising 33 monthly magazines, concert programmes, calendars, photograph books and other related publications dating from around 1963.

4. Three photographs of the Beatles rehearsing in the Cavern Club (one duplicated), a fan club photograph signed on the back by the group, and a card similarly signed on the front.

5. 'The Beatles For Their Fans', a hand-out leaflet – measuring 6" x 9" – illustrating John, George, Paul and Pete, and inviting you to a concert at the Cavern on 5 April 1962. On the reverse, in his own handwriting, Paul gives his forwarding address as 'The Twist Club' in Hamburg. Circa 1961.

6. Printed material relating to the Cavern comprising a booklet detailing the club's history, a photograph of Manfred Mann, a signed postcard of Billy J Kramer, a Christmas card to the club from members of the Merseybeats and from the club owner, Ray McFall, and DJ Bob Wooler. Circa 1963.

7. A signed photograph of the Beatles, depicting the group with three guitars. Framed and glazed, 14½" x 11½". Circa 1965.

8. A collection of 24 stock transfer forms relating to Triumph Investment Trust Limited signed by Lennon, McCartney, Harrison and Richard Starkey – six apiece. 1969.

9. A programme for the 1963 Royal Variety Performance, signed on the inside cover by George Harrison, Paul McCartney, Ringo Starr, John Lennon, Wilfrid Brambell, Harry H Corbett, 'Pinky and Perky', Buddy Greco, Dickie Henderson, and others. 11¾" x 8¼".

10. A collection of Beatle souvenirs, including a Lowell Toy Authentic Beatle wig, seven badges, an unused diary for 1965, four plastic figures, two cut-out tickets, a plastic ring, and other printed material. Circa 1965.

11. A poster of a Richard Avedon photograph of the Beatles taken for *Look* magazine, 15" x 40".

12. A Richard Avedon photographic poster of John Lennon, 30" x 22".

13. *Yellow Submarine* film poster, in two sections, 78" x 41". 1968.

14. *Help!* film poster in two sections, 78" x 41". 1965.

15. *A Hard Day's Night* film script, dated 28 June 1964.

16. *Let It Be* United Artists film poster, 30" x 40"; a French handbill for *Yellow Submarine;* and a *Let It Be* publicity hand-out.

17. Eight front-of-house stills from *Yellow Submarine*, each measuring 8" x 10". Circa 1968.

18. Italian advertising poster for *Yellow Submarine*, 54½" x 39". Circa 1968

19. *Help!* poster, advertising the film, 30" x 20".

20. A signed photograph of the Beatles, taken while on location for *The Magical Mystery Tour,* 6½" x 8½".

21. A one-page letter with envelope, signed by John Lennon and countersigned by Yoko Ono, thanking Baldwin Bass for his "piece (. . .it hangs. . .)". This was a statue of John and Yoko, now owned by Kate Bush.

22. A ticket to the Beatles Christmas Concert at the Gaumont, Bradford – signed by the group and contained in an autograph book alongside signatures from members of the Barron Knights, Tornadoes, King-size Taylor and the Dominoes, Joe Brown, Pirates, Hollies, Bachelors, Dave Clark Five and the Downbeats. Circa 1963.

23. Beatle fan club material, comprising 34 posters, the majority in original envelopes, 75 photographs with imitation signatures and 73 copies of the *Beatles Monthly,* the *Beatles News* and the *Beatles Newsletter,* variously dated.

24. The Beatles Posters. The four Beatles photographed in full colour by Richard Avedon for *Look* magazine. 29¾" x 21¼". Circa 1968.

25. The Cosset Pop Poll Award 1970, presented to the Beatles as the most popular group in the International Section, bronze, 10" high.

26. *In His Own Write,* signed first edition of John Lennon's book, published by Jonathan Cape in 1964.

27. Four painted plastic models of the group playing guitars and drums, 9″ high. Circa 1965.

28. A poster of Paul McCartney, signed by the photographer, Richard Avedon, and dated '68. Framed and glazed, 30¼″ x 22¼″.

29. A poster of Ringo Starr, signed by the photographer, Richard Avedon, and dated '68. Framed and glazed, 30¼″ x 22¼″.

30. *The Beatles Book,* 27 copies numbered 1 - 27, dating from August 1963 to October 1965.

31. The marriage certificate of John Lennon and Cynthia Powell from Liverpool South Register Office, dated 23 August 1962, witnessed by James Paul McCartney and Marjorie Joyce Powell and signed by Eric Williams on behalf of the Borough. Framed and glazed.

32. A TWA flight bag, one of a limited edition named for members of the Beatles' tour to America. Circa 1965.

33. A celluloid from *Yellow Submarine,* depicting the four Beatles with their instruments, 14″ x 10¼″.

34. Paul McCartney and Jane Asher in Scotland. Six black-and-white photographs, including shots of Jane at the sink, and Paul, with his dog Martha, sweeping the front step. Each 3½″ square. Circa 1968.

35. The Beatles, with Roy Orbison and Gerry and the Pacemakers, photographed in their dressing-room during their first British tour in 1963. Mounted on card.

36. John Lennon and Yoko Ono, portrait heads against a representation of a revolver blast, 19½″ x 15¼″. Oil on board, framed. 1980.

37. Ringo Starr's black hand-stitched silk necktie, 50″ x 2″, and a letter of authenticity signed by Ringo. 1964.

38. The Beatles, photographed in 1963 on the BBC Radio *Pop Inn* programme while promoting their first single, 'Love Me Do'. Mounted on card.

39. George Harrison's twelve-string harptone guitar, Model L/12NC, Serial No. 2004/27, contained in a rexine case lined in blue velvet, together with a letter of authenticity from Harold J Harrison, Director of Harrisons Limited.

40. John Lennon's stage suit – a tan silk, collarless jacket edged with brown velvet, with buff lining, small pocket containing a plastic plectrum and inner pocket bearing tailor's label and handwritten 'John Lennon' label, with matching trousers. Circa 1964.

41. John Lennon's black jacket with satin finish, green and cream lining and inner pocket bearing tailor's label and handwritten 'John Lennon' label.

42. John Lennon's stage jacket – a collarless self-striped black jacket, with black velvet edging, maroon lining and small pocket at one side holding plastic plectrum and inner pocket bearing tailor's label and handwritten 'John Lennon' label. Circa 1964.

43. John Lennon's stage jacket – black silk, collarless, edged in black velvet, with a sky-blue lining, small pocket holding plastic plectrum, and inner pocket bearing tailor's label and handwritten 'John Lennon' label. Circa 1964.

44. John Lennon's stage jacket – grey silk, with black velvet collar and sky-blue lining, small pocket at one side holding plastic plectrum, and inner pocket bearing tailor's label and handwritten 'John Lennon' label. Circa 1964.

45. A Raleigh Super-50 moped, once owned by John Lennon, with black finish and canvas pannier bags and complete with registration book detailing the ownership of

the vehicle by Brian Epstein Automobiles, and then by John Winston Lennon in 1967 and 1968. 69" long. Circa 1965.

46. A teak-veneered radiogram, with four hinged sections and a top opening that reveals Stereo 30 amplifier controls, Garrard record deck and two storage compartments, the four lower sections for storage. 35½" x 72½" x 21". English. Circa 1960. This radiogram originally included a tape-deck and was used by John Lennon in the early sixties at his aunt Mimi Smith's house to record songs that he then played back over the telephone to Paul McCartney for his comments.

47. John Lennon's upright piano by Steinway and Sons, Hamburg, 1970, inscribed on the nameboard Steinway & Sons and on the frame Steinway Maker, Germany, bearing the serial number 417139. Teak case, seven-octave keyboard with ivory naturals and ebony accidentals, two pedals controlling forte and piano stops, height 44¾", width 57¼".

48. 'Bag One' by John Lennon, No.292 from a limited edition of 300, comprising 14 erotic and other lithographs, each signed in pencil by John Lennon. Contained in white plastic portfolio with catalogue, dated 1970 from the exhibition at the Lee Nordness Galleries, New York. Lithographs 30" x 23". Items purchased from Sotheby's York Avenue Galleries, New York, 9 June 1982.

49. Seventy-seven black-and-white, and three colour press photographs.

50. Beatles wrist-watch, with sweep second hand, the face printed with a photograph of the Fab Four. Dated 1964.

51. John and Yoko's *Two Virgins* album – Apple Records, May 1968 – signed on the front by John Lennon and with one of his cartoon figures; dated 1979; complete with the brown over-sleeve in which it was sold (to cover John and Yoko's nakedness).

52. Four animation celluloids from Beatles cartoons.

53. A 22-coloured poster of Yoko Ono as the Mona Lisa. Untrimmed, 42" x 30".

54. Two Italian posters for *Yellow Submarine,* prima edizione Italiana 1969. One of flying sharks, the other of John Lennon, 18½" x 26½".

55. Beatles memorabilia, comprising a 'Make a date with the Beatles' calendar; a blue cotton table-cloth printed with portraits of the boys, surrounded by their instruments; a jigsaw, 'Illustrated Lyrics Puzzle', 1970, designed by Alan Aldridge; a set of six coasters.

56. Sheet music for 'I Should Have Known Better' and 'She Loves You', each signed by John Lennon and each with a caricature and dated 1974 – the second inscribed "(really 63)".

57. Hirschfeld caricature of Ringo Starr, numbered 127/150, signed by Ringo in pencil, printed in green, matted and framed. 20½" square.

58. Miscellaneous ephemera, 1963 to 1977, including a *Yellow Submarine* press-out book and press invitation; four biographical booklets, 1963; four *Teen Screen Life Story* issues, each featuring one of the Beatles; John Lennon, 'Man of the Year' issue of *Rolling Stone,* 1970; a Paul McCartney and Wings press kit, 1973; Northern Songs Limited shareholder information; *Out Of The Mouths Of The Beatles,* Dell, 1964; a small poster, 'Look Who's Joined The Apple Club Now'; various early Beatle magazines – an Apple pamphlet including biographical, release and tour information and a 1962-1969 chronology – as well as other magazines with relevant features and programmes.

59. Complete set of *The Beatles Book* monthly fan magazines, August 1963 – December 1969. The first issue signed on the cover by George Harrison, John Lennon and Paul McCartney, other numbers with other signatures.

60. Promotional material for John Lennon's *Walls And Bridges,* comprising four matchbooks, a press kit, a cash register placard, and black cotton T-shirt, each inscribed "Listen to this. . ."

61. A 1969 Citation of Achievement presented by Broadcast Music Inc to John Lennon for the number of broadcast performances attained by 'Yesterday'. Purchased from Mr A J Gillam.

62. Souvenir programme from 1964 première of *A Hard Day's Night,* purchased from Rensburgs, Liverpool.

Items 63-66 were purchased from a private individual.

63. Hammond dual keyboard electronic organ that the Cavern Club bought for approximately £700 from Rushworths Music Stores, Liverpool, and which was used by the club from 1968-70.

64. A black-and-white photograph of the Beatles, signed by all four on the reverse.

65. A leather-bound visitors book dating from July 1967 (when the Cavern Club was reopened by its new owners) and signed by, amongst others, Harold Wilson, John Moores, Ken Dodd, Jimmy Savile, Valentine Dyall, Spike Milligan, three members of the Scaffold (John Gorman, Roger McGough and Mike McGear, Paul McCartney's brother) and by Paul himself, on 23 November 1968, with the caption "Second time around".

66. Two Reslo RBTL microphones, part of the public address system on stage at the Cavern Club, which were used by virtually all the visiting groups who appeared there during the sixties, including the Beatles.

Itesm 67-73 came from various sources.

67. Six-wheel, 52-seat Bedford coach, Registration Number URO 913E, extensively featured in the Beatles film *Magical Mystery Tour.* Purchased October 1982.

68. Complete limited edition of 500 prints of a portrait of the Beatles commissioned to commemorate the appearance of the group on the *Ed Sullivan Show.* The prints were never issued because Sullivan objected to 'commercialisation'. Bought privately in New York.

69. Collection of 48 original and reproduction posters and playbills promoting Beatles films and records in the United States and other countries. Purchased from various private sources in New York and Los Angeles.

70. Gretsch Les Paul lead guitar used by George Harrison between about 1962 and 1964. The instrument was subsequently given to a local school fund-raising project and bought and sold several times. A minor alteration to the head has been made. Purchased from Lendwick of New York.

71. John Lennon's Rickenbacker six-string guitar, Model No. 320, Serial Number UK 4186. One of two used by John in New York between 1977 and 1979, and donated by him to the World Health Organisation for fund-raising. Purchased privately in Los Angeles.

72. Framed photograph of James Rushworth, Chairman of Rushworths Music House, with John Lennon and George Harrison; he is handing over their new guitars flown in from Chicago in 1962. Donated by Mr Rushworth.

73. The second front door from the Apple Corporation in Savile Row (the first is owned by Yoko Ono). It hung there during the late sixties and early seventies and has hundreds of carved messages from fans as well as carved drawings of the famous four.

The following items were bought at Sotheby's, Belgravia, on 22 December 1982:

74. Four inflatable plastic polychromed figures of the Beatles. 12" high. Circa 1965.

75. A Beatles airline bag for British European Airways with the three-letter logo BEA incorporated into the word Beatles. Circa 1964.

76. Paul McCartney's drumkit, comprising 14" snare drum, 20" bass drum, 10" tom-tom, 15¾" side base tom-tom, 18" Zyn cymbal, two 13" hi-hat Krut special cymbals, 12¼" clash cymbal, with one snare drumstand, an Olympic bass pedal, two drumsticks, one hi-hat stand and later editions of a 10" tom-tom and two cymbal stands. Letter of authenticity from Mike McCartney and photograph from his book, *Thank U Very Much,* showing Paul McCartney using the drums.

77. Apple, designed by The Fool (three Dutch artists), a brightly-painted panel depicting a semi-reclining figure with exotic birds, sun and clouds. Oil on board, 28½" x 48". Circa 1967.

78. An Audiotek/Cadec mixing console, circa 1970, used by John Lennon to record *Imagine.* The console was custom-built by Eddie Veale of Audiotek for Acorn Studios, modified for 24-track use, and installed in John Lennon's private studio. A small plaque at the front is inscribed with an acorn and "John & Yoko Ascot Sound Studios Audiotek – England". Letter of authenticity from Starling Studios, Tittenhurst Park, Ascot, (formerly Acorn Studios).

79. Ringo Starr's stage suit. A grey pocketless jacket, with large black velvet collar and plum-coloured lining and no plectrum pocket, 1966.

80. Three early Beatles posters advertising Merseyside venues including one for the Beetles (*sic*) together with Rory Storm, Gerry and the Pacemakers and other local groups, 30" x 20". 1962.

81. 'Our First Four'. First four singles – the Beatles , Black Dyke Mills Band, Mary Hopkin and Jackie Lomax – produced by Apple Records Limited. Each in explanatory folder, 13½" x 9". 1968.

82. *Evening News* and *Standard* newspaper placards, one entitled "Paul Not Quitting Beatles Yet", the other "Beatles Split – Paul's Statement". Each 29" x 17½".

83. Twenty-seven photographs and negatives relating to the Beatles, including shots of George Harrison's Claygate bungalow and of vehicles belonging to the Beatles, as well as portraits, one signed, dating from circa 1967.

84. Astrid Kirchherr photograph of Stuart Sutcliffe and John Lennon, on the beach near Hamburg. Original print, measuring 7" x 9½", with Kirchherr stamp on the reverse, Hamburg, 1961.

85. A seven-page airmail letter, with envelope, from Stuart Sutcliffe to his sister Pauline. Writing from Hamburg in 1961, Stu discusses the chances of playing bass for a German band, a new suit made for him by Astrid, and relationships within the group. The letter is illustrated with two line drawings of Astrid's suit designs.

86. Astrid Kirchherr double-image portrait of Stuart Sutcliffe, original print (with torn borders). 15½" x 12". Hamburg, 1961.

87. A contract for the Beatles concert at Comisky Park, Chicago, between Nems Enterprises and Triangle Theatrical Productions Inc., signed by Brian Epstein and Frank Ifield, together with a three-page rider, similarly signed, dated 31 April 1965.

88. Photograph of the Beatles at the *NME* Poll Winners Concert, Wembley, 1964, with copyright and negative, 9½" x 12".

89. Two photographs of Ringo Starr, one alone and one with his aunt and uncle, complete with negatives and copyright.

90. Six early photographs, circa 1962, of the Beatles with Pete Best, in action at the Cavern. Each 3½" x 5½".

91. Four photographs, sold with the negatives and copyright: George Harrison with Freda Kelly of the Beatles Fan Club, Mr and Mrs Harrison (George's parents) and two of George's brother, Harry.

92. Five photographs of the Beatles preparing for *Juke Box Jury* with David Jacobs on 7 December 1963. Complete with fifteen negatives and copyright.

93. George Harrison's guitar and amplifier, and two letters of authenticity.

94. The Beatles At Shea Stadium concert ticket and programme. 1966.

Beatles Shop Mail Order

Beatle City has a range of goods that can be purchased by post. The address for mail order enquiries is: Department H, Beatle City Limited, PO Box 12, Liverpool L69 1RA, England.

Please ensure that your name and address are written clearly on all correspondence. All cheques and postal orders should be made payable to 'Beatle City Limited'. Allow 21 days for delivery if you live in the UK or Europe, and 28 days if you live in the US. If you haven't received your order in that time, then write giving full details of the order.

Republic of Ireland and overseas orders must be paid in pounds sterling and 25 per cent added to the total amount to cover postal charges. Only certified bank or Post Office cheques can be accepted. Eire cheques will not be accepted. Master Card (Access), Visa, American Express and Diners card are all accepted, but credit card orders must include the full card number, the expiry date and the registered address of the cardholder.

All the quoted prices were correct at the time of going to press, but I would strongly suggest that you double-check with Beatle City to make sure they are still current.

Badges	CODE	PRICE
Abbey Road	0723	.45
Beatle City logo	0211	.25
Beatles plastic guitar	0542	1.75
Button badge	0523	.20
I Love the Beatles – Apple	0728	.35
Mathew Street sign	0724	.45
Paul's bass guitar	0729	.35
Penny Lane street sign	0725	.45

Books

Beatle: The Pete Best Story (hb)	5502	9.95
Beatle: The Pete Best Story (pb)	5503	4.95
Beatles – Helen Spence	0601	2.95
Beatles England – Bacon & Maslor	6701	2.50
Beatles Illustrated Record – Roy Carr and Tony Tyler	4606	4.95
Beatles Who's Who – Bill Harry	0901	4.95
Book of Lennon – Bill Harry	0902	5.95
Childrens Colouring Book	0401	1.30
Exhibition Guide Book (Second Edition)	0103	2.95
Give My Regards To Broad Street – Pictures	3201	5.95
In The Footsteps of The Beatles – Mike Evans and Ron Jones	1801	1.50
John Lennon – Richard Wooton (pb)	4601	3.95
John Lennon – Richard Wooton (hb)	4602	5.95
John Lennon – The Lost Tapes	6002	1.75
John Lennon, Summer of 1980	3101	4.95
John Ono Lennon (Vol 2) – Ray Coleman (hb)	4302	9.95
John Winston Lennon (Vol 1) – Ray Coleman (hb)	4301	9.95
Lennon (Liverpool Post & Echo)	4401	1.99
Lennon In My Life – Pete Shotton	4603	5.95
Lennon Tapes Book	2701	1.99
Linda's Photographs – Linda McCartney	3203	6.95
Linda's Pictures – Linda McCartney	3202	5.95
Liverpool – the 60s (photographs)	3901	5.95
Liverpool: The Book	0801	1.95
Loving John – May Pang	6003	5.95
Ocean View – Wings Tour Pictures (hb)	5501	9.95
One Day At A Time – Anthony Fawcett	4605	2.50
Paul McCartney, Composer/Artist	3204	6.95
Playboy Interviews – John and Yoko	4604	2.50
Shout! – Philip Norman	6001	2.50
Thank U Very Much – Mike McCartney	5101	5.95

Calendars

Calendar 1984	0539	1.95
Calendar 1985	4004	3.95
Calendar 1986 – John Lennon	6901	3.95

Clocks

Beatles Carriage Clock	0718	19.95
Clock Black Framed (5½″ × 6″)	0702	12.95

Clock Black Framed (6″ × 8″)	0704	14.50
Clock Silver Framed (5½″ × 6″)	0701	13.50
Clock Silver Framed (6″ × 8″)	0703	14.95

Clothing

Baseball hat	0720	3.50
Beatle jacket – 30″	5301	34.95
Beatle jacket – 30″ (braided)	5302	35.95
Beatle jacket – 32″	5303	34.95
Beatle jacket – 32″ (braided)	5304	35.95
Beatle jacket – 34″	5305	34.95
Beatle jacket – 34″ (braided)	5306	35.95
Beatle jacket – 36″	5307	34.95
Beatle jacket – 36″ (braided)	5308	35.95
Beatle jacket – 38″	5309	34.95
Beatle jacket – 38″ (braided)	5310	35.95
Beatle jacket – 40″	5311	34.95
Beatle jacket – 40″ (braided)	5312	35.95
Kitchen apron (PVC)	4502	3.25
Knickers ('The Beatles')	0300F	1.25
Knickers (various song titles)	0719	1.00
Scarf (nylon)	0300G	1.95
Scarf (wool)	0503	2.95
Sweat shirt – logo	0300J	8.50

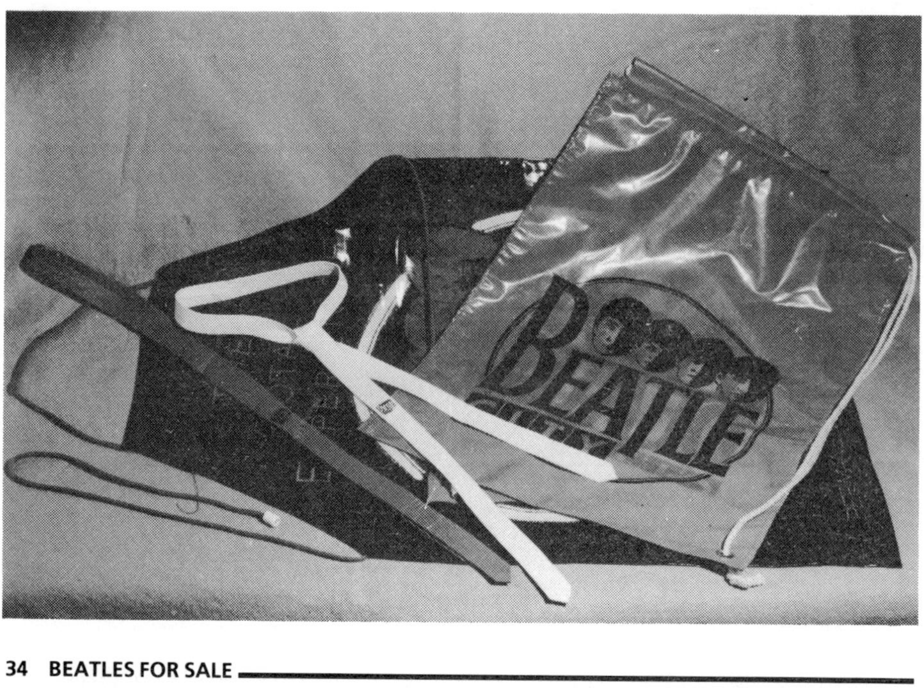

Sweater – 'Help!' (hand-knitted acrylic)	4701	26.95
Sweater – long-sleeved with logo	2301	18.45
Sweater – 'Penny Lane' (pure wool)	4702	34.95
Sweater – slip-over with logo	2302	16.45
T-shirt (adult) – 40 various designs	0300A	4.95
T-shirt (children) – 5 various designs	0300B	2.95
Tie (leather) 'Echo' – black on white	1606	4.25
Tie (leather) 'Echo' – red on black	1607	4.25
Tie (leather) 'Echo' – white on black	1608	4.25
Tie (leather) with logo – black on white	1601	4.25
Tie (leather) with logo – white on black	1602	4.25
Tie (leather) with logo – red on black	1603	4.25
Tie (leather) with logo – grey on white	1604	4.25
Tie (leather) with logo – blue on white	1605	4.25
Tie (satin)	0510	1.95

Cups and mugs

Beatle City logo	1501	1.25
Beatle City logo (stoneware)	6201	2.25
Character mug – Harrison	6404	22.50
Character mug – Lennon	6402	22.50
Character mug – McCartney	6401	22.50
Character mug – Starr	6403	22.50
Penny Lane	1502	1.25
Sgt. Pepper, John and Ringo	1504	1.45
Sgt. Pepper, Paul and George	1505	1.45
Strawberry Fields	1503	1.25

Cushions

Cushion – 2 designs	0527	2.50

Jewellery

Earrings	0511	1.95
Enamel brooch	0532	1.50
Locket	0517	1.95
Name necklace	0529	1.50
Pendant	0515	.95
Pendant	0516	.95
Photo necklace	0530	1.50
Ring	0512	1.75
Stone logo brooch	0514	1.95
Stone logo necklace	0513	1.95

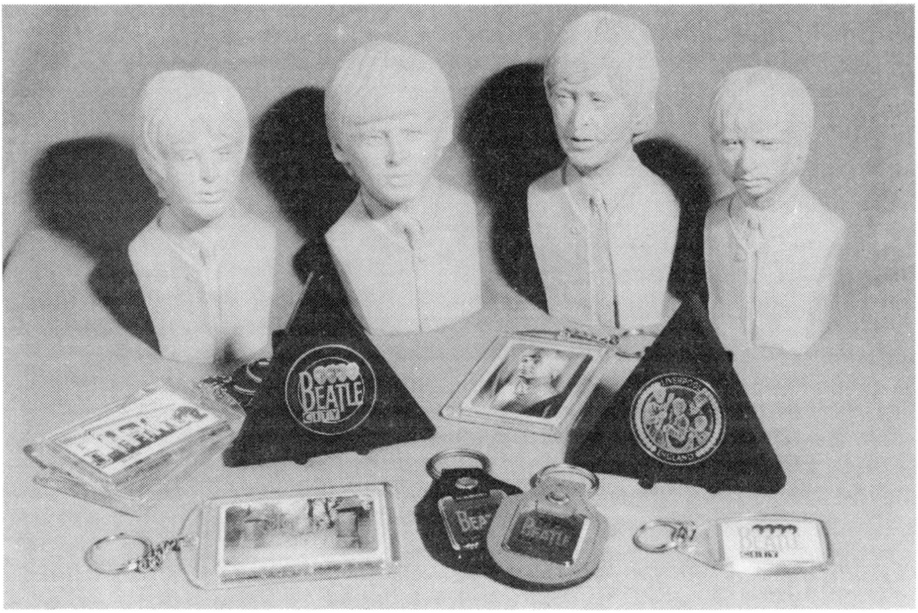

Jigsaws

Guitar (wooden)	2001	19.50
Penny Lane (wooden)	2002	19.50
Yellow Submarine (wooden)	2003	16.50

Key-rings

Acrylic – large (various designs)	1325	1.75
Black leather and gilt key fob	0714	1.75
Nickel-silver key-ring	2902	2.25
Photo keyring	0509	.70
Red leather and gilt key fob	0715	1.75

Magazines

Beatles Now	2501	1.00
Beatles Unlimited	3551	1.00
Starclub Magazine	0531	1.95

Maps

50 Miles Around Manchester	2805	1.65
A-Z Atlas of Liverpool	2801	1.45
Liverpool – Beatle Guide/Map	3001	.85
Liverpool/Birkenhead/Wallasey	2803	.65
London – Beatle Guide/Map	3002	1.00
Main Road Map of Manchester	2804	1.85
Merseyside A1 Street Atlas	4801	1.75
Premier Map of Liverpool	2802	1.95

Mirrors

Beatle City mirror (small)	0535	1.95
Beatle City mirror (medium)	0536	2.95
John Lennon	0300H	1.95
Mirror – various designs (medium)	0521	2.95
Mirror – various designs (small)	0520	1.95
Union Jack mirror (medium)	0537	2.95

Miscellaneous

Apple – glass ornament	1101	3.25
Ashtrays with Beatle City logo (two in box)	0726	1.95
Beatle City pennants	0711	.60
Beatles birth certificates pack	0101	7.50
Bookmark	0733	.65
Bronze medallion	2901	1.95
Candy rock	0519	.25
Coasters (logo)	0727	1.95
Dishes – various designs	0546	1.95
Duvet cover	0300E	22.50
Glass tumbler (Beatles faces)	1202	4.95
Glass tumbler (logo)	1201	4.95
Guitar – glass ornament	1102	14.75
Hanging wall pictures	0300C	1.95
Handkerchief	0300I	1.25
Logo puzzle	0722	.85
Nickel-silver pendants	2905	4.95
Paperweight logo	0734	2.95

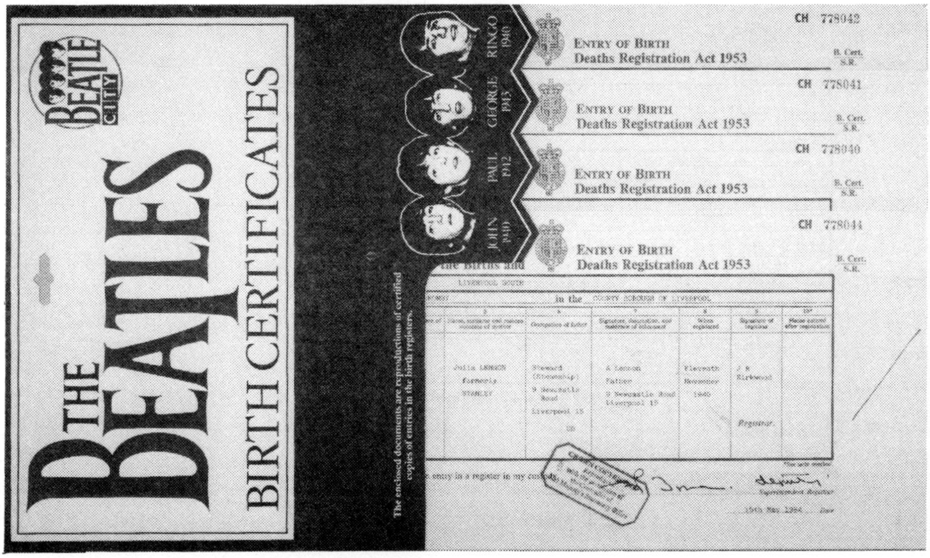

Penny Lane dish	0540	1.95
Pillow slip	0300D	1.95
Rosettes (large)	0526	1.95
Rosettes (medium)	0525	1.50
Rosettes (small)	0524	.95
Silver logo balloons	0208	1.25
Silver spoons	5801	2.00
Slate triangle paperweight (Beatles picture)	2903	2.50
Slate triangle paperweight (logo)	2904	2.50
Strawberry – glass ornament	1103	3.95
Street Signs (set A)	0533	1.50
Street Signs (set B)	0534	1.50
Street Signs (set 1)	0721	1.50
Sunglasses (green)	0544	3.95
Sunglasses (mirror)	0543	3.95
Union Jack flag (large)	0545	8.25
Writing pad holder (A5)	5901	7.95
Writing pad holder (A4)	5902	14.25
Yellow Submarine – glass ornament	1104	7.25
Yellow Submarine – pottery money box	1322	4.99
Yellow Submarine – pottery ornament	1323	4.99
Yellow Submarine – wooden plaque	4101	18.50

Patches

Beatle City – sew-on patch	6101	.50
Beatle City patch (black)	3801	.45
Beatle City patch (red)	3802	.45
Patch – various designs	0501	.50
Photo patch – various designs	0538	.60

Pens and pencils

Ballpoint	0731	.30
Calculator pen	0541	.60
Letter-opener pen	0547	.60
Pencil	0730	.20
Rollerball	0732	.80

Postcards

By Mike McCartney (c)	5001	.20
By Mike McCartney (bw)	5002	.20
By Mike McCartney (bw)	5003	.20
By Mike McCartney (bw)	5004	.20

BEATLE

By Mike McCartney (bw)	5005	.20
By Mike McCartney (bw)	5006	.20
By Mike McCartney (bw)	5007	.20
By Mike McCartney (bw)	5008	.20
By Mike McCartney (bw)	5009	.20
By Mike McCartney (bw)	5010	.20
By Mike McCartney (bw)	5011	.20
By Mike McCartney (bw)	5012	.20
By Mike McCartney (bw)	5013	.20
By Mike McCartney (bw)	5014	.20
By Mike McCartney (bw)	5015	.20
By Mike McCartney (bw)	5016	.20
By Mike McCartney (bw)	5017	.20
By Mike McCartney (bw)	5018	.20
By Mike McCartney (bw)	5019	.20
Art of the Beatles (c)	1803	.20
Beatle City memorabilia (A) (bw)	0413	.20
Beatle City memorabilia (B) (bw)	0414	.20
Beatle City Total Experience logo (c)	0411	.20
Beatles (c)	1833	.20
Beatles – In Snowy Washington (bw)	6602	.20
Beatles – night picture (bw)	1802	.20
Beatles – on stage (c)	6501	.20
Beatles – on stage (bw)	6603	.20
Beatles – on the beach (bw)	6601	.20
Beatles and fans	1830	.20
Beatles at NME Poll Winners Concert 1964	0407	.20
Beatles at the Empire	1831	.20
Beatles on Juke Box July 1964 (A) (bw)	0408	.20
Beatles on Juke Box Jury 1964 (B) (bw)	0409	.20
Beatles on Juke Box July 1964 (C) (bw)	0410	.20
Beatles – their homes (c)	1809	.20
Birthplaces of the Beatles (c)	1804	.20
Boys from Liverpool (c)	1835	.20
Broad Street – Paul (c)	6502	.20
Broad Street – Paul (bw)	6503	.20
Broad Street – Paul and cast (c)	6504	.20
Broad Street – Paul and Ringo (c)	6505	.20
Broad Street – Paul and Tracey Ullman (bw)	6506	.20
Caricature face – Harrison (bw)	4903	.20
Caricature face – Lennon (bw)	4901	.20
Caricature face – McCartney (bw)	4902	.20

Caricature face – Starr (bw)	4904	.20
Commemorative 'Can't Buy Me Love'	1815	.60
Commemorative 'From Me To You'	1811	.60
Commemorative 'I Want To Hold Your Hand'	1814	.60
Commemorative 'Please, Please Me'	1812	.60
Commemorative 'She Loves You'	1813	.60
Eleanor Rigby	5402	.20
Eleanor Rigby commemorative envelope	5401	1.50
George Harrison Close (c)	1824	.20
John Lennon (bw)	1704	.20
John Lennon (bw)	6604	.20
John Lennon – pastel drawing (c)	1324	.20
Lennon Liverpool (c)	1807	.20
Light Impressions (c)	1001	.25
Liverpool (c)	1810	.20
Liverpool, Beatles' birthplaces (c)	1834	.20
Mathew Street (c)	1827	.20
Mathew Street statue (c)	1832	.20
Old Liverpool – (bw)	5201	.25
Old Liverpool – (bw)	5202	.25
Old Liverpool – (bw)	5203	.25
Old Liverpool – (bw)	5204	.25
Old Liverpool – (bw)	5205	.25
Old Liverpool – (bw)	5206	.25
Old Liverpool – (bw)	5207	.25
Old Liverpool – (bw)	5208	.25
Original Magical Mystery Tour coach (c)	0412	.20
Paul McCartney by Bratby (c)	3701	.20
Paul McCartney Way (c)	1825	.20
Penny Lane (M Cockrill) (c)	1828	.20
Penny Lane street sign (c)	1823	.20
Penny Lane street picture (c)	1808	.20
Postcards 16 various (bw)	0508	.15
Ringo Starr Drive (c)	1826	.20
Silver Beatles (c)	5701	.20
Strawberry Fields and John (bw)	1320	.20
Strawberry Fields (line drawing)	1319	.20
Strawberry Fields Forever (c)	1806	.20
Strawberry Fields 'Nothing is real' (c)	1805	.20
Strawberry Lane (M Cockrill) (c)	1829	.20
The Beatles (bw)	1703	.20

Posters and prints

'The Beatles' – original lithograph (limited edition)	0102	27.50
A-Z of Beatle song titles	5601	1.75
Art of the Beatles	1816	1.50
Beatles print set	2601	1.00
Cavern poster 1	1401	1.95
Cavern poster 2	1402	1.95
Colouring poster (in tube)	0406	2.25
Colouring sheet (4 designs)	0402	.10
Giant colour picture	1403	2.50
John Lennon (bw)	6605	.95
John Lennon (c)	1702	2.50
Liverpool Beatle trail poster	5403	.50
Penny Lane (framed print)	0716	19.95
Penny Lane print	0403	2.50
Strawberry Fields (framed print)	0717	19.95
Strawberry Fields (line drawing)	1318	1.25
Strawberry Fields print	0404	2.50
The Beatles (bw)	1701	2.25
The Beatles (c)	4001	2.00
The Beatles (c)	4002	2.00
The Beatles (c)	4003	2.00
Yesterday (c)	0405	2.75

Records and cassettes

Liverpool Guided Tour (cassette)	4201	3.99
Oh John! by Gerry Markey (record)	2400	1.40
Much Missed Man (record)	2401	1.40

Statues and busts

Lennon – 130mm high bronze	1302	29.95
McCartney – 130mm high bronze	1303	29.95
Harrison – 130mm high bronze	1304	29.95
Starr – 130mm high bronze	1305	29.95
Lennon – 130mm high ivory plaster	1306	15.65
McCartney – 130mm high ivory plaster	1307	15.65
Harrison – 130mm high ivory plaster	1308	15.65
Starr – 130mm high ivory plaster	1309	15.65
Lennon – 130mm high pottery	1321	9.95
Lennon, 'Imagine' – bronze 180mm high	2402	39.95
Harrison – bronze plaque	1312	15.65
Lennon – bronze plaque	1310	15.65
McCartney – bronze plaque	1311	15.65
Starr – bronze plaque	1313	15.65
Harrison – dark resin statue	1328	15.65
Lennon – dark resin statue	1326	15.65
McCartney – dark resin statue	1327	15.65
Starr – dark resin statue	1329	15.65
Harrison – dark resin mask	1332	5.50
Lennon – dark resin mask	1330	5.75
McCartney – dark resin mask	1331	5.50
Starr – dark resin mask	1333	5.50
Lennon – ivory plaster plaque	1314	15.65
McCartney – ivory plaster plaque	1315	15.65
Harrison – ivory plaster plaque	1316	15.65
Starr – ivory plaster plaque	1317	15.65
Lennon – life size bronze	1301	999.00

Stickers

Beatle City	1817	.35
Birthplaces of the Beatles (blue)	1821	.35
Birthplaces of the Beatles (red)	1822	.35
Boys from Liverpool (blue)	1818	.35
Boys from Liverpool (red)	1819	.35
Liverpool Loves the Beatles	1820	.35
Logo (large) with sticky back	0705	.25

Logo (large) with sticky front	0706	.25
Logo (small) with sticky back	0707	.10
Logo (small) with sticky front	0708	.10
We've Visited Beatle City – with sticky back	0709	.30
We've Visited Beatle City – with sticky front	0710	.30

Tea towels

Beatle City – Total Experience	1901	2.25

Videos

Beatles Live – 12 classic tracks (BetaMax)	3410	17.95
Beatles Live – 12 classic tracks (VHS)	3409	17.95
Compleat Beatles (BetaMax)	6302	19.95
Compleat Beatles (VHS)	6301	19.95
A Hard Day's Night (BetaMax)	3302	29.95
A Hard Day's Night (VHS)	3301	29.95
Ready, Steady, Go! – Volume 1. (VHS)	3403	24.95
Ready, Steady, Go! – Volume 1. (BetaMax)	3404	24.95
Ready, Steady, Go! – Volume 2. (VHS)	3405	24.95
Ready, Steady, Go! – Volume 2. (BetaMax)	3406	24.95
Ready, Steady, Go! – Volume 3. (VHS)	3407	24.95
Ready, Steady, Go! – Volume 3. (BetaMax)	3408	24.95
Wings – Rock Show (BetaMax)	3402	24.95
Wings – Rock Show (VHS)	3401	24.95

THE CAVERN CLUB
Cavern Walks, Mathew Street, Liverpool 2

As a one-time habitué of this world-famous club, I was asked to write a brief and colourful history of it for the publicity brochure accompanying its second reopening in 1984. It reads in part:

"The heat, the noise, the condensation dripping from the walls, the boys in the leather jackets, the girls with the bouffant hair-styles and laddered fish-net stockings, the babble and chatter, the euphoria, the sheer atmosphere, the soggy cheese rolls and bottles of Coca Cola, the cheery buzz as packed youngsters shared the communal sound while a band pounded away on a tiny wooden stage: that was the Cavern in the early sixties. Unique, never-to-be-forgotten and yet, miraculously, reborn in the 1980s. . .

"It all came from an idea which germinated in the mind of Alan Sytner, a Liverpool doctor's son, during a visit to Paris. He was enchanted by the atmosphere of a Parisian cellar club called Le Caveau, and returned home determined to recreate the experience. The vision took shape, Alan scoured Liverpool for an equivalent site, discovered the old warehouse cellars in Mathew Street, named it the Cavern and announced the opening date as 16 January 1957. . .

"Jazz had found a unique showplace in Liverpool, but Sytner moved on to other things and in October 1959 the club was transferred to the hands of former accountant Ray McFall. During those early days, the jazz purists would settle for support bands who played skiffle, but they spurned rock and roll. . .but Ray soon realised that Liverpool was creating a unique sound of its own. Word had reached him of the many exciting Merseyside groups at venues such as Aintree Institute, Litherland Town Hall, Holyoake Hall and Hambelton Hall. By the summer of 1960 he decided to switch to the new music. The first time this occurred was on 25 May 1960, when Cass and the Cassanovas and Rory Storm and the Hurricanes appeared.

Cavern-dwellers at a Saturday afternoon 'Under-16s' session

"In 1961 a music paper *Mersey Beat* was launched in Liverpool and the groups then began calling themselves 'beat groups'. Among them was a dynamic outfit called the Beatles who had made their biggest impact at Litherland Town Hall on 27 December 1960, following a trip to Hamburg. They made their debut at the Cavern on 21 March 1961, on a special 'Swinging Blue Jeans Guest Night' bill. The impact of the groups was phenomenal, the queues in Mathew Street became a fact of life. Ray began to book beat music as the main attraction, with occasional jazz bands livening up the bill. . .and still the crowds poured in. The club began to open on more evenings, started lunchtime sessions, and then all-night sessions. Ray was even to introduce a Junior Cavern Club at lunchtime on Saturdays.

"By this time he had employed an enterprising local compère called Bob Wooler, a well-loved figure at the local jive hives with a mellifluous voice, a fund of puns, and an astute knowledge of the music the groups wanted to play and the fans wanted to hear. It was Bob who introduced the Beatles on stage more than any other person in the world and who, checking the Cavern booking lists, discovered that the Fab Four had graced the Cavern stage no less than 292 times. . .

"It was also the home of a powerhouse of groups, too many to name, but Gerry and the Pacemakers, the Swinging Blue Jeans, the Merseybeats, Kingsize Taylor and the Dominoes, the Escorts and the Searchers will give you some idea. . .

"The Cavern continued to expand, although the Beatles and the Mersey Sound had by this time reached the four corners of the world and the Beatles had made their final bow on 3 August 1963. Ray bought the next-door premises to extend the club, incorporating a recording studio on the premises. Unfortunately, financial problems raised their head and the bailiffs moved in. A new owner, Joe Davy, relaunched the club in July 1967 and Prime Minister Harold Wilson attended the opening ceremony. By the early seventies Liverpool was undergoing drastic changes and the club was bulldozed to make way for a vent for an underground railway. It closed on 27 May 1973.

"Yet the debris of the original club still lay beneath the car-park in Mathew Street; the original bricks, the original aura were still below the packed earth. Folks remembered the original club's stage being cut up into 'Beatleboard' and sold around the world with the proceeds going to Oxfam, they remembered the charity Caverncade around the city, they remembered so much of the vitality of those unique years. . .it was apparent that bulldozers could not erase a memory.

"Like a sleeping giant, the guts of the original club lay dormant underground, waiting for more Mersey enterprise to surge forth. It was inevitable: Royal Life came to the rescue and, using the original bricks, rebuilt the club in its entirety for a grand opening in 1984."

And another piece, this one on the cover of the brochure, reads:

"Whilst acknowledging its famous roots, the Cavern will not rest on its laurels, but slams into the eighties with vibrant enthusiasm.

"Enterprising architect David Backhouse, depressed by the death of John Lennon, decided that a great memorial, a living, breathing complex, could be erected at the old Cavern site. With the support of the Royal Life Insurance company he set out to work on an architectural structure which is a combination of the old and the new – with its Cavern Walks, its Cavern Mecca, its shops, its tribute to the Beatles. . .and the resurrection of the Cavern itself.

"The heritage of the club has passed into the willing hands of three Merseyside men who see the club as a showcase for talent both old and new, a home for Merseyside youngsters eager to listen to new bands as well as tourists from around the world who wish to capture the excitement of the Mersey Beat. George Downey, Tommy Smith and Stuart Granger, as Cavern Entertainments Ltd, will be injecting a special brand of magic into an underground cellar which, with merely six letters CAVERN, has earned its place in twentieth-century history."

Every attempt was made to see that the new club resembled the original as much as possible. Former doorman Pat Delaney made sketches of the original wall at the rear of the stage which sported signatures of the various Mersey Beat groups who played there. Several former band members attended a private reception at the Cavern Club and once again signed their names on the wall at the rear of the stage. Fifteen thousand bricks from the original Cavern were used in the reconstruction, although the club now occupies a different site, parallel to Mathew Street. The familiar straight stone staircase at the entrance has been changed into a spiral, decorated with murals of the Beatles at different stages of their career – and portraits of some of the Royal Life staff! A passageway designed to look like the Mersey promenade leads to the Abbey Road pub and a Nems souvenir shop.

The reopening took place immediately after the Cavern Walks opening. A crowd of Mersey Beatsters, including Gerry Marsden and members of the Swinging Blue Jeans, took to the stage for a photo session. That evening many acts appeared live, including Billy J Kramer, The Merseybeats, Gerry and the Pacemakers, Beryl Marsden, Jimmy Tarbuck and a new Liverpool group called Mojo Filter, who played Beatle-style music.

Over the weekend Cavern Mecca threw a three-day party, with films and live groups, including Faron's Flamingos, Karl Terry and the Cruisers, the Beryl Marsden Band and Cavern. Among the guests were Ray McFall, Victor Spinetti, Tony Barrow, Charles Lennon, Alistair Taylor, Cynthia Lennon, Father Tom McKenzie, Freda Kelly, John 'Duff' Lowe, Clive Epstein and Pete Shotton.

Comparing the new club with the original, Billy J Kramer commented: "The dressing-rooms are luxurious compared to what they used to be. I couldn't believe it.

The Beatles take the stage with American singer Davy Jones

In the old club it was like trying to change in a telephone box. It's hard to tell if it will end up with the same atmosphere. There used to be seats right up to the stage and there was sweat running down the walls."

The Cavern received a further promotional boost when the Liverpool Playhouse presented a musical, *Cavern Of Dreams,* by Carol Ann Duffy, based on Spencer Leigh's book *Let's All Go Down The Cavern.* The play ran from 3 August to 22 September 1984 and was a great local success. The programme read: "It is 1957. Rock'n'roll has put a spell on Billy and the Dingles. So it's goodbye school, goodbye work. Fired by the music of Little Richard, Chuck Berry, and the immortal Buddy Holly, they'll be on the road to fame and fortune – just as soon as they get *that sound.*

"*Cavern Of Dreams* captures the magic of the Mersey Beat era with the story of Billy and the Dingles as they move from washboards and a tea-chest bass to the electrifying beat of rock'n'roll. They'll play anywhere, all around Liverpool, in Hamburg, even Southport, but the Cavern becomes home. *Cavern Of Dreams* features songs made famous by Kingsize Taylor and the Dominoes, Faron's Flamingos, the Swinging Blue Jeans, Gerry and the Pacemakers, and the Beatles. Billy and the Dingles played with them all!!"

The Swinging Blue Jeans sign the Cavern wall at the 1984 reopening

A Playhouse Theatre musical attempts to recapture the Mersey Beat days

Tribute to the Cavern

A compilation album with cover photo, taken by Les Chadwick, showing a typical Cavern crowd

This 16-track album was compiled by EMI Records exclusively for sale at the Cavern Club when the new premises opened in April 1984. The cover features the famous black-and-white photograph taken by Les Chadwick for the Peter Kaye studio. Les took the photograph standing on top of a parked car. In the foreground, Cavern 'bouncer' Pat Delaney is seen whispering into the ear of a policewoman. The crowd seems to be comprised of young children – Les took the shot on a Saturday lunchtime when the Junior Cavern Club sessions were held for under-16s only.

The photographs on the reverse of the sleeve depict the Beatles, the Swinging Blue Jeans, Billy J Kramer, Cilla Black, the Fourmost and Gerry and the Pacemakers. The sleeve notes were penned by Tony Barrow who acted as press officer for all these acts – with the exception of the Swinging Blue Jeans – during the sixties. All the tracks on the album were recorded in the 1963-4 period.

Side one contains hits from five Mersey artists who appeared at the Cavern: 'Bad To Me' (Billy J Kramer and the Dakotas); 'Hello Little Girl' (the Fourmost); 'You'll Never Walk Alone' (Gerry and the Pacemakers); 'Hippy Hippy Shake' (the Swinging Blue Jeans); 'Little Children' (Billy J Kramer and the Dakotas); 'You're No Good' (the Swinging Blue Jeans); 'It's For You' (Cilla Black) and 'Ferry 'Cross The Mersey' (Gerry and the Pacemakers).

Side two is exclusively composed of Beatles hits: 'Love Me Do', 'I Saw Her Standing There', 'Twist And Shout', 'She Loves You', 'Money', 'I Want To Hold Your Hand', 'Can't Buy Me Love' and 'A Hard Day's Night'.

With the exception of the Beatles and the Fourmost, all the acts represented here are still actively performing (although the membership of Gerry's Pacemakers has changed since those early days and Billy J no longer fronts the Dakotas).

None of the tracks contained on *Tribute To The Cavern* were actually recorded at the club. However, an album entitled *Liverpool Today: Live At The Cavern* – issued on Ember NR 5028 in September 1965 – was recorded there, by Cavern Sound. This recording studio, run by Peter Hepworth and Nigel Greenberg, had been built into a Cavern extension by Ray McFall. The album contains dialogue from Cavern DJ Bob Wooler as he introduces some of the Liverpool bands – recently signed to the Cavern Agency – who performed on the record. They include Earl Preston's Realms, the Michael Allen Group and the Richmond.

In March of the previous year, Decca had issued an album on Decca LK 4597 called *At The Cavern.* Altogether nine bands were featured, but only four came from Liverpool: the Big Three with 'Bring It On Home To Me', Lee Curtis and the All Stars with 'Jezebel' and 'Skinny Minnie', the Dennisons with 'Devoted To You' and 'You Better Move On', and Beryl Marsden with 'Everybody Loves A Lover'.

The Big Three were the first band to immortalise the club with their song 'Cavern Stomp', featured on the B-side of their minor hit 'By The Way' (issued on Decca F 11689 in June 1963). The following year in July the group brought out an EP entitled: *The Big Three Live At The Cavern.* It included four tracks: 'What'd I Say?', 'Don't Start Running Away', 'Zip A Dee Doo Dah' and 'Reelin' and Rockin' '.

On the Scene at the Cavern

Originally published in the sixties as a one-off magazine, price 2/6d (12½p), this official Cavern souvenir was written by Tony Barrow, using the pseudonym Alistair Griffin. Tony was the publicist for Nems Enterprises and handled the Beatles as well as other bands. He told me that he used pen-names when undertaking freelance work in order not to forfeit half his fee to Nems. He adopted the pen-name Frederick James (his middle names) to write articles for *Beatles Monthly.*

On The Scene At The Cavern became such a collectors' item that, following a meeting with former Cavern owner Ray McFall, Tony decided to republish it. He borrowed an original copy of the magazine from Jim and Liz Hughes of Cavern Mecca, and the souvenir booklet was issued in April 1984 to coincide with the club's reopening. It is a special, limited edition. Mail order copies (while stocks last) can be purchased directly from Tony Barrow International, 10 Buseph Drive, Torrisholme, Morecambe, Lancs LA4 6PQ.

Apart from a different cover, a centre spread of additional pictures and an introduction from Tony, the publication is an exact replica of the one published 20 years ago.

The new cover is a collage featuring thumb-nail photos of the Beatles and a picture of Gerry Marsden and Cilla Black doing the Twist. It is a 44-page publication with more than 60 photographs of such artists as Kingsize Taylor, Casey Jones, the Swinging Blue Jeans, Pete MacLaine and the Dakotas, Gerry and the Pacemakers, the Searchers, the Undertakers, the Merseybeats and, of course, the Beatles.

Ray McFall, owner of the Cavern during the Mersey Beat years, contributes a foreword. There are biographical articles on both Ray and Cavern DJ Bob Wooler. There is also a two-page 'Caverner's Diary', with highlights from the club's history. We learn that Johnny Kidd and the Pirates were the first southern group to visit the Cavern; Wednesday, 26 July 1961 produced the bill – the Beatles, Gerry and the Pacemakers, Johnny Sandon and the Searchers, and the Four Jays; the first Birmingham group to appear was Gerry Levene and the Avengers; and London singer Simone Jackson sang with the Beatles on 12 September 1962.

Tony Barrow's original Cavern booklet, now available in reprint

Cavern Beat

Following the success of *The Beatles At Abbey Road,* a compilation video of the Beatles recording career made by and shown at Abbey Road Studios during 1983, the Cavern asked if they could provide a special programme for exclusive viewing at the club.

The production was planned over a nine-week period – to include research – but it was eventually completed in four weeks to meet the reopening date of 26 April 1984. This proved to be an extremely tight schedule for a very small production team working round the clock.

In February 1984, John Barrett, who directed *The Beatles At Abbey Road,* sadly died and the small production unit had to be reorganised. Ken Townsend, general manager of Abbey Road Studios, steered the project as executive director. Paul Bates, who produced the 1983 programme, directed *Cavern Beat.* It was written and produced by Kathy Varley, who had acted as production assistant/co-ordinator in 1983, and Mike Jarratt, a balance engineer and cutter at Abbey Road Studios. Audio production was by Chris Blair, who also worked on the 1983 programme, and Mike Jarratt.

The programme traces the music scene in Liverpool from 1957 – when Alan Sytner transformed a gloomy cellar into a thriving jazz club – through the Mersey Beat era, to 1965. Footage has been taken from archive material and stills of the era, capturing the atmosphere of the music as it evolved. The programe features many of the famous Liverpool groups of the sixties who played at the Cavern. The Escorts perform 'Dizzy Miss Lizzy', and there is also footage of the Beatles at the club playing 'Some Other Guy', a song they never actually recorded.

With narration by Terry Sylvester, a former member of the Escorts and, later, of the Hollies, the 45-minute programme was screened twice a day at the Cavern Club during the summer of 1984. Its running order was as follows:

SONG	COMMENTARY
'HMS Pinafore'	Liverpool, home now of one of the finest orchestras in the world, was, in the early sixties, birthplace of a kind of music that was to take the world by storm.
	In 1957, Alan Sytner turned a dark gloomy cellar in Mathew Street into a thriving jazz club. During the first few years many famous artists performed there, amongst them Mr Acker Bilk and his Paramount Jazz Band, Alex Welsh and his Band, Terry Lightfoot, Ken Colyer and, of course, Merseyside's own Merseysippi Jazz Band.
'I Can Tell' **Rory Storm and the Hurricanes**	Rory Storm and the Hurricanes started their career as the Alan Caldwell Skiffle Group. They never achieved national success but were essential to the development of the Mersey Sound. Rory was one of the greatest showmen of all time. Probably his most famous stunt was jumping from the balcony at the Majestic Ballroom in Birkenhead. He broke his leg.
'Some Other Guy' **The Beatles**	In August 1962 Rory's drummer joined a group who were starting to gain national interest...
'Love Me Do' **The Beatles** **'A Little Loving'** **The Fourmost**	It wasn't only the music scene that was changing. Hair-styles and clothes were looking very different too, and at Brian Epstein's record store, the North End Music Shop, business was booming.

Emile Ford borrows the sticks while Pete Best and Paul McCartney look on in amusement

'Please Please Me'
The Beatles

'Hippy Hippy Shake'
The Swinging Blue Jeans

'Please Please Me' reached No.2 in the national chart in 1963; so did this one from the Swinging Blue Jeans.

'Cavern Stomp'
The Big Three

(Bob Wooler) On stage right now are the boys with the Benzedrine Beat, a trio of talent called the Big Three.

'She Loves You'
The Beatles

'It's Gonna Be Alright'
Gerry and the Pacemakers

The first three singles released by Gerry and the Pacemakers made the No.1 position in the British charts, an unsurpassed achievement. They had their own monthly magazine and starred in their own film, *Ferry 'Cross The Mersey.*

'Twist and Shout'
The Beatles

'Sugar and Spice'
The Searchers

'I Feel Fine'
The Beatles

Of course the most famous group to come from Liverpool were the Beatles. Between May 1961 and August 1963 they played at the Cavern 292 times. Not only were they great performers – the song-writing skills of Lennon and McCartney penned no less than 26 No.1 hit singles.

'Dizzy Miss Lizzy'
The Escorts

By now the Cavern was attracting as much attention as the Beatles. Lunchtimes and evenings, the place was packed. One of the youngest and most popular groups were the Escorts, seen here playing at a lunchtime session.

'A Hard Day's Night'
The Beatles

'Little Children'
Billy J Kramer and the Dakotas

Billy J Kramer's original group were the coasters, but when he started his recording career Billy teamed up with a band from Manchester called the Dakotas. Following his three hits in 1963, a change of style brought him his second No.1.

'Penny Lane'
The Beatles

'Strawberry Fields'
The Beatles

The Beatles started a revolution, leading the way through a very important transitional period from Mersey Beat to psychedelia. They were without doubt the biggest single influence on popular music.

'Ferry 'Cross The Mersey'
Gerry and the Pacemakers

The video is now held by EMI Records.

CAVERN WALKS
Mathew Street, Liverpool 2

The narrow brick street known as Mathew Street gained a great deal of fame in the sixties as the site of the Cavern Club. In the seventies, in a local decision to provide an air-vent for an underground railway, the original warehouses perched above the club were destroyed and the club itself disappeared. The site was turned into a car-park, surrounded by corrugated iron. The only attractions of the street seemed to be the Grapes pub, the Dooley Madonna statue and a club called Eric's across the street from the original Cavern. Eric's became to the contemporary bands what the Cavern had been to the Mersey Beat groups. It spawned a new breed of Liverpool bands – 'scallies' – outfits such as Echo and the Bunnymen and Orchestral Manoeuvres In The Dark. This led to a musical renaissance which has so far continued unabated; there are a reputed 850 bands in the area, such as Teardrop Explodes, Frankie Goes To Hollywood, China Crisis, Cooka Da Books, 3D, Dead Or Alive, The Icicle Works and This Island Earth.

Shortly after John Lennon's death, a local architect, Dave Backhouse, happened to walk down Mathew Street, was shocked at the mess, and decided to design a great tribute to John. He would create a new building on the site: not just an ordinary building, but something with character and style – a fitting monument to the street's achievements during the sixties.

The Royal Life Insurance company provided him with the means to realise his dream. The company, operating within Britain, the Republic of Ireland, Australia, Canada and New Zealand, had a revenue by 1982 of £431 million, and funds under their control of £1,956 million. Their head office was in Liverpool. They decided to back the Cavern Walks scheme (originally referred to as the Eleanor Centre, after 'Eleanor Rigby') to the tune of £9 million.

Backhouse designed the basic plans for the complex in only two days, producing an original design of a structure seven stories high with an almost Victorian look to it. He also included provision for the restructuring of the original Cavern Club. The complex was also to have a shopping centre, offices, a pub, a restaurant, a Beatles museum and a central atrium where the shopping malls merged, and an eye-catching Beatles statue.

A competition to choose a title for the venture was held in conjunction with the *Liverpool Echo.* It was reader Mrs Jean Myers who came up with 'Cavern Walks'. Construction on the project began in October 1982, with the aim that the opening should coincide with the major events occurring in Liverpool during 1984.

Cynthia Lennon was asked to provide a design for the terracotta tiles that would

Cynthia Lennon and Dave Backhouse

face parts of the new building. On 25 April 1984 she unveiled a small commemorative plaque, placed on an outside wall. It is inscribed "To John" and contains the lyrics to 'In My Life'. "That says it all," commented Cynthia at the unveiling.

In the centre of the atrium itself – which reaches up past the entire seven floors, with a wall-climber lift, candy-pink lamp-posts, vaulted ceilings and hanging gardens of foliage – is the controversial statue of the Beatles, sculpted by John Doubleday. John, who lives in Essex with his wife Isabel and their three sons, was 35 when he completed the work. He had already gained himself an international reputation; he had works in many galleries, including the Tate, and statues in places as far away as Fiji. His other noted works include the Charlie Chaplin statue in Leicester Square, the Brunel piece at Paddington Station and the Dylan Thomas statue in Swansea. John has this to say about the statue: "It is the largest figurative group in bronze commissioned in Britain for twenty-five years, in fact since Epstein's Bowater House Group. It has been a considerable professional challenge. Above all, I have tried to capture the raw energy of the Beatles as they were when they were playing at the Cavern."

Dozens of people from the original Mersey Beat days were present at the unveiling, including Lee Curtis, Faron, Pete Best, Johnny 'Guitar' Byrne, Freda Kelly, Joe Flannery, Pat Delaney, Cynthia Lennon, Gerry Marsden, Adrian Henri, members of the Swinging Blue Jeans, the Merseybeats, the Dennisons, the Coasters and the Undertakers. There were gasps of amazement from many of them when the statue was unveiled: the £40,000 sculpture bore no resemblance to the Beatles. It was after all a figurative work. The individual bronze figures had detailed faces, so that it seemed logical they should bear some resemblance to the Beatles. Had Doubleday just made them up, or were they the faces of anonymous models?

Paul's brother, Mike McCartney, who unveiled the sculpture, attempted to conceal his surprise. However, he later remarked: "From close up I didn't recognize any of them, not even my own brother. I think you have to get away from it so that distance will lend perspective." Former promoter Sam Leach was less polite: "It's a disgrace. The only one I recognized was Ringo and that is because he was sitting down and holding a drumstick."

When told of people's reaction John Doubleday commented: "I particularly did not want a close likeness." He certainly succeeded!

MERSEYSIDE COUNTY COUNCIL
29 Lime Street, Liverpool LI IJG

Much of the tourist office's success in promoting the heritage of the Beatles lies with Ron Jones, the Tourist Development Officer. Ron was born in 1941 and, with the exception of two or three years, he has spent his whole life living and working on Merseyside. He was brought up in the Liverpool 8 area, went to Granby Street School in Toxteth, failed the 11-plus exam, passed at 13, and then transferred to Evered Avenue High School. He left in 1957 with six O levels. "Incidentally," he comments, "I showed some early promise in art and was sent to the Junior Art School in Gambier Terrace when I was eleven to sit their entrance exam. However, I was obviously not good enough because I failed that one too! Early influences were the same as the

Heinz and Ann Roll, the 25,000th visitors to the Art of the Beatles exhibition, receive an award from Ron Jones

Beatles' and most other Liverpool schoolboys' and teenagers' in the mid-fifties: 'Rock Around The Clock', Elvis, Fats Domino, James Dean, Jerry Lee Lewis, Little Richard and Lonnie Donegan. I played in a college skiffle group when I was seventeen and even had genuine Levi jeans which were virtually unobtainable in Britain then! However, my best friend's sister was courting a Yank from Burtonwood who drove a '57 Chevy with a hood and passed American clothes, records, comics (real DCs!) and chewing-gum to my friends and me. While in a skiffle group playing college gigs, labour clubs, etc, I auditioned along with many other local skiffle groups (perhaps even the Quarrymen?) for Lonnie Donegan one Saturday afternoon at the Cavern. He thought we–all of us–were rubbish. Dispirited, my group disbanded in the middle of Mathew Street at the end of the afternoon!

"I retained an interest in the guitar, skiffle and rock'n'roll and started going to the Cavern and watching the Blue Genes [later the Blue Jeans] playing between jazz sets. I got friendly with Don Andrew and the Remo Four and regularly watched them and the Beatles for a number of years at the Cavern.

"I first got involved with promoting Liverpool via the Beatles in 1972 when I started to prepare the first-ever official souvenir of the group. This was something I felt strongly about and eventually in 1974 the double album concept *The Beatles Collection* was launched. Ten thousand copies were produced and it is now something of a collector's item–wish I'd kept a few! However, by then I had moved to the Public Relations office of Merseyside County Council and left others to continue the Liverpool/Beatles promotion. But it all went flat again until eventually, by default, I had to get involved once more." Ron then goes on to summarise his involvement in recent years:

Secured funds to enable Bob Wooler and Allan Williams to stage the first Liverpool Beatles Convention at Mr Pickwick's in 1977.

Secured funds to enable Jim and Liz Hughes to get their first two Mersey Beatle Extravaganzas off the ground.

Produced the first local Beatles postcard (apart from the set I did for *The Beatles Collection* in 1974) and then produced an extensive range of original postcards. Also introduced a range of commemorative postcards, starting with 'Love Me Do', to mark the twentieth anniversary of the release of various Beatles singles.

Conceived the idea of *In The Footsteps Of The Beatles,* a tourist guidebook; wrote it in conjunction with Mike Evans, author of the small booklet which accompanied *The Beatles Collection*.

Introduced guided Beatle tours–on foot, by coach or car.

Introduced trained Beatleguides, Mersey Beatle Weekend Holidays on special weekends in the summer and Go As You Please Beatle weekends *every* weekend in the year.

BRITAIN
Liverpool '84
THE
BEATLES
BTA

Beatles '85
Beatles '85
Beatles '85
Beatles '85
Your 1985 guide
to Beatle happenings
in
LIVERPOOL
Birthplace of the Beatles
Merseyside County Council Tourism

MerseyBeatle
Weekends
1984

City of Liverpool
MATHEW
STREET
L2

THE BEATLES:
Their Liverpool Homes

"Penny Lane is in my ears and in my eyes,
there beneath the blue suburban skies."
Lennon and McCartney
PENNY LANE, LIVERPOOL

THE BEATLES

Produced a wide range of exclusive Beatle souvenirs, all designed to promote Liverpool as the Birthplace of the Beatles.

Helped get funding for Beatle City, in which Merseyside County Council has a major financial stake; assisted with the Cavern Walks project. My offices's grant – £15,111 – helped to get Cavern Mecca set up.

Conceived and staged The Art of the Beatles exhibition at the Walker Art Gallery, May – September 1984. It was the best-attended exhibition in the recent history of the Walker, with 46,000 paying visitors. The exhibition will be staged in Japan in 1985 and possibly in the US after that.

Promoted Liverpool/Beatles at a number of the top US Beatlefests, and appeared as a special guest. Also gave slide presentations on the theme 'The Beatles' Liverpool'.

Participated in numerous media interviews on this theme, and was directly responsible for bringing dozens of press, radio and TV reporters to Liverpool to cover Beatle developments.

Produced a 20-part action plan for developing Beatles tourism in Liverpool.

Assisted in creating a climate on Merseyside in which Beatle developments and promotional activities could thrive – no easy job!

Endeavoured to set up a John Lennon museum in Liverpool, though there's been a recent set-back – Yoko tells me she's setting up one in New York in 1986. I'm working on another idea for a tribute to John.

It is a great shame that *The Beatles Collection* is no longer available. It was packaged in an album-sized double folder, printed with 15 of their album covers. The items inside included a large, illustrated fold-out map of the 'Beatles Liverpool' detailing their homes and schools and Merseyside venues. A giant 'Back-Track' poster followed their lives and careers from 1955 to 1971. 'Beatles Tours 1963-1966', another fold-out on tinted paper, provided a visual souvenir of the Beatles' touring activities. A circular Beatles discography – designed to look like an actual record – listed all their album and singles releases. There was also a bookmark with a bibliography, a reproduction of the last Beatles Offical Fan Club release, a large poster of a Beatles portrait, a selection of postcards of the Beatles in their Liverpool days, and a book by Mike Evans entitled *Nothing To Get Hung About.*

Souvenirs and Postcards

In recent years the tourist office has produced an exclusive range of Beatles memorabilia. All the souvenir items on the following list are available to personal callers only at the Tourist Information Centre. The *Art of the Beatles* catalogue and *In the Footsteps of the Beatles,* however, may be ordered by mail order.

The *Art of the Beatles* catalogue is a wonderful souvenir for disappointed fans who were unable to attend the exhibition itself. A large-format 80-page book with semi-stiff covers, the front cover depicts David Oxtoby's *Yesterdays* painting. Inside there are over 130 illustrations – many in colour – ranging from an oil painting by Stuart Sutcliffe to bronze masks by David Wynne. Photographers whose works appear in the catalogue are Astrid Kirchherr, Don Valentine, Graham Spencer, Peter Kaye, Mike McCartney, Angus McBean, Robert Freeman, Michael Cooper, Ian McMillan, Richard Avedon, Dezo Hoffmann and Linda McCartney. Painters include Sam Walsh, Adrian Henri, Maurice Cockrill, Franklin Wilson, John Bratby, Peter Blake, Cynthia Lennon, David Oxtoby, James Marsh, Sue Butler and Steve Gublin. There are drawings by Paul McCartney, Klaus Voorman, James Thompson and John Lennon. Other material includes Beatle comic-strips as well as book, magazine and album covers. The text was penned by Mike Evans.

In the Footsteps of the Beatles, sporting the Maurice Cockrill *Penny Lane* painting on the cover is a lavishly illustrated guide, written by Mike Evans and Ron Jones to all the places of interest on Merseyside associated with the Beatles. The original print order of 5,000 sold out very quickly and a further 10,000 were printed.

The memorabilia available from the tourist office is as follows:

Ashtry, long black	1.75
Badges:	
Button	.20
Guitar	.70
Original Fan Club	3.75
Bookmark, leather	.60
Bronze head, John Lennon	19.95
Car stickers	.20
Coasters, set of four	1.65
Key-rings:	
Leather	.50
Enamel	.85
Leather items:	
Comb in case	.60
Fruit knife in case	.95
Comb and nail-file in case	.75
Scissors in case	.95
Medallions (Beatles, or Lennon):	
Boxed	1.50
Keychain	1.95
On neck-chain	1.95
Mirror, round	.70
Mug	.95
Paperweight	4.50
Pen, multi-coloured	2.95
Pennant	2.45
Plaques	5.00
Plaques, enamel (street names)	1.25
Records	
Beatle City	1.20
Much Missed Man	1.10
Picture disc	1.99
Rock	.25

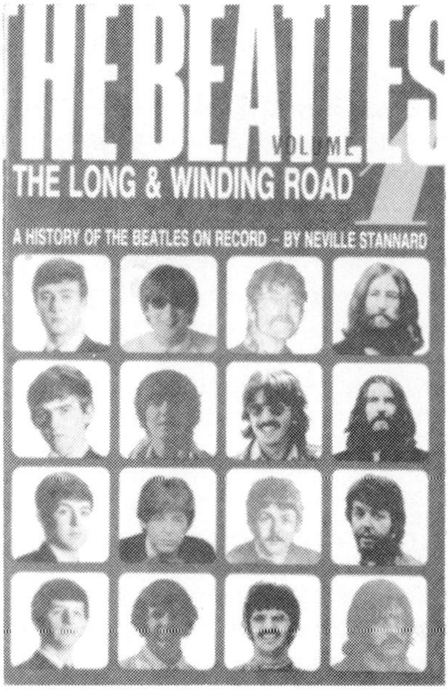

Strawberry Fields picture (framed):	
Red lacquer	39.95
Metal	34.95
Real wool designer sweater	25.00
Sweatshirt	7.95
T-shirt	3.50
Tea-towel	1.40
Ties, leather	3.50
Tankards:	
Glass	4.50
Black and gold	2.95
Videos:	
Compleat Beatles	19.95
A Hard Day's Night	24.95
Wall-hanging	1.50
Clock (picture disc)	7.95

Beatles prints and posters

Artboard	.99
Art Of The Beatles poster	.95
Beatles map	.30
John Lennon poster	2.25
Strawberry Fields, limited edition print	15.00
Beatles '84 poster	1.50
Mathew Street statue print	.99
Beatles logo with street names print	.50
Small coloured logo print	.95
Black and white print of Beatles	.95
Engravings on hessian (framed)	5.50
Framed prints	9.95

Beatle books

In the Footsteps of the Beatles	1.50
Art of the Beatles catalogue	1.95
Sunday Times supplement	.30
History of Rock	.70

Beatles England	2.50
Thank U Very Much	5.95
The Man Who Gave the Beatles Away	3.50
The Beatles Apart	4.95
All You Need Is Ears	7.95
The Ballad of John and Yoko	6.95
Behind the Beatles Songs	3.95
PS We Love You	1.25
The Beatles at the Beeb	2.25
John Lennon's Secret	5.95
The Beatles Who's Who	4.95
Beatle Lyrics	1.95
Apple to the Core	1.50
The Long and Winding Road	5.95
Complete Lyrics	4.95
Mersey Beat	3.95
Beatlemania	5.95
Paperback Writers	5.95
The Lennon Tapes	1.95
Lennon – Echo Tribute	1.99
The Book of Lennon	5.95
Beatles Map of Liverpool	.85

Postcards (10p each)

Gold cards (3 designs)	
Street names (6 designs)	
Penny Lane: painting	
Strawberry Fields: painting	
Mathew Street: Dooley statue	
Eleanor Rigby statue	
Silver Beatles painting	
Black and white photos of Beatles in Liverpool (3 designs)	
Beatle cartoons (4 designs)	.20
Glossy colour Liverpool cards (8 designs)	
Commemorative cards, limited edition, Beatles No. 1 hit singles	.50

The two paintings *Penny Lane* and *Strawberry Fields* which are available as postcards were executed by Maurice Cockrill, who was born in North Wales in 1936 and moved to Liverpool at the beginning of the sixties. *Penny Lane* was originally commissioned in 1977 by Alexander Howden, the insurance company. Maurice based it on a photograph by Don McCullin. The street sign contains several girl's names scrawled in graffiti: astute observers will notice that the names are all characters from Beatle songs. The Merseyside Tourist Office commissioned the next Cockrill work, *Strawberry Fields*, in 1981. The same McCullin photograph has been used as a basis for the four faces, seen in torn strips of a photograph before the leaf-stewn gates of the Strawberry Fields children's home.

The commemorative cards pay tribute to each of the Beatles singles exactly twenty years after they were first issued in Britian. On one side of the 'Please Please Me' card, for instance, are the words "The Beatles' Hit Singles, 1961-1983. PLEASE PLEASE ME, 11 January 1963 – 11 January 1983. 20th Anniversary." There is a print of their four heads with the words "The Beatles. The Boys from Liverpool." The informative text reads: "On 11 January 1963, EMI released, on the Parlophone label (R.4983) 'Please Please Me' with 'Ask Me Why' on the B-side. It was to be the first of twelve consecutive No.1 British hit singles.

"'Please Please Me' was written by John in the bedroom of 251 Menlove Avenue, the neat semi-detached house in Liverpool where he lived with his Aunt Mimi.

"Just before his death in 1980 he was to recall the exact day, even remembering the colour of the coverlet on the bed and Roy Orbison's 'Only The Lonely' which, along with an old Bing Crosby song, 'Please, Lend Your Little Ears To My Pleas', gave him the inspiration for 'Please Please Me'."

On the reverse side is a post office stamp, "Liverpool 11.1.83", and a further stamp in red "From the Birthplace of the Beatles", which incorporates the four faces. Across the 15½p postage stamp is a further impression from the "Liverpool Philatelic Counter", dated 11 Jan. '83, with a symbol of the Liver Buildings. Stamped in red is the address "The Beatles C/o the Cavern Club, 10 Mathew Street, Liverpool." Further text reads: "No.1 in a series of special collectors' cards issued by Merseyside Tourism to commemorate the 20th anniversay of the release of each of the Beatles hit singles. This series is limited to 2,000 cards per edition."

The six street signs are for John Lennon Drive, Ringo Starr Drive, George Harrison

THE BEATLES AT THE LIVERPOOL EMPIRE

"Strawberry Field" by the Liverpool artist Maurice Cockrill

Close, Paul McCartney Way, Mathew Street and Penny Lane. Street signs for such places as Abbey Road in London and Penny Lane in Liverpool have caused headaches for local authorities: the originals were pilfered long ago by fans, who continue to disappear with the replacement signs. These postcards have proved a legal way to obtain a souvenir of the signs. Mathew Street, of course, is the site of the Cavern and now includes the new Cavern Walks complex with the Doubleday Beatles statue, an Abbey Road pub, a John Lennon bar, Cavern Mecca and the Dooley madonna statue. Penny Lane is the street immortalised in the songs. The four Liverpool streets named after the boys are in the Liverpool 6 area, in a new estate near West Derby Road. The first of the homes in the new estate was officially opened by Michael Heseltine, then Minister of the Environment, on 27 November 1981. The estate was finally completed at the end of 1982.

The Mathew Street, Dooley statue postcard details the Beatles' birthplaces and sports a colour photograph of the famous Beatles madonna sculpted by Arthur Dooley. This was erected in Mathew Street in April 1974, opposite the site of the old Cavern. It is appropriate that the statue now faces the new, rebuilt Cavern. Above the bronze madonna is the sign "Beatles Street", below is the legend "The Four Lads Who Shook The World". An additional statue, dedicated to John, has been placed on the wall to one side of the madonna; it depicts a baby with a halo on which is written "Lennon Lives", while below are the lyrics to 'Imagine'.

The Eleanor Rigby statue was donated to the city by entertainer Tommy Steele for the symbolic sum of half a sixpence. The statue was unveiled in Stanley Street on 3 December 1982.

The three gold cards are designed in black. The first is a drawing of the Beatles' heads, with the Liverpool seafront in the background and an arched design with the words "Liverpool. Birthplace of the Beatles". The second is a black ink rendition of the Fab Four based on a Dezo Hoffmann photograph, the third a drawing of their heads with the words "The Beatles. The Boys From Liverpool".

The black-and-white photographs of the Beatles in Liverpool in the early sixties were taken by the late Graham Spencer for *Mersey Beat* during the hectic years when the group began to conquer the world. The *Art of the Beatles* postcard reproduces David Oxtoby's painting, and is the same basic design as the exhibition poster and catalogue cover.

The glossy Liverpool cards include colour photographs of places such as Strawberry Fields and Penny Lane. One, called "Their Liverpool Homes", features the houses in Menlove Avenue, Forthlin Road, Arnold Grove and Admiral Grove; "Lennon's Liverpool" depicts Strawberry Fields, Liverpool College of Art, Gambier Terrace, Quarry Bank School, Newcastle Road and John Lennon Drive. The colour photographs on most of the cards were taken by Ron Jones; the designs were produced by Alphabet Design Partnership.

The Art of the Beatles

Ron Jones must be particularly proud of his brainchild, The Art of the Beatles exhibition; during its five-month run (4 May-30 September) it attracted the largest-ever crowds of recent times to Liverpool's famous Walker Art Gallery. It was opened officially by Cynthia Lennon. Such was its success that Merseyside County Council is hoping to organise a further travelling exhibition on Beatle art.

In addition to the exhibition catalogue already described, there is *The Art of the Beatles,* a lavish book with a 40,000-word text by Mike Evans, which takes an in-depth look at the exhibition. Published jointly by Anthony Blond and the Merseyside County Council, it uses coated art-paper to enhance reproduction. A more ambitious project than the catalogue, the book introduces lots of items not actually shown in the Walker exhibition, such as material from *Mersey Beat,* concert programmes and advertisements.

There is a set of four 'family group' paintings by Cynthia Lennon – rather over-romanticised images of the Beatles as children with their parents; there is a portrait of John in his art college days by fellow-student Ann Mason, and various pages from John's *Daily Howl* book, which was in the possession of Rod Murray before he auctioned it at Sotheby's in 1984. A black-and-white illustration by Cynthia, first used in her book *A Twist of Lennon,* shows her waiting for John underneath the clock at Lewis's store. John liked her to dress sexily, and here she portrays herself wearing a

very, perhaps exaggeratedly, short skirt. There is a self-portrait by Stuart Sutcliffe, an oil in the style of Vincent Van Gogh, and a photograph of him, taken by Astrid Kirchherr, which well conveys his brooding character.

In his accreditation of some early photos of the Beatles in Liverpool, Mike Evans unfortunately and mistakenly credits pictures by Albert Marrion and Harry Watmough to Les Chadwick; on the other hand, he at last gives Les credit for all the photographs he took for *Mersey Beat* while working at the Peter Kaye studio. A detailed study of the making of the Sgt. Pepper sleeve includes a number of the original sketches by Peter Blake. A set of Iain Macmillan photographs shows us what John's 'You Are Here' and the 'Yoko At The Indica' exhibition were like. Black ink drawings of the Fab Four, include the Jimmy Thomson cartoons from *Melody Maker,* John Cornelius' sketch from his book *Liverpool 8* and the Max Ernst 'Beatles, 1969'. Among my personal favourites are the two paintings of John by James Marsh and the painting-on-glass of all four in their Sgt. Pepper outfits by Yugoslavian artist J Generalic. Tex O'Hara, brother of Brian O'Hara of the Fourmost, is represented by a rough sketch of his design for the Beatles drumkit logo and by an abstract sculpture called 'Beatles, 1962'.

Walks and Tours

Mendips in Menlove Avenue where John was reared by his Aunt Mimi.

The Merseyside County Council organises a number of tours, several of them concerning the Beatles. From Easter until the end of September there is a series of guided walks with about thirty different themes. They include:

Oriental Mystique: Liverpool has the longest established Chinatown in Europe and even today Merseyside's Chinese community is more than 10,000 strong. This walk takes you right through the heart of Chinatown and tells the story of its development.

Ale Trail: Concentrates on some of Liverpool's resplendent Victorian and Edwardian gin palaces.

Liver Birds and Other Surprises: Introduces some of Liverpool's curiosities such as the 'friendly doors', the sanctuary stone and the origin of the famous Liver Bird shrouded in mystery and conjecture.

In the Footsteps of the Beatles: Of most interest to readers, this takes you through the City Centre and points out the many places associated with the Fab Four and the amazing story of their rise to fame. It culminates with a visit to Mathew Street, site of the Cavern Club and the new Cavern Walks development.

There are also a series of guided coach tours, which include:

Singing City: A tour focusing on Liverpool's rich musical heritage, from sea-shanties to Mersey Beat. Feel free to sing along!

Murders and Mysteries of Bygone Liverpool: A light-hearted look at the unexpected side of Liverpool's colourful past. The city abounds in tales of ghosts, famous criminal cases and unsolved mysteries which will all be revealed as the tour makes its way from one haunt to another (adults only, as a visit to a pub may be included).

City Sightseeing Tour: An excellent introduction to Liverpool with its rich history, grand buildings and numerous other attractions.

Beatles Magical History Tour: A must for Beatles fans, old and young. Re-live the early days of the 60s with this nostalgic look at some of the places associated with those 'four lads who shook the world': Penny Lane, Strawberry Fields, Mathew Street and many more.

Mersey Beatle Weekends: Usually take place between June and September and include two nights accommodation at a three-star hotel in Liverpool City Centre with dinner and full English breakfast, a social evening with Beatles sounds on the Friday, a visit to Cavern Mecca, a guided ale trail to some of Liverpool's spectacular pubs, the guided walk 'In The Footsteps of the Beatles', and a ticket to ride on a Magical History Coach Tour.

A report on a Mersey Beatles weekend was published in the special Beatles edition of the *Sunday Times* magazine on 27 February 1983. Writer Gordon Burn described how the group met on the first evening, all displaying suitable name-tags, and had a sherry get-together in the hotel, with Beatles music in the background. The ubiquitous Bob Wooler was their host on this occasion, and told them many stories of the early days in Liverpool when he was Cavern compère. Ron Jones tested the tourists knowledge in a Beatles quiz. On the Saturday, the group set out from Mathew Street and Cavern Mecca on their Magical History Coach Tour, visiting the various former homes of the individual Beatles, ranging from 'Rembrandt', the house in the Wirral which Paul bought for his father in 1964, to Madryn Street where Ringo was born, and also taking in other notable Beatles sites, such as Penny Lane and Strawberry Fields.

The County Council is constantly introducing fresh ideas to its tours and during 1984 launched weekends dedicated to individual Beatles (a 'John Lennon Weekend' etc) and a Beatle Holiday Week.

Beatleguides are a special corps who lead visitors around the Merseyside Beatle tours. At peak tourist times, the Merseyside Tourist Board may have upwards of 50 general Merseyguides. Beatleguides undergo a six-month training course on the Beatles before being presented with their badge and certificate. One of the new Beatleguides hired in April 1981 was Bernadette Boyle, a former Cavern habituée and ex-girlfriend of Paul McCartney.

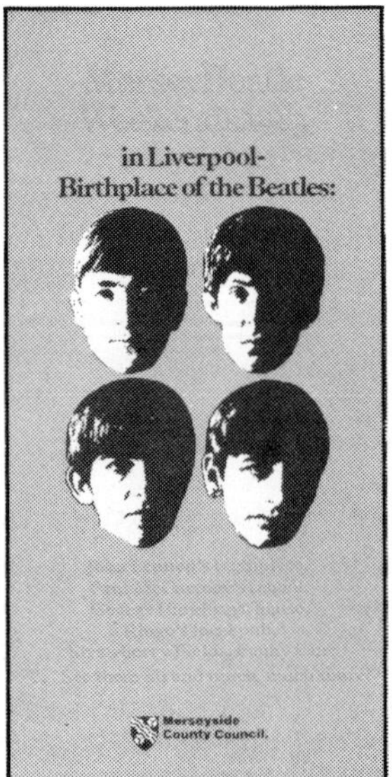

BEATLE WALK

The first guide to the Beatles sites in Liverpool was written by me and appeared in the August 1979 issue of *Beatles Monthly* under the title 'The Beatles' Liverpool'. I also included a Beatle Walk, a description of places of interest in a set route around the City Centre.

Arriving in a strange city with nothing but a lot of Beatle memories to guide you can be very confusing. But any good street map of Liverpool will enable you to find all the places on the short Beatle Walk described below.

Lime Street station has been completely restructured and is not as dark and grimy as it was when the Beatles first caught their trains to London to find fame and fortune. When you emerge from the station with its large 'Welcome To Liverpool' sign you notice the new St George's Precinct facing you, with the Top Rank Ballroom, site of Allan Williams' third Beatles convention. To the right is St George's Hall, which closed in 1984, its last event being the last Beatles convention organized by Jim and Liz Hughes. The imposing structure, which houses a unique mosaic floor, was also the setting for an Allan Williams promotion – a 1959 Arts Ball. Opposite the hall is the Empire Theatre, site of so many major rock concerts. Here, Paul McCartney queued up to see Wee Willie Harris, eager to obtain the rock'n'roll singer's autograph. Here as Johnny and the Moondogs, the group entered a Carrol Levis 'Discoveries' competition and made their first major appearance as the Beatles on a bill with Little Richard in 1962. Other appearances followed, including their all-Beatles edition of *Juke Box Jury* and a televised concert for the BBC, *It's The Beatles.* They made their final bow at the Empire on 5 December 1965.

To the right of St George's Hall, divided by William Brown Street, is the Walker Art Gallery, originally opened in 1877 under the sponsorship of Andrew Barclay Walker, the Lord Mayor of Liverpool at the time. This is the setting for the annual John Moore's Exhibition and it was at such an exhibition in 1959 that Stuart Sutcliffe sold a painting, enabling him to buy a bass guitar and join the Beatles. The gallery's most successful exhibition was, of course, The Art of the Beatles.

At the side of the Empire Theatre, leading north, is London Road, where you will find the Odeon cinema where the première of *A Hard Day's Night* took place on 10 July 1964. Twenty years later, Paul McCartney once again graced the premises for the première of *Give My Regards To Broad Street* in November 1984. Opposite the Odeon in Camden Street is the former Gaumont cinema where Fred and Julia Lennon took their honeymoon – it was called the Trocadero then and the couple went there after their wedding and then left for their separate homes! Further up London Road, running parallel to Camden Street, is Fraser Street where the New Shakespeare Theatre stood until it was burned to the ground in the seventies (like so many other Mersey venues). Several clubs, including Pickwick's where two Beatles conventions have been held, and venues, such as the Peppermint Lounge, that played host to the Mersey Beat groups in the sixties, are also to be found in Fraser Street.

Returning to Lime Street, next door to the Walker Art Gallery is the Picton Library where Paul McCartney was officially made Freeman of the City of Liverpool in November 1984.

Heading south towards the Mersey Tunnel you enter Dale Street, off which branch several smaller streets that were the sites of Beat venues in the early sixties, such as the Iron Door club and the Casanova club. On the right hand side of Dale Street is Moorfields, where Brian Epstein set up a branch of Nems Enterprises, opposite Harry Watmough's photographic studio. Harry took some of the earliest Beatles photos after the Epstein signing. Dale Street becomes Water Street, the site of the grandiose Town Hall where the Beatles were guests at a Civic Reception on 10 July 1964.

Off Dale Street to the left is North John Street. Walk along here and you will find Mathew Street on your left-hand side. This is probably the most popular street with Beatles fans because it is the site of the rebuilt Cavern Club, as well as the Abbey Road pub, Cavern Walks and the Doubleday Beatles statue, Cavern Mecca, the Dooley madonna, the Grapes and the White Star (two pubs where the Beatles used to imbibe), the Beatle Shop and the John Lennon Memorial Club (a bar for members only). One opening at the end of Mathew Street leads to Stanley Street, where Frank Hessy's music store is still open for business. Frank Hessy died a few years ago, but Jim Gretty, who sold the Beatles some of their first guitars, still works there. Also in Stanley Street are to be found Radio City, the most successful independent radio station in Britain, and the Eleanor Rigby statue.

Another exit from Mathew Street brings you into Whitechapel, almost directly opposite Brian Epsteins' Nems Record store (which, at the time of writing, is a Rumbelow's store). To the left along Whitechapel is Rushworth & Dreapers, another store where the Beatles purchased guitars. We turn right, past Lord Street and into Paradise Street, where Radio Merseyside now has its new HQ. Branching off on the left are two streets, Hanover Street and Duke Street. Walk along Hanover Street and you will reach Seel Street on your right-hand side.

The first sight which should greet you as you turn into Seel Street is the imposing structure of Beatle City. Continue walking straight up Seel Street and you will find Slater Street on the left-hand side, home of Allan Williams' Jacaranda coffee-bar in the cellar of which the Silver Beatles performed a couple of early gigs. In 1983, after several years under different names, the club was renamed the Jacaranda and during redecoration Stuart Sutcliffe's original murals were found. The original Jacaranda sign is now in Beatle City. Continue up Seel Street and at the top of the road you will come to the Razamatazz Club on the right. Long ago it was the Wyvern Social Club, where the Beatles auditioned for Larry Parnes, hoping for a job as Billy Fury's backing group. In 1962, Allan Williams took it over and it became the famous Blue Angel, the happy hunting ground for so many Mersey Beatsters.

Parallel to Seel Street, is Duke Street, where Joe's Café used to be. Brian Epstein, the Beatles and various Mersey groups used to frequent this late-night eating place for curries, cups of tea and chat. The host, Joe Davy, even compiled a 'wall of fame' in the upstairs room with photographs of local groups. Joe was later to buy the Cavern.

Continue walking north up Duke Street, with the Anglican Cathedral to your left, and you will come to Hope Street. To your right is Gambier Terrace, where John, Stuart and Rod Murray had a flat at No.3 and where Cynthia Lennon (she was Powell then) and I once studied at the Junior Art School. Immediately to the left is the playground of the Liverpool Institute where Paul, George and Neil Aspinall studied. Further up Hope Street you will pass the front of the Liverpool College of Art, which, although a polytechnic now, is structurally unaltered. The huge top-floor art-rooms saw many an early Beatles rehearsal and the basement canteen many a gig before they turned professional. John, Stuart, Cynthia, Rod Murray and I were among the students there in the late fifties and early sixties.

Continue along Hope Street and you will come to Rice Street on your left, where stands Ye Cracke, the pub frequented by John and Stu and other art students. Further along the street is the Everyman Theatre, which held the premiers of the plays *John, Paul, George, Ringo and Bert* and *Lennon*.

Turn left at Hardman Street and, walking south, you will come to Renshaw Street (passing Rodney Street on your left, where Brian Epstein was born). I set up the *Mersey Beat* offices at No.81a Renshaw Street in 1961. Continue walking and you come to Lewis's store, where Cynthia and John used to meet on their dates. To the right is the Adelphi Hotel, site of several Beatles conventions. The street branching north to the right is Mount Pleasant where, at No.64, Fred and Julia Lennon and, many years later, John and Cynthia were married. Walk left at Lewis's a short way down Ranelagh Street and you will see Great Charlotte Street to your left. Nems opened their first central record store here, opposite Blackler's store where George Harrison first worked. In front of you you will see St John's Precinct and, opposite that, Lime Street station, completing a compact, but interesting tour of the City Centre.

A green Liverpool Corporation bus will take you to other important Beatles landmarks, such as their birthplaces – 9 Madryn Street in the Liverpool 8 district (Ringo, 7 July 1940), Liverpool Maternity Hospital, Oxford Street (John, 9 October 1940), Walton General Hospital (Paul, 18 June 1942) and 12 Arnold Grove, Wavertree (George, 25 February 1943).

Ringo was to spend his youth in a small terraced house in the Dingle, at 10 Admiral Grove, near the docks. His future music partners lived in more fashionable areas, where the houses had bathrooms and the streets were tree-lined. George lived at 174 Mackets Lane, John at 251 Menlove Avenue, both in Liverpool 25, and Paul at 28 Forthlin Road, Liverpool 18. Paul and George, however, had both lived in various other houses, including council premises in the Speke area.

Ringo's schooldays must have been quite depressing, spent as they were at St Silas' Primary School and Dingle Vale Secondary Modern, both in the grimy dockland area. In recent years the docklands have witnessed major reconstruction and renovation and Ringo would hardly recognise the area – but it is still not a pretty sight. Far more picturesque is Dovedale Primary School in Dovedale Road where George and John were taught the three Rs (in different classrooms).

Of peripheral interest are the many jive hives that the Beatles played in before their Cavern debut – Litherland Town Hall, the Aintree Institute, Holyoake Hall and the rest – most of which still exist. A pilgrimage to West Derby is definitely worth the journey, for there, at Heyman's Green, you will find the Casbah, site of their first solid residency, in the basement of Mona Best's house.

A few of the larger venues that they played as their local fame grew can also still be visited – the Grafton and the Locarno (now a bingo hall) in the West Derby Road, and, of course, the lovingly reconstructed Cavern. Others have vanished forever: the Tower Ballroom, destroyed by fire in 1969; the Rialto in Upper Parliament Street, razed to the ground in the Toxteth riots of 1982, and the Mardi Gras, demolished to make way for a car-park.

Strawberry Fields children's home (recipient of a generous donation from Yoko, who visited it with Sean in 1984) still stands in Beaconsfield Road, Woolton, although I have been told it is to close as a result of cuts in the Council's grant. And Penny Lane in Allerton still boasts a barber's shop.

To Beatle buffs, Liverpool is the centre of the universe, the vibrant city which surrounded the group in their formative years and nurtured their music. If you wish to make a nostalgic trip that includes the largest number of Beatles shrines within any compact area, then the 'Pool is the place to visit.

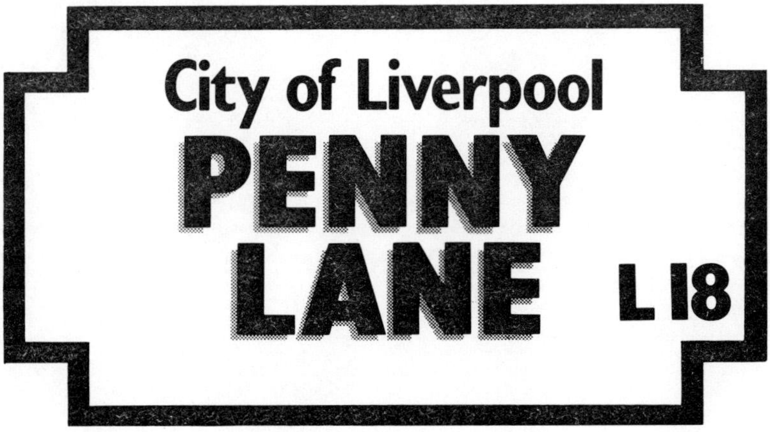

THE BEATLES SHOP
31 Mathew Street, Liverpool 2

Brothers Ian and Muir Wallace are the men with the vision behind the world's major Beatles merchandising outlet. Ian told me that he had always liked the Beatles music since the early sixties when he met them at the Queen's Hall, Leeds: "My pal's father was promoting an all-night dance and they were the headline attraction."

In the late seventies, Ian and his brother had been running a successful record shop in Liverpool: "We always sold a lot of Beatles records and there were always enquiries for Beatles merchandise, so we sent the people down to Mathew Street, but apart from Liz and Jim Hughes there was nothing there. Since we knew there was a demand, we decided to start the Beatles Shop and agreed that it had to be in Mathew Street – that's the best address in the world for selling Beatles gear.

"It took me a long time to find a suitable building. When we did, it was a six-floor warehouse, which we bought. We had to completely re-do it: there were no windows on the top three floors; we had to have a new roof fitted; and we removed 3½ tons of pigeon shit from the top two floors. The building had been an old fruit warehouse with big metal doors and a pulley, which were still there when we bought it. The basement wasn't very high (in fact your head touched the roof), so we had to dig two feet down into the floor to get headroom. We'd decided that to have the right atmosphere, the shop had to 'feel' the sixties, which wouldn't suit first or second floors – we just had to have it in the cellar and we kept all the original brick walls and

brick arches. We even spent six months looking for a 1962 juxe-box.

"To get it right, we also felt we had to have more Beatles gear than anyone else in the world. We wanted people to walk down the stairs and be confronted by such a sight they'd say "Wow, where did all this come from?" The actual shop is not very large but we have 100 different posters, 1,000 different photographs and 200 different button-badges displayed on the walls. We also stock every legitimate Beatles-related record currently on the market – and in most cases they're cheaper than they are even in record shops, and that's including the posting and packaging costs.

"Initially, I went around everywhere I knew to buy merchandise – badges, posters, magazines and stuff, which gave me a start. Then I began to buy stuff advertised in magazines, from dealers around the world. Later, I began buying negatives and manufacturing from my own design and now I've got so much stuff that other dealers buy from me.

"The top floor of the warehouse is used for mail order and we have let the others off. On the second floor there is a ladies and gents hairdressers, A Head of Hair, who do Beatle haircuts. The statue of the Beatles is in the hoist-well in the front of the building." Ian refers to the piece of sculpture situated above the doors of the shop, noticeably lifelike. It is the work of Liverpool artist David Hughes RA, who actually trained at the same art college as John Lennon (Liverpool College Of Art) before gaining entry to the Royal Academy. The statue was unveiled at a low-key ceremony on Tuesday 2 April 1984.

The range of goods is simply staggering and when I met Ian he had just arranged to have a special Beatles chess set made exclusively for the shop. He did mention, however, that he wasn't in the business of selling individual items of special memorabilia. "We're not geared for selling one-offs, although I do buy a lot of original items which are good to display in the shop. I also take a number of original one-off items to sell at Beatlefests."

The shop is a member of the North-West Tourist Board and Ian commented: "Most merchandise available in the Beatles Shop is sold mail order exclusively in the Beatles City magazines. Very many items are made exclusively for the Beatles Shop and are therefore not available elsewhere. We have always aimed to have goods of high quality at value-for-money prices.

"The future looks good as the magazine has been launched successfully and will shortly be available, not only on subscription, but through the newstands. New merchandise is being introduced constantly and always to a high standard.

"We have come a long way fast, but we hope that our shop, magazine and statue is being looked upon as a tribute to the world's greatest group."

The Beatles City Magazine

In January 1984, Ian Wallace launched his glossy publication *The Beatles City Magazine* from his address at the Beatles Shop. The publication has no specific publication dates but is issued roughly every quarter. The magazine is basically a catalogue of items available in the Beatles Shop and is very similar in style to *Elvishly Yours,* the Presley magazine/mail order catalogue. The publication also contains an order form to enable subscribers to purchase by mail order.

The magazine features several colour pages and issue No.1 is now unobtainable. Alistair Taylor, former personal assistant to Brian Epstein and general manager of Nems from 1960-1967, provides a lively column of memories, which include many previously unpublished anecdotes and stories concerning the Fab Four. Steve Phillips is the main editorial contributor, providing a 'Beatles News' round-up, with the accent on Liverpool, and a question and answer column. There is also a pen-pal section and a Beatles quiz and crossword. Copies are obtainable by post at £1.25 each.

The Beatles Shop Catalogue

Framed prints and mirrors

A1 John Lennon mirror	2.95
A2 Autographed Beatles mirror	2.95
A9-A12 Beatles framed colour print	1.95

Badges

B1 1″ button badges, new Beatles designs (set of five)	1.95
B2 Ringo Starr 1″ badges (set of five)	1.95
B3 George Harrison 1″ badges (set of five)	1.95
B4 Paul McCartney 1″ badges, new designs (set of five)	1.95
B5 John Lennon 1″ badges, new designs (set of five)	1.95
B6 Metal pin badges (set of three)	1.95
B7 Pair of metal Beatles guitar badges	1.50
B9 New set of four Yellow Submarine 1″ badges	1.95

Key-rings and fobs/sew-on patches

DPI Exact replica in enamel of street signs	2.50
DP2 Enamel street-sign key-rings	1.25
DP3 Large Abbey Road enamel street sign	17.50
DK6 Pair of Beatles metal key-fobs	2.95
D1 Pack of four sew-on patches	2.50
D4 Authentic copy of original fan club sew-on patch	1.25
D5 Sgt. Pepper sew-on patch	1.00

Stationery

S1 Set of eight street names postcards	1.25
S2 Set of eight Beatles photo postcards	1.50
S4 Three greetings cards, blank	1.50
S5 Beatles ballpens (set of three)	1.95
S7 Beatles letterheads, ten sheets of writing paper plus six envelopes	.75
S8 1968 *Yellow Submarine* pop-up book, made in USA	12.50
S9 Beatles Shop book-matches	.75
S10 Colour postcards, imported from France, large	2.95
S11 Wooden paper-weight with all four faces finished in gold or silver	4.95
S12 Magnificent desk pen set, marble-type base	6.95

Clothing

K1	Woollen Beatles scarf	2.95
K2	Beatles wristband	1.95
K3	Beatles headband	2.50
K4	Beatles boots, absolutely original in design, black leather or suede, sizes 6-11	29.50
K5	Beatles panties, two pairs	2.50
K6	Delux tie, commemorating Beatles twentieth anniversary, various designs	2.95
K7	Autographed satin square	2.95
K8	Beatles sun visor	3.50
K9	Black long-sleeved, V-neck jumper with Beatles logo (32″-44″)	10.95
	Slip-over in same design (32″-44″)	10.25
K10	Satin scarf	1.75
K11	Sgt. Pepper satin jacket with silver or gold braid, various colours available (S, M, L)	34.95
K13	Round-neck, collarless, medium-grey Beatles jacket, edged in velvet, (32″-44″)	34.95

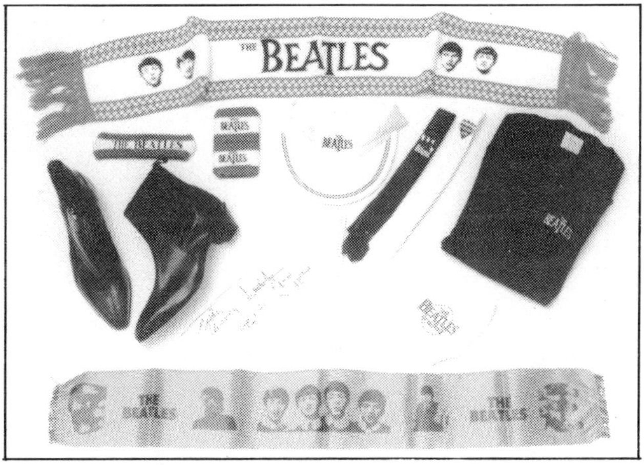

K14	Black cord Lennon cap (S, M, L)	7.50
K15	New design top quality mirror or black Lennon glasses	4.95
K16	Rectangular black sunglasses	4.95

T-shirts and sweat shirts 4.50/7.25

J1 Four heads on dark shirt
J2 Let It Be design
J5 Sgt. Pepper full colour
J6 The Official Beatles Shop, Liverpool
J8 Small John Lennon motif
J9 Twist And Shout
J10 Working Class Hero (new design)
J11 Small Paul McCartney motif
J12 Yellow Submarine
J15 The Beatles logo
J16 Large Beatles Forever
J18 Large designs with autographs
J19 Beatles, Liverpool, England, with Union Jack flag
J21 John Lennon – Bag One
J22 Lennon – All You Need Is Love
J23 John, George, Paul, Ringo
J24 The Cavern
J25 Abbey Road
J26 Beatles heads and autographs on left breast
J27 A Hard Day's Night

Photos

	Colour photo 10″ × 8″ in presentation wallet	3.25
L1	1964 Christmas show	
L2	In Paris	
L3	From *Help!*	
L4	Paul in the studio	
L5	John in the studio	
L6	At the seaside	
L7	The Beatles	
L8	'All You Need Is Love'	
L9	TV show special	
L10	Ringo	
L20	Set of five colour photos, 5½″ × 3″	3.25
	Set A Comedy shots	
	Set B Psychedelic shots	
	Set C Studio poses	
	Set D Lennon, mixed	
	Set E Around the world	
	Set F Paul	
	Set G Concert shots	
	Set H TV specials	
	Set I Seaside fun	
	Set J New York and Paris	
	Set K Sixties Lennon	
	Set L Lennon solo	
	Set M John and famous people	
	Set N John and Yoko	
	Set O John at the movies	
	Set P Paul solo	
	Set Q Group poses	
	Set R Candid Beatles	
	Set S Beatles with the famous	
	Set T Ringo (I)	
L21	Set of six black-and-white photos, 10″ × 8″	4.95
	Set A John	
	Set B George	
	Set C Paul	
	Set D Ringo	
	Set E Beatles	
	Set F Beatles on tour	
	Set G Beatles in USA	
	Set H Beatles in late sixties	

Bits and pieces

Bub 1	Sixteen mini US album covers, containing bubblegum; imported, set of four	2.50
P1	Beatles pennant	1.95
P3	Bag tag double-sided with photos, Beatles signatures and all the famous Liverpool place-names, printed with your name on	2.95
P4	Set of three car or window stickers	1.50
P5	Two sticks of Beatles rock	.95
P6	Black-and-white Beatles bag with autographs (plus free bag tag personalised with your name)	7.95
P7	Beatles jigsaw puzzles, set of three	3.95
P9	Apple bag with Union Jack in centre	4.95
P10	Beatles comb with full colour picture – two assorted	.95
P12	Hardback notebook with colour picture of John on the cover	3.00
P13	Small colour photograph mounted in black frame	3.95

Jewellery

Q1	Photo-rings	2.50
Q2	Beatles double photo-locket on chain	2.75

Q3	Lapel or tie-pin with Beatle photo	2.50
Q4	Beautiful envelope necklace with your favourite Beatle inside	2.50
Q5	Photo earrings	2.50
Q6	Sparkling Beatles brooch or tie-pin	2.95
Q7	Sparkling Beatles necklace	3.50
Q8	Beatles necklace with John, Paul, George and Ringo's names on	2.95
Q9	Original sixties Beatles necklace	1.95
Q11	Digital watch, plays two Beatles tunes, gents style	36.95
Q12	Digital watch, as above, for ladies	31.95

LP clocks

N2	Unique Sgt. Pepper clock with quartz movement	16.95
N3	Timeless 1 picture disc clock with quartz movement	16.95
N4	Timeless II picture disc clock with quartz movement	16.95
N36	Silver Beatles clock with quartz movement	16.95
N37	New release silver Beatles clock	16.95

Singles clocks

N32	I Want To Hold Your Hand, 7" picture disc clock, quartz movement	8.95
N33	Love Me Do, 7" picture disc clock, quartz movement	8.95
N38	Timeless 2½, 7" picture disc clock	8.95
N39	Help! 7" picture disc clock	8.95

Square framed clocks

N34	Let It Be	9.95
N35	Abbey Road	9.95
N28	Street sign (Beatle Street or Abbey Road)	1.50

Wood blocks in natural pine

N14	John	2.20
N15	Lennon	3.30
N16	George	3.30
N17	Ringo	2.75
N18	Paul	2.20
N19	Beatles	3.75

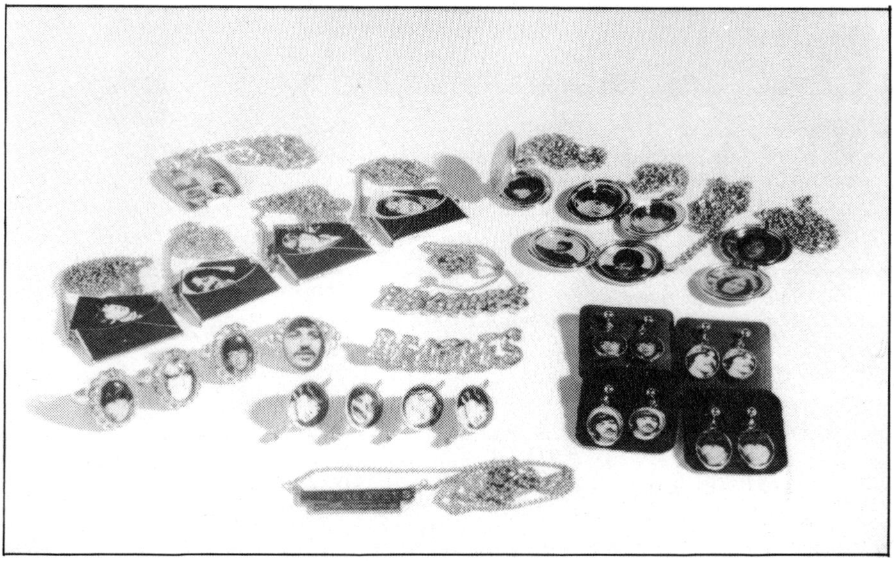

Household items

N38 Colour wall hanging, complete with hanger, 16″ × 16″	2.95
A Beatles heads	
B Yellow Submarine	
C John, All You Need Is Love	
D Abbey Road	
E Liverpool, England	
N21 Paper-weight, commemorating the Beatles at the Cavern 1962	6.95
N22 Beatles ashtray	1.95
N23 Set of six half-pint glass tankards	8.95
N24 Single duvet cover with the fab four	19.95
N25 Beatles pillow-case. Also individual John, George, Paul, Ringo available	3.50
N27 Real satin Beatles cushion	3.25

Posters

Sent in protective tube	2.95 each
R1 John, an art poster	
R2 Colour Beatles collage	
R4 Alistair Taylor's shot of John in Greece, exclusive	
R5 John, Rockers by Bob Gruen	
R6 Colour poster of 1963 Beatles show	
R8 Beatles at the London Palladium	
R9 An early poster of John	
R11 US import in full psychedelic colour	
R12 John and Yoko, Rockers by Bob Gruen	
R13 Early TV studio shot in colour	
R14 A famous Beatles pose in black-and-white	
R16 Beatles getting ready for a show	
R18 All four faces in psychedelic colour on flock paper	
R19 Full colour stage shot of the Beatles	
R20 Black-and-white shot of John	
R22 John, collage	

Beatle coffee mugs

Sent in polystyrene container	1.95
M1 The Beatles Shop logo	
M3 The original sixties Cavern design	
M6 Abbey Road – the original sign	
M7 Sgt Pepper's Lonely Hearts	
M8 Yellow Submarine	
M9 I Love Liverpool	
M10 Tug Of War – the original album promotion design	

Beatle graphics

A range of blank greeting cards, with Beatles song titles in full colour on front, with envelopes, 24 designs – two cards	1.50

Sweaters

Exclusively designed thick, woolly, round-neck sweaters in three woven designs (S, M, L, XL)	25.00
Jump 1: Help! design in navy blue	
Jump 2: John, Paul, George & Ringo across the front (white lettering on black)	
Jump 3: Yellow Submarine in blue, and small sub on sleeve	

Beatles calendar

Exclusive 1985 calender with full colour photographs	3.50

Royal Doulton mugs

Hand-made, hand-decorated Royal Doulton figure mugs, 5½″ high. Exclusive Beatles figures modelled by Stanley James Taylor. Set of four	89.50

Videos

F1 McCartney Rockshow	21.00
F2 Lennon – A Legend (includes his last interview)	31.00
F3 The Compleat Beatles	24.95
F4 The Rutles	24.95
F5 A Hard Days Night	31.00
F6 Ready Steady Go! Vol 1	21.00
F7 Ready Steady Go! Vol 2	21.00
F8 The Beatles Live, 20 minutes	17.50

With all videos add £2.00 to cover insurance. Please state system, VHS or Beta. No videos suitable for US

Cavern club membership card

A limited-edition replica of the original 1962 membership card. Each one carries the original numbers and space is left for you to put your name and address 2.50

Bronze figures

A set of cold-cast bronze figures of John, George, Paul and Ringo, 5″ tall

The Set	95.00
Individual figure	25.00

Books and magazines

The Beatles Shop has a range of approximately 70 different titles of Beatles books and magazines available.

Beatles Monthly magazines can also be obtained. Issues 1-103 (excluding 2, 8, 9, 13, 14 and 15), any three	2.95
Beatles Now, a bi-monthly, issues 1-13 available	1.00

Records and cassettes

The shop also has a large range of Beatles records and cassettes available, approximately 22 different records, including boxed sets, picture-discs and albums of the Mersey Beat groups.

All prices quoted by the Beatles Shop are inclusive of postage, packing and VAT. Ian Wallace makes these suggestions if you wish to order goods:

1 Make sure your name and address are written clearly.
2 Check the prices and total amounts.
3 Make all cheques and postal orders payable to Beatles City Magazine, ensuring all details are correct, including date.
4 Remember to send your payment with the order.
5 Allow 21 days for delivery of your order in the UK and Europe (USA – see paragraph 13). If by chance you have not received your order by then, please write giving as many details as possible.

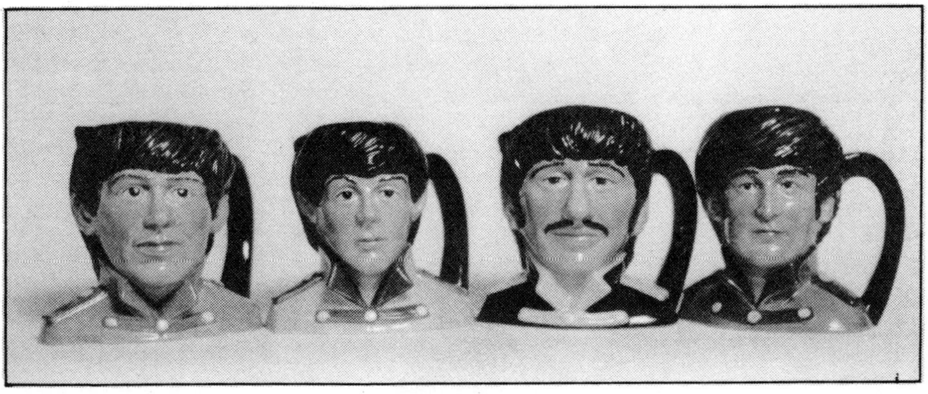

6 If when you receive your goods you have any queries, please inform us as soon as possible.
7 Never send bank notes through the post, unless in an official Post Office registered envelope.
8 Overseas orders must be in pounds sterling and 25 per cent added to total amount to cover extra postage charges.
9 Republic of Ireland orders should be in pounds sterling. However, Eire postal orders can be accepted provided 25 per cent has been added to cover exchange rates. Eire cheques will not be accepted.
10 All orders are sent by certified mail.
11 All US orders are acknowledged by airmail. Payment in dollar bank draft, postal or money orders payable to Beatles City Magazine as listed prices. No personal cheques please, only certified cheques, plus 30 per cent extra for airmail.
12 Credit card orders – full numbers plus card expiry date.
13 USA orders allow four weeks for delivery from our despatch date quoted on your airmail card.

THE BEATLES BAZAAR
55 Breck Road, Liverpool L4 2QS

1985 has been a year of change for the Beatles Bazaar. The company moved from Tynwald Hill, where it had been based for several years and has now settled in Breck Road, Anfield, just opposite the Cabbage Hall pub, only five minutes from the City Centre.

The company has also decided to specialize in the production of T-shirts. The Bazaar originally sold a range of items from pillow-cases to bags, but Dave Finler tells me: "In the past we sold a whole range of Beatles souvenirs, but from now on we will be specialising in T-shirts of which we have over 50 different designs. The price this year (1985) will be £4.25 plus 50p p&p per T-shirt and £8.25 plus 50p p&p for each sweatshirt. They are all top-quality garments and carry a full money-back guarantee if you are not satisfied. People can order by sending a cheque or postal order to the above address."

THE BEATLES' LONDON

There are no organised tours in London equivalent to those provided in Liverpool by the County Council. Beatles fans wishing to visit London sites with a Beatles association are advised to make their own arrangements. In the January and February 1980 issues of *Beatles Monthly,* I contributed a two-part series called 'The Beatles' London', which was an aid to those fans wishing to trek around the big city. I have updated and added to the articles in the following information guide.

The first important London date for the Fab Four took place on 1 January 1962. Decca A&R man Mike Smith had accepted Brian Epstein's invitation to see the Beatles at the Cavern in Liverpool and, as a result, authorised a recording audition. The group cut approximately fifteen numbers, including 'To Know Her Is To Love Her' 'Memphis, Tennessee'; 'Love Of The Loved'; 'Hello Little Girl'; 'Money'; 'Three Cool Cats'; "Till There Was You'; 'Please Mr Postman'; 'Red Sails In The Sunset'; 'Like Dreamers Do'; 'The Shiek Of Araby' and 'What'd I Say'. Some writers have suggested that Brian Epstein requested them not to play any of their own compositions, but there were three Lennon and McCartney numbers cut during the sessions, which have been available on various bootleg albums.

Unfortunately, Mike Smith's enthusiasm for the group didn't cut any ice with his boss Dick Rowe who turned them down. Then Brian Epstein sent me a telegram: "Have secured contract for Beatles to record for EMI on Parlophone label 1st recording date set for 6 June." That was their first session at Abbey Road studios (in No.3 studio) where they were to spend so much of their recording life. On Tuesday 4 September 1962, they flew down to London, without Pete Best, to record with George Martin at Abbey Road's No.2 studio.

The Beatles were also to find themselves in film, radio and TV studios in London on dozens of occasions over the years. Their first radio and TV appearances had, in fact, been in Manchester – radio shows at the Playhouse Theatre and Granada TV's *People And Places* (even *Top Of The Pops* was filmed in Manchester, only moving to London later in the sixties). But they soon found themselves bustling from one London studio to another to record such shows as *Saturday Club, Top Gear, Talent Spot, From Us to You,* and *Easy Beat.* They even had their own BBC radio series *Pop Go The Beatles.*

However, apart from the filming of concerts at the Palladium and Wembley, and some *Ready, Steady, Go!* shows for Rediffusion TV, London didn't dominate television pop music then. In addition to their London-based shows, the Beatles guested on shows televised from the ABC, Blackpool, did some specials for Granada TV, some documentaries on the road, made their *Top Of The Pops* appearances from Manchester and their *Thank Your Lucky Stars* gigs from ABC TV's studios in Birmingham.

As far as their live tour and concert appearances are concerned, I have limited the following list to venues in central London.

During 1963 they appeared at the ABC, Croydon on 23 March and at the *New Musical Express* Poll Winner's Concert at the Empire Pool, Wembley on 28 April (the same venue and occasion being the scene of their last major British appearance on 1 May 1966). They also appeared that year at the Granada, Walthamstow (24 May); Granada, Tooting (1 June); Fairfield Hall, Croydon (7 September); London Palladium (13 October); Prince of Wales Theatre (4 November); Grosvenor House (2 December); Palace Ballroom, Wimbledon (14 December) and Finsbury Park Astoria (24 December-11 January 1964)

The London Palladium gig was the setting for their triumphant *Sunday Night at the London Palladium* ATV show, televised live. They performed 'I Want To Hold Your

Hand'; 'This Boy'; 'All My Loving'; 'Money' and 'Twist And Shout', and hit the headlines of the national newspapers the next day, firmly establishing themselves as the new British phenomenon. The Prince of Wales appearance was a Royal Command Performance attended by the Queen Mother and Princess Margaret; it was televised and screened on 10 November. The Grosvenor House gig was a Charity performance in aid of Spastics. Their Wimbledon show was the special Southern Fan Club Convention attended by over 3,000 fans. The short season at Finsbury Park was the occasion of 'The Beatles Christmas Show' and artists on the bill included fellow Liverpudlians Tommy Quickly, Billy J Kramer and Cilla Black. Rolf Harris and the Barron Knights were also among the guests.

World tours and numerous TV and radio appearances throughout 1964 limited their live London shows during the year. They appeared at the London Palladium (12 January); Empire Pool, Wembley (26 April); Prince of Wales Theatre (31 May); London Palladium (23 July); Granada, Walthamstow (24 October); Finsbury Park Astoria (1 November) and Odeon Hammersmith (24 December–12 January 1965). The first Palladium appearance was their second ATV *Sunday Night at the London Palladium* show, the second a special charity show called 'The Night Of 100 Stars' in which fellow guests included Sir Laurence Olivier, Max Bygraves and Shirley Bassey. The Empire Pool concert saw them take the *NME* Poll Winner's prize for the second time.

The Walthamstow and Finsbury Park gigs were part of their fifth British concert tour in which they were supported by Mary Wells, Michael Haslam, the Rustiks, Sounds Incorporated and Liverpool friends Tommy Quickly and the Remo Four.

The Beatles Christmas Show at Hammersmith had a supporting cast of Jimmy Savile, Mike Cotton Sound, Yardbirds, Freddie and the Dreamers, Elkie Brooks and Ray Fell. Among the numbers the Beatles performed were: 'She's A Woman'; 'I'm A Loser'; 'Everybody's Trying To Be My Baby'; 'Baby's In Black'; 'Honey Don't'; 'A Hard Day's Night'; 'I Feel Fine'; 'Twist and Shout' and 'Long Tall Sally.'

1965 saw only three live London shows. On 11 April they made their third appearance in the *NME* Poll Winner's Concert at the Empire Pool, Wembley, an occasion which was filmed by ATV and screened on 18 and 25 April. The Odeon, Hammersmith (10 December) and Finsbury Park Astoria (11 December) appearances were both part of the sixth British concert tour, when their support acts included the Moody Blues, the Paramounts and Liverpool acts Steve Aldo, Beryl Marsden and the Koobas. Within a matter of months they made their final live concert appearance in Britain as the Beatles at the *NME* Poll Winners Concert at Wembley.

The Beatles' first trips to London found them staying at hotels in the Bloomsbury area, such as the President in Russell Square, WC1. Brian Epstein then decided to move his offices to the capital and opened a branch of Nems Enterprises in Argyle

Street, W1, next to the London Palladium. The headquarters of the Beatles Fan Club was later established at 13 Monmouth Street, WC2, near Cambridge Circus.

Within an area a couple of square miles wide there are numerous sites a Beatlefan might visit. Close to Monmouth Street is Shaftsbury Avenue, site of the former Saville Theatre, which Brian bought as a venue for concerts. The Avenue leads to Piccadilly Circus where you will find the London Pavilion, the cinema in which the Beatles film premières were held. Almost opposite the Pavilion is the Prince of Wales Theatre where the group made several live appearances. From the Circus, a short walk up Regent Street leads to Savile Row where, at No.3, the Apple empire had its base. Not far away at 94 Baker Street was the Apple Boutique which once sported the giant mural designed by the Fool (three Dutch artists) and painted by 40 helpers, the gaudiness of which caused an outcry among local traders. Above the boutique were the offices of Apple Music.

A few hundred yards away, at 95 Wigmore Street, was the building where the original Apple office was established prior to the move to Savile Row. Running north from that street is Wimpole Street where Jane Asher's parents lived. Paul stayed in their house for a time during the sixties when he was courting Jane. A mile further west is the Royal Lancaster Hotel in Bayswater Road, overlooking Hyde Park. Beneath the hotel is a discothèque which was formerly the Yellow Submarine, a club which the Beatles attended following the première of their cartoon film.

Within the area I've described were the various clubs which the Beatles frequented during their club-going days. Initially they were members of the Ad Lib Club in Leicester Street, off Leicester Square, one of the original 'in' clubs of the Swinging Sixties. Another 'in' club was the Scotch of St James, in Mason's Yard, near Jermyn Street. Another club of note was the Bag O' Nails, which opened in Kingley Street (behind Liberty's department store in Regent Street) in the mid-sixties, where Paul originally met Linda.

When Brian Epstein and his boys moved into the big city, they initially lived in central London. John, Cynthia and Julian moved into a flat at 13 Emperor's Gate, Knightsbridge. Paul remained at the Asher's house at 57 Wimpole Street before buying his own house at 7 Cavendish Avenue, St John's Wood. George and Ringo lived at Whaddon House in William Mews and Ringo also rented a flat in Montague Square. Brian Epstein bought a house at 12 Chapel Street, Belgravia, and later a mansion at Kingsley Hall, near Heathfield, Sussex. Following the tremendous success of their American trip, the boys began to buy luxury houses in the stockbroker belt of Weybridge, Surrey. John and family moved into Kenwood, a house in Cavendish Road, Weybridge, while Ringo spent £35,000 on Sunny Heights, a pleasant residence in St George's Road, Weybridge. George moved into a luxury bungalow in Claremont Drive, Esher.

THE THEATRE MUSEUM
Victoria and Albert Museum, London SW7 2RL

The Theatre Museum, a branch of the Victoria and Albert Museum, will be moving to Covent Garden late in 1986.

In 1980 Danny Friedman filled me in on the background to future plans, particularly the Beatles aspect of the Museum: "The idea of having a specific Beatles exhibition at some stage evolved almost accidentally, in that news about my attempts to expand our items relating to the Beatles got into the press, since when

I've been inundated with donations and offers of loans. Though it was always planned to exhibit some of our Beatles material as part of the Pop Collection when we opened, I now have the makings of what could be a very exciting exclusive exhibition.

"The address of the Theatre Museum will be the Flower Market, Covent Garden. The idea for the Beatles exhibition is mine (and the fans!) though the setting up of the Pop Collection is the work of my predecessors, especially Lola Michael, who started the collection, and the present Curator, Alexander Schouvaloff.

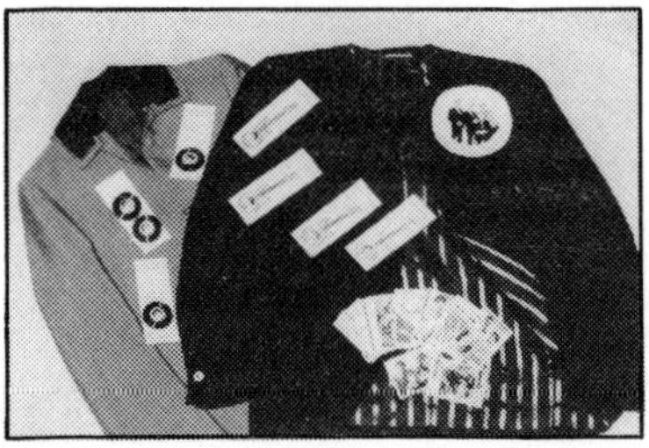

"The development of the Beatles Collection (and of the Pop Collection as a whole) is largely dictated by the amount of material available. Our policy is to expand our own collection, so we prefer donations to loans. Apart from obviously wanting to build up a national Pop Collection, loans raise all sorts of insurance problems, and are not usually considered, except on a short term basis for exhibitions.

"Specifically on the Beatles, we have: six early stage suits, 1963-64, worn by John Lennon and Ringo Starr; a number of programmes from early concerts, in Britain and abroad, some of them autographed, and tickets for the concerts; early adverts for the Beatles at the Cavern; and literally thousands of press-cuttings, including some uncut issues of *Mersey Beat.* Dezo Hoffmann has offered some of his photographs, a lot of which are unpublished. We also have much of the fan club material, a nearly complete set of *Beatles Monthly,* and many books; much of the range of promotional material which came out in the sixties (stockings, wigs, badges, plates, bowls, bubblegum cards etc), and offers of loans of more. We also have the uniforms worn by the usherettes at the première of *A Hard Day's Night,* which are Beatles mini-dresses in various colours, and the Beatle-covered wall hangings that formed part of the decor of the cinema.

"The majority of the material came from the fans, except the stage suits which were donated via Apple.

"There are major gaps in the actual properties used and owned by the Beatles, such as instruments and costumes. I'd love to get hold of the Sgt. Pepper costumes for example. I also need more documents and letters relating to their career."

Danny left the museum in November 1984 and Leela Meinertas took his place. Since Danny originally wrote to me, various auctions have spotlit original Beatles documents and souvenirs, pushing them beyond the limited financial resources of the museum.

Leela writes: "The final content of the displays has not been decided for the twentieth century but I am certain there will be at least one thing – probably John Lennon's jacket – in the permanent display. The rest of the Beatles collection will be stored but accessible to those who wish to see things. Hopefully, it will be part of the archive collections, at least the paper things: mags, photographs, programmes etc. It may be more difficult with the three dimensional material.

"I am not entirely sure yet, but we may have to operate an appointment system as we do at the V&A.

"We have not really acquired anything outstanding to add to the Beatles material over the last few years. The last thing was a set of tiles, with the usual early Beatles images of John, Paul, George and Ringo. We have plates and other bits in the same range. I bought them at the recent Rock and Pop sale at Sotheby's. Unfortunately, the George Harrison guitar was out of our price range."

ABBEY ROAD STUDIOS
3 Abbey Road, St John's Wood, London NW8

Because of its Beatle associations, Abbey Road is recognized as the most famous recording studio in the world; but in fact this EMI recording complex has always been the home of hit records, producing a stream of No.1 recordings since charts first appeared in 1952. The premises initially became a recording studio in 1929 when it was purchased by the Gramophone Company, which eventually evolved into EMI Records.

The entire history of the studio has been documented in a highly entertaining book *Abbey Road,* first published by Patrick Stephens Limited of Bar Hill, Cambridge CB3 8EL, in 1982. The book was written by EMI executive Brian Southall, who is an authority on Beatles recordings.

Of tremendous interest to Beatles enthusiasts was the 'Beatles At Abbey Road' event which took place between 18 July and 11 September 1983. The No.2 Studio, where the Beatles recorded between 1962 and 1969, was opened to the public and a compilation video of their recording career was shown.

However, there are no plans to repeat the event and there are no longer any souvenirs to be purchased. Now under the general managership of Ken Townsend, Abbey Road concentrates on its activities as a busy recording studio and does not offer access to visitors at the moment – Beatles enthusiasts will have to make do with taking photographs of the exterior. A few yards from the studios is the most photographed zebra-crossing in the world, that which was immortalised on the cover of the *Abbey Road* album.

The *Abbey Road* cover photograph was taken by Iain Macmillan at approximately 10am on 8 August 1969: He was to comment: "It was a nerve-racking experience. I had never met all four Beatles together before that day. I had to climb up a step-ladder in the middle of the road to take the shot and a friendly policeman held up the traffic for me. Surprisingly there was no great gathering of fans, most people hardly seemed to take any notice."

Interestingly enough, one of the first Beatles-related auctions took place at the studios. The auctioneers Phillips, Son & Neale presented their 'Sale Of The Century' at Abbey Road Studios on Thursday 16 October 1980. Among the items for sale were: a pair of Studer J37 4-track tape recorders used by the Beatles on *Sergeant Pepper;* the loudspeaker used on the Beatles EMI audition by Paul McCartney; Mellotron tape organ used by the Beatles on various recordings, with original tapes; metal positive ('silver disc') with original Beatles signatures; a standing brass ashtray used by Ringo Starr on EMI sessions; and a roll of loo paper stamped 'EMI Ltd', the last one of a batch rejected by the Beatles.

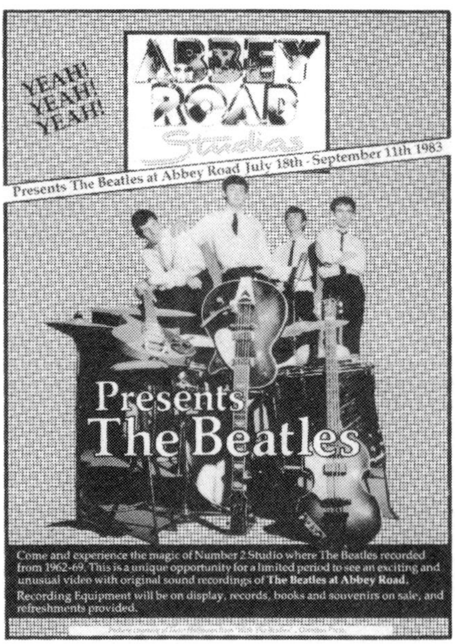

THE CONVENTIONS

THE MERSEY BEATLE CONVENTIONS

The first real Beatles convention in Britain took place in London at Alexandra Palace, on the weekend of 18-19 December 1976. Former Cavern DJ Bob Wooler, was Master of Ceremonies, assisted by Peter Lord; other DJs included Tony Prince, Roger Scott and Paul Gambaccini. Special guest was Allan Williams, and groups included Gerry and the Pacemakers, Faron's Flamingos and Abbey Road. There was an exhibition of Stuart Sutcliffe's works, which were on sale for as little as £40 a painting, a Beatle flea-market and several other events. Low attendance figures ensured the event was not repeated.

However, the following year, Allan Williams and Bob Wooler ran Liverpool's first Beatles convention, with the financial help of Ron Jones. It took place at Mr Pickwick's club in Fraser Street on the week-end of 8-9 October 1977, was organised along similar lines to the London event – groups, competitions and film shows – and proved to be a modest success, encouraging Allan and Bob to stage a further convention the next year. With the rather cumbersome title of 'The Year Of The Liverpool Beatles Statue Festival 1978', the convention was again held at Mr Pickwick's club, on Saturday 15 July from noon until 2am and on Sunday 16 July from 10am until 1am to commemorate the commissioning of the Beatles statue to be sculpted by Brian Burgess. A flea-market, a Beatle ballet, a Magical Mystery Tour around Liverpool, performances by local groups and a visit to Brian Burgess at his studio (where he was working on the model for his statute) were all part of the entertainment laid on.

Allan Williams organised one more convention at the Top Rank Ballroom in St John's Precinct, but it turned out to be a frustrated affair: the series of Beatles films that were advertised as being the main attraction of the event, to be shown in nearby cinemas, didn't materialise. Furthermore, the under-16s who had paid their convention fees were refused admittance to the main venue after eight o'clock because alcohol was on sale.

The next major conventions were organised by Liz and Jim Hughes of Cavern Mecca. The first, called 'Mersey Beatle', was held at the Adelphi Hotel, Lime Street, on Saturday 29 August 1981, and was part-financed by sponsorship arranged by Ron Jones. Master of Ceremonies was Bob Wooler again, who welcomed conventioneers at 10am. The dealers' room, with bar, was opened and a film was shown in one of the rooms. In another, the band Mojo Filter, who specialize in Beatle numbers, performed. Speeches by Tony Tyler, co-author of *The Beatles Illustrated Record,* Brian Southall of EMI, and Philip Norman, author of *Shout*, were separated by disco intervals and a performance by the Profumo Affair. Another film was screened in a side-hall and at five o'clock the Grand Final of the Beatle Brain Competition and Raffle Draw was held. The evening continued with performances by the Federals, the Skitters and Broadway, the unveiling of Allan Curran's statue of John Lennon, another film, another disco and a second appearance by the Profumo Affair. Finally a 'goodnight talk' brought the one-day event to an end at midnight.

The second 'Mersey Beatle Extravaganza' was a two-day affair which took place on the weekend of 28-29 August 1982. The Adelphi Hotel once again played host to the conventioneers and the theme of the occasion was the twentieth anniversary of 'Love Me Do'. This presented a mixture of guest speakers, special guests, films, videos (in two separate rooms), live music, quizzes and competitions, expert panels, exhibitions and a flea-market.

The Cavern was the theme of the third convention at the Adelphi, a three-day event (27-29 August 1983) with Bob Wooler again as MC, Stephen Baker as quiz-master and Ron Jones co-presenter and DJ. Groups included Mojo Filter, Avion and Cavern; the film and video shows were organised by Fenno Werkman and the main guests were Pete Shotton and members of John Lennon's first group, the Quarrymen. Other guests included former Cavern owner Ray McFall, photographer Les Chadwick, and myself; panel-experts included Mark Lewisohn and Joel Glazier, and various special guests, such as Charles Lennon and Pat Delaney, were to be found roving around.

Saturday 27th, Sunday 28th, Monday 29th August.

We request the pleasure of your company at this year's Beatles Convention as our Special Guests.

M*E*R*S*E*Y
*B*E*A*T*L*E*
*** EXTRAVAGANZA ***
1983
Britannia ★ Adelphi Hotel, Liverpool.

From Jim and Liz,
"Cavern Mecca", 18, Mathew Street,
Liverpool, L2 6RE, Merseyside. R.S.V.P.
Tel: 051 - 227 1026. Mon. to Sat. 10-30 to 5-00 p.m.

The fourth annual Cavern Mecca Beatles Convention took place at St George's Hall, Lime Street on Sunday 26 August 1984 from 11am to 11pm. Bob Wooler and Ron Jones shared the MC duties and Fenno Werkman once again handled the film and video shows. Groups included Faron's Flamingos, Karl Terry and the Cruisers, Mojo Filter, Beryl Marsden and the Premiers; star guests were Tony Barrow, Ray McFall, Mike McCartney and Ray Coleman. Special guests included Johnny 'Guitar' Byrne, Pat Delaney, Charles Lennon, Spencer Leigh and Father Tom McKenzie.

Liz and Jim Hughes obviously found running the conventions too much of a strain on top of their work-filled days at Cavern Mecca itself and the many other Beatles events that they have been producing in Liverpool for several years, almost singlehanded and without adequate financial support. As from 1985 the Mersey Beatles Conventions are to be run jointly by Ron Jones at the Merseyside CC and Beatle City, although Liz and Jim will be on hand to offer their expertise in an advisory capacity. The first event under the new management is to be held during the first-ever Beatles Festival Week which is to run from Friday 23 August to Friday 30 August 1985 (eight days in this week!) Apart from the two-day convention, there is to be a series of special events, including a Cavern party night and a Beat Music cruise on the *Royal Iris.*

Beatles Conventions are now held regularly in several other countries, including America, Japan and Holland. Souvenirs and memorabilia are to be found in abundance at the various dealers' stands and in special auctions. Items for auction at the 6th Annual New York Beatlefest in 1980, for instance, included a gold record of *With The Beatles*, a plaster-cast face mask of Ringo used for the Ognir Rats character in the 1978 TV special *Ringo*, a hand-made Blue Meanie puppet and a silk tie of Ringo's.

BEATLEFEST

As an example of the type of events which take place at Beatles conventions, I shall quote excerpts from the promotional literature for Beatlefest '83 at the Meadowlands Hilton in New Jersey.

"**Beatles Films and Videos.** Beatlefest '83 features more than 50 Beatles films dating back to the Cavern Club in 1962. This year, with special thanks to film producer Walter Shenson (a guest at Beatlefest '81), we will once again be showing everyone's favourite Beatles movie, *A Hard Day's Night*. Of course, we will continue to show all the other features: *Help!, Yellow Submarine, Let It Be, Magical Mystery Tour,* plus *Concerts of the Beatles at Shea Stadium, Washington Coliseum* and *Tokyo*; promotional videos such as *Hey Jude, Revolution, Strawberry Fields Forever, Give Peace A Chance, Mull Of Kintyre, Crackerbox Palace, Only You*; and newsreels, documentaries, Beatles cartoons etc. In addition there are many new surprises in the six Beatles video rooms, where we will be showing nearly 30 hours of non-stop Beatles videos (mostly from the outstanding collection of Ron Cuoco), including *The Beatles In Paris 1965, The Beatles In Melbourne 1964,* promotional videos of *Hello Goodbye, Ballad Of John And Yoko, We Can Work It Out, Imagine, Helen Wheels,* the first four *Ed Sullivan Show* appearances, and much more.

"**Special Guests.** We are very proud to be presenting Pete Shotton and Nicholas Schaffner as our special guests. Pete and Nick have co-authored a brand new book called *John Lennon: In My Life*. Pete's association with the Beatles dates back to his school-days when he was pals with John. John and Pete were the founding (and only two) members of the Quarrymen in 1957. This is the group that Paul and later George joined, and the rest is history! Pete's long-standing friendship with John continued: he became John's personal assistant for a few years and, later, director of Apple Retail. He is still good friends with George. Nick has appeared at many Beatlefests and has three previous Beatles or Beatles-related books to his credit: *The Beatles Forever, The Boys from Liverpool* and *The British Invasion*. Our Master of Ceremonies, WPJL's Jimmy Fink, has expanded his horizons greatly since the last show. Jimmy is now the producer of the nationally syndicated radio programme, *Rolling Stone's Continuous History of Rock and Roll.*

BEATLEFEST '84—20th ANNIVERSARY SHIRTS *AND MORE!*

ALL BEATLEFEST '84 DESIGNS ARE SILKSCREENED ON HIGH QUALITY SHIRTS, MADE IN THE U.S.A.

A & D*-$7.00 - 50 poly/50 cotton Adults S, M, L, XL
B & C -$7.00 - 100% cotton Adults S, M, L, XL
E & F -$13.00 - 50/50 Adults S, M, L, XL
G - $4.50 - 50/50 Childs XS(2-4), S(6-8)
H - $7.00 - 50/50 Childs T 1-2, T 3-4, S(6-8)
I & J*-$10.00 - 50 poly/50 cotton Adults S, M, L, XL

*D & J also available in Childs M(10-12) and L(14-16) with Adults size design

FROM LYRIC ART
K - 1984 BEATLES CALENDAR
12 Color illustrations inspired by Beatles songs. Suitable for framing.
Orig. $8.95 **ONLY $5.00**
While they last!

36 Different Greeting Cards sold in three sets of 12
L - $10.00-12 Cards (#101-112)
M - $10.00-12 Cards (#113-124)
N - $10.00-12 Cards (#125-136)
LMN - $27.00-All 3 sets (36 Cards)

TO ORDER BY MAIL:
USE ENCLOSED FORM OR JUST SPECIFY ITEMS & SEND CHECK, MONEY ORDER, OR CREDIT CARD INFO (CARD #, EXPIRATION DATE & SIGNATURE)
TO:
BEATLEFEST '84
P.O. BOX 436
WESTWOOD, NJ
07675

PHONE ORDERS (CREDIT CARD ONLY) **CALL TOLL FREE: 1-800-B E A T L E S** IN NJ-(201) 666-5450

SHIPPING CHARGES: $1.50-ANY ONE ITEM. 50¢-EACH ADDITIONAL ITEM.

"Live 'Beatles' Music by Liverpool. Ever since Beatlefest first began in 1974, each evening has been highlighted by a live concert of Beatles music. We have been very fortunate to have found the very finest of Beatles sound-alike bands – Liverpool. They've played at every Beatlefest all across the US since 1979 and have been 'getting better all the time'. You can surely expect some new and exciting surprises from Liverpool this year. The talents of Drew, Neal, Jonathan and Chris have taken them into a recording studio where their first single was recorded, on Caromar Records (Beatlefest's own label). One side is a Liverpool original called 'No Regrets' and the other side is 'Bad To Me', a Lennon/McCartney song that the Beatles themselves never recorded. Liverpool have recorded it the way they imagined the Beatles might have done.

"Giant Beatles Flea Market and Beatles Auctions. Just about everybody who attends Beatlefest collects at least some kind of Beatles memorabilia, whether it be Beatles records, photos, magazines, books, T-shirts, posters, trading cards, Beatles dolls, autographs, or thousands of other items for sale in the Giant Beatles Flea Market. Dealers from all across America are constantly on the look-out for those rare and hard to find Beatles collectibles to bring to Beatlefest. Plus, there are always first time dealers who will be selling their own collections.

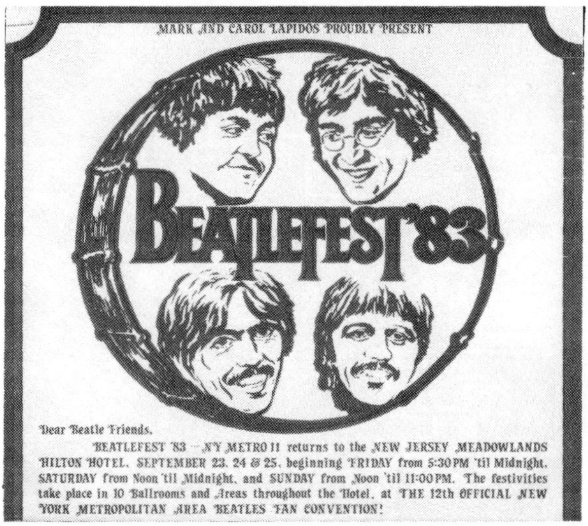

"Beatles Museum and Art Contest. Over two decades of Beatles history is traced in the Beatles Museum, which is being updated to 1983, with newspaper and magazine articles, photos, posters, etc. Some pieces of artwork shown here were winners in last year's art contests in various cities.

"Sound-Alike and Other Contests. After seeing its success at last year's conventions in Los Angeles and Chicago, we have decided to have a Battle of the Bands here for the very first time. Any professional or amateur band is welcome to enter this contest. Each group will perform three Beatles' songs. For Beatles Trivia experts, this year we are going to have a live Trivia Competition, where Al Sussman will be asking the questions. Prizes are awarded to all winners of all contests. Panel discussions: besides the special guests, *Beatlefan* publisher Bill King and senior editor Al Sussman will be joining these discussions. When discussions and sound-alike try-outs are going on, the piano is available to anyone who wishes to join in."

The Beatlefests, the most professional, highly-organised and regular Beatle Conventions in the world, are run by Mark and Carol Lapidos, who have now notched up a total of approximately 40 such major events in America.

In the February/March 1980 issue of *Beatlefan*, Mark talked about the history of the Beatlefests, and about the initial impact the Beatles had made on his life in 1964, turning him into a 'Beatlemaniac'. He eventually met John Lennon in June 1969 and, as a result, decided to work in the music business. He found a job at Sam Goody's record store in New Jersey where he became known as the shop's 'Beatle fanatic'. It was in November 1973 that he came up with the idea of a Beatles fans convention and began sending letters to all and sundry asking for support. Harry Nilsson proved a great help and Mark was able to get in touch with all four former members of the Beatles. John had responded to Mark's idea with the comment: "I'm all for it, I'm a Beatles fan, too."

Mark launched the first Beatlefest in September 1974 and it was a sell-out. Fans demanded more, so Mark ran a second. Soon, with the help of his wife Carol, he was running annual Beatlefests in New York, Chicago and Los Angeles and organising special events in cities such as Philadelphia, San Francisco and Atlanta.

In addition to the conventions, Mark and Carol also run a Beatlefest Mail Order service, which stocks books, records, T-shirts and bags. For details of the items available, send an SAE to Beatlefest Mail Order, PO Box 436, Westwood, New Jersey 07675.

The Dutch Conventions first began in 1976 and are organised by the staff of *Beatles Unlimited*. They are generally one-day events held in various theatres in Holland, the very first being held at the famous Paradise Club in Amsterdam. Guests at the conventions include such personalities as Allan Williams and Horst Fascher.

MEMORIALS

In addition to listening to the Beatles' music, visiting their many haunts, attending conventions and collecting souvenirs, some of you might like the opportunity to contribute actively to keeping alive their memory, in particular that of John Lennon and what he stood for. Here I offer two means of doing this; if anyone knows of any other similar projects, please let me know via the publisher.

THE JOHN LENNON PEACE FOREST

Jill Goldman, 141 Carlton East, Wembley, Middlesex HA9 8PU

In January 1981, the Israeli Government announced that it would be planting a John Lennon Peace Forest in Galilee, near Safed. Fittingly, both Israeli and Arab youths attended the ceremony that marked the planting of the first tree. A special dedication ceremony, in which Yoko has been invited to participate, will take place when 10,000 trees have been planted.

In the UK the project is promoted by Jill Goldman, who was recruited by the American promoter Joel Glazier (see Courses) and who can be contacted at the above address. Actual orders for trees can be placed with Edmond Cohen of the Jewish National Fund at Harold Poster House, Kingsbury Circle, London NW9 9SP.

The brochure from the JNF fills in some background to the project: "After the murder of John Lennon in December 1980, a group of young people from the Middle East decided to create a living memorial to their favourite Beatle in the form of a new forest. . .They identified with John Lennon's strong desire for World Peace and felt that the purchase of trees to benefit the environment, for a project neither profit-making nor politically motivated, was a positive way for people all over the world who still enjoy his songs to remember John's contribution to music – which like the trees themselves will live on. . .

"The Galilee region of Israel was the chosen location – an area linked with several major world religions, rich in Biblical history, where intellectual mystics and prophets lived and are buried. . .

"Many forests have been planted in Israel in the names of well-known personalities and in memory of such world leaders as the late President John F Kennedy. More recently established is a forest dedicated to the Late Lord Louis Mountbatten of Burma."

Should you wish to buy a tree, contact your nearest JNF office. Prices start at £2.50 a tree, and you can buy any number, dedicating them to a friend or relative and including a special message. Once the trees have been bought, a Tree Certificate, with a photograph of John Lennon and printed with the name and message requested will be sent to the recipient. The certificates, which verify that the trees will be planted in the John Lennon Peace Forest, make unique and lasting gifts for special occasions such as births, marriages or anniversaries. Trees can also be given as an expression of sympathy. Four trees cost £10; forty, £100; a garden of trees (100), £250; a copse (400), £1,000; and a grove (1000), £2,500. When a grove is purchased, the prepared site will be marked with a special, individual plaque.

Other offices of the Jewish National Fund can be found at Harold House, Dunbabin Road, Liverpool L15; Herzog House, Zion Road, Rathgar, Dublin 6; Abraham Links House, 43 Queen Square, Glasgow G41 2BD; 411a Harrogate House, Leeds LS17 7TT; and at Mamlock House, 142 Bury Old Road, Manchester M8 6HD.

When Joel Glazier was authorized to promote and collect for the forest, he commented: "The idea of a living memorial to John Lennon is one that should appeal to many Beatles fans and Lennon admirers. Some people are satisfied to possess a bronze medallion or metal bust of John as a memorial, but I believe a living memorial in the form of trees provides something more practical and lasting, especially for those who desire a tribute to John other than a government sponsored memorial or statue."

WORLD PEACE PARK
2049 Century Park East, Suite 5287, Los Angeles, California 90067

This non-profit making organization began originally as a project to raise money for a John Lennon statue; the response was so great that its aims have been raised. The organization release to contributors to the project states: "The original concept and idea has grown to proportions beyond our wildest dreams. It is no longer a monument dedicated to hopes and dreams of one man, but to all the advocates of world peace, such as Ghandi, Martin Luther King, and others; and of course to the one who inspired many of us – John Lennon.

"It is now going to be a park which, when completed, will contain statues and symbols and the names of all people who want the world to know of their awareness and dedication to the concept of peace on earth.

"Your participation will permit this organization, which has merged with the non-profit Love Foundation run by Beach Boy Mike Love and other entertainers who are organizing a series of musical concerts, to promote the World Peace Park internationally. This allows us to send you a newsletter periodically informing you of what the United Nations is doing and what the great number of other world peace and world hunger organizations are doing. Your name in bronze opens the communication line with people world-wide with major movements dedicated to help our world grow in peace with goodwill amongst all people of all nations.

"Because of the size and scope of this project, we are now in the process of finding a much larger and more accessible location in Malibu. If you wish to participate your contribution will be used to cast your name in bronze with other peace followers around the John Lennon statue. The World Peace Park Monument location was changed from New York to Malibu, California, due to Pepperdine University's co-operation in pursuing peace through education."

COURSES

For those who enjoy reading there are numerous books on the Beatles (see Publications). If you prefer a more disciplined and structured environment in which to soak up information, there are even a number of courses that you could attend. At present the American educational establishment is well ahead of its British equivalent and all the courses here described are in the US, although one does have a tie-up with an English university.

BEATLES AND HUMANITIES

420 Darland Administration Building, Univ of Minn, Duluth, Minnesota 55812

Joseph Gallian, Professor of Mathematics at the University of Minnesota, is in charge of this intriguing course. He told me: "The University of Minnesota, Duluth, offers an upper division three-credit Humanities course on the Beatles every year. The course was offered for the first time in 1983. Enrolment was 263. In 1984, the course was taught as a radio course. All lectures were broadcast from the university radio station: KUMN, 100,000 watts FM.

"During the summer of 1984 (8 July – 4 August) Duluth offered the Beatles course at the University of Birmingham in England as part of the 'Study in England' programme. The students received credit from the University of Minnesota, Duluth.

"I was the instructor. In addition to the regular classes we took field trips to Liverpool and London to see the Beatle-related sights. We will offer the Beatles class in England again – probably in the summer of 1987."

Applications for the English course were also obtainable from Carol Threinen of the Administration Building. The details concerning the 1984 course were: "The University of Minnesota, in co-operation with the University of Birmingham in England, will offer a course on the music and lives of the Beatles. The cultural, musical, and political impact of the Beatles will be studied. The course includes lectures, videotapes, audiotapes, and field trips to Liverpool and London. Weekends will be free for relaxation and touring.

"Students can receive three credits in the Humanities from the University of Minnesota if they wish. These credits are applicable towards a degree at another institution under the policies determined by that institution.

"The cost for the programme is $1,550, including round-trip airfare from Minneapolis to London, group transportation from London to Birmingham, single-room accommodation on the University of Birmingham campus, full English breakfast daily, all tuition costs, and field trips. Breakfast is the only meal included in this expense."

Professor Gallian describes his course by borrowing an apt quotation: "If any one person or group defined that whole spectrum of dreams, accomplishments, failures, and creative confusion that we call the sixties, it was the Beatles. For all their epitomization of their time, they seem to have tapped some secret of universality". *New York Times* 24 October 1982. He then goes on to give further details of the course:

"**Their Cultural Impact.** It was more than 20 years ago when 75 million Americans tuned into the *Ed Sullivan Show* for their first glimpse at four cheeky, mop-top musicians with a fresh sound and a new look. Over the seven-year period from 1964 to 1970, the lives and music of the Beatles had a profound impact on our society. They changed every aspect of the popular music industry. Their films, *A Hard Day's Night* and *Help!* influenced the way present-day films are shot and edited. Today's ubiquitous rock videos began with *Penny Lane* and *Strawberry Fields Forever.* Following the examples of the Beatles, men let their hair grow long, and wire-rim glasses became fashionable. Millions experimented with 'mind-expanding' drugs after the Beatles had done so. Transcendental meditation, Eastern religions, and Eastern music became popular when George Harrison expressed interest in them. Pop art exploded when the film of *Yellow Submarine* was released. The important role that youth culture has in our society was accentuated by the Beatles. John Lennon gave the Vietnam peace movement an anthem with his song 'Give Peace A Chance', while 'Imagine' encapsulated the dreams of many that one day 'the world will be as one'. The Nixon administration so feared the political potential of John Lennon that it employed wire-taps and undercover surveillance for two years to check on his activities. Even four years after Lennon's death, the Reagan Administration argued in court that keeping secret 90 per cent of the FBI file on Lennon was vital to our national security. John Lennon also made a significant contribution to the Women's Movement by spending the last five years of his life raising his son and acting as a househusband while his wife managed their fortune. These topics and the music of the Beatles are the content of the three-credit Humanities course that I teach.

"**Interdisciplinary Connections.** The centrality of the Beatles to the events and attitudes of the sixties offers an ideal vehicle for interdisciplinary connections. Indeed, the variety of their interests and endeavours encompasses not only the arts, but social, political, and popular intellectual movements as well. Their music and lives both shaped and reflected the values of their generation.

"Although people who witnessed the Beatles exploits have vivid memories of the phenomenon, today's students were just young children when the group broke up. To most of these students, the Beatles are more a myth than a historical relic. They are often viewed in the same category as Albert Einstein, Babe Ruth, Willie Mays, Wilt Chamberlain, Ghandi, John Kennedy, Martin Luther King, Notre Dame football teams, and the New York Yankees – subjects of reverential tales of yesterday's heroes. But popular music typically plays a more important role in the lives of today's students than athletics or politics, so that their curiosity about the Beatles is far greater than it is for these other idols of bygone days. They are eager to know the basis for this idoltry.

"Let me emphasise that one need not be an expert in music theory to teach a humanities course on the Beatles. I am certainly not an expert; I might add that none of the Beatles can read or write music (for that matter, neither can many great jazz musicians). Nevertheless, some musical understanding is important, so I asked music professors to analyse musical technique (one of whom is an accomplished classical pianist who has performed in Carnegie Hall, as well as being a jazz musician and teacher of music theory); a historian to lecture on the Lennon-FBI story; an English professor to discuss the social significance and poetic imagery of Beatles lyrics; a music critic to detail the influence of the Beatles on the music business (everything from recording methods to sleeve design); and a Beatle fan club president to decribe Beatle conventions and fan magazines. My experience hardly exhausts the possibilities. One could have a sociologist or psychologist speak on the group dynamics of Beatlemania or the world-wide interest in the rumour that Paul McCartney had died, with the attendant 'clues' found on album covers and lyrics; a TV or film critic or a communications professor could evaluate the influence of the Beatles films and videos; someone with expertise in women's studies could examine Lennon's feminist activities. These guest lecturers need not be fans or experts on the

A Beatles Retrospect

PUBLIC LECTURES

presented by The University of Minnesota, Duluth

■ Monday, March 21, 1983 Chemistry 200

"Transforming Mass Culture: The Beatles as Brahmins."
Thomas Bacig,
Associate Professor of English, University of Minnesota, Duluth
7:30-8:30 p.m.

■ Monday, March 28, 1983 Chemistry 200

"Beatlemania"
Al Sussman
Senior Editor of *Beatlefan* 7:00-8:00 p.m.

"Beatlefandom"
Barbara Fenick
Founder of Beatles' fan club "The Write Thing" 8:15-9:15 p.m.

■ Wednesday, April 13, 1983 Chemistry 200

"A Hard Day's Night: An Historical Perspective on the Beatles and Sixties"
Lary May
Associate Professor of American Studies, University of Minnesota
7:00-8:00 p.m.

"The Musical Importance of the Beatles"
Henry Gwiazda
Assistant Professor of Music, Moorhead State University
8:15-9:15 p.m.

■ Monday, April 18, 1983 Chemistry 200

"The Music of the Beatles"
William King
Publisher of *Beatlefan*, Music Critic for *Atlanta Constitution*
7:30-8:30 p.m.

■ Monday, April 25, 1983 Chemistry 200

"The Paul is Dead Rumor"
Joel Glazier
Teacher, writer 7:00-9:00 p.m.

■ Monday, May 2, 1983 Chemistry 200

"John Lennon the Activist"
Jon Wiener
Associate Professor of History, University of California, Irvine
7:30-8:30 p.m.

■ Monday, May 9, 1983 Chemistry 200

"Let it Be" Movie 6:00-7:30 p.m.
"Listening to the Beatles"
Thomas Wegren
Associate Professor of Music, University of Minnesota, Duluth
7:30-8:30 p.m.

ALL LECTURES ARE INTENDED FOR GENERAL AUDIENCES.
THERE IS NO ADMISSION CHARGE. *EVERYONE IS WELCOME.*

The University of Minnesota is an equal opportunity educator & employer.

This Program is sponsored, in part, with funds from The Minnesota Humanities Commission in cooperation with The National Endowment for the Humanities, the UMD Kirby Program Board, the College of Letters and Science, the Vice-Provost's Office, and Continuing Education and Extension.
For more information, write to Joseph A. Gallian, Department of Mathematical Sciences, University of Minnesota-Duluth, Duluth, Minnesota 55812.

Beatles *per se.* Their objectivity may even enhance the humanistic perspective. There is a plethora of available source material that can be used in preparation for a guest lecture.

"Resources For Teaching. Fortunately, there is an enormous wealth of resource material available to anyone interested in teaching such a course. Indeed, over 200 full-length books and 10,000 newspaper and magazine articles have been written about the Fab Four – many by scholars. On film or videotape are: *A Hard Day's Night, Help!, Magical Mystery Tour, Yellow Submarine, Let It Be, The Beatles at Shea Stadium* and *The Cream of the Beatles.* There are numerous Beatle fan magazines that carry advertisements for a wide variety of Beatle videos, unreleased songs, audiotapes and memorabilia. The two-hour video documentary, *The Compleat Beatles,* provides an excellent introduction and overview of the Beatles' career. Several outstanding series of audiotapes prepared as syndicated radio programmes are available (one of these runs for 30 hours). Naturally, a course on the Beatles must prominently feature their music. For this, I recommend the complete British set of 13 albums (available for about $100.00) plus the *Magical Mystery Tour* LP. The book, *The Beatles Forever,* by Nicholas Schaffner, is wonderfully effective as a textbook.

"A course on the Beatles is ideal for those who enjoy using a variety of teaching materials and methods. I have employed photographs, slides, videos, films, audiotapes, newspapers, magazines, and exhibitions. The campus newspaper ran articles about the course and conducted a survey of favourite Beatles songs; the campus record shop offered special prices on Beatles records; the School of Fine Arts sponsored a Beatles-related art contest; the local news media gave the course extensive coverage – in fact, newspapers and radio stations in many parts of the state picked up the story.

"On one occasion, I taught the course entirely by radio. The lectures focused on the music, while the reading assignments concentrated on the Beatles' lives and their cultural influence. Students who missed the broadcasts were able to hear them on cassettes in the library.

"The most challenging, and rewarding undertaking in my 13-year teaching career was an Elderhostel course on the Beatles. A series of five, 90-minute lectures was part of a package designed for 40 retired people ranging in age from 55 to 83. Nearly everyone reported that he/she was apprehensive about the Beatles portion of the programme, fearing "loud electronic music". Fortunately, they were willing to give the Beatles an "audition". Songs like 'Till There Was You', 'Michelle', 'Eleanor Rigby', 'When I'm 64', 'She's Leaving Home', 'Penny Lane', 'Strawberry Fields Forever', 'Mother Nature's Son', 'Honey Pie' and 'Yesterday' completely won them over (one lady wept while listening to this last song). Of course, these students were aware of the great impact the Beatles had had on the youth of the sixties, and they were eager to know why. They were surprised to hear of Lennon's efforts for peace and his commitment to the feminist cause. They were especially interested in the reasons for the break-up of the Beatles and amused by the bizarre business dealings of the group. The course concluded with everyone gathered round a piano singing 'All You Need Is Love'. This song perfectly captured the mood of the class. This delightful scene was filmed and shown on public television stations in Minnesota.

"Although the student response has been overwhelming, reaction from colleagues has been mixed. Whereas some have been enthusiastically supportive, one traditionalist (noting that there were not enough courses in the art of composition) wrote in the student newspaper: 'So one can only conclude that writing well is deemed less important than studying Ringo Starr'. Criticism like this should be anticipated, and it should be listened to reasonably – and equally critically. However, it can be minimized by setting rigorous working standards and by setting a substantial amount of background reading and essay writing."

Here is a short list of selected reference material suggested and described by Professor Gallian:

Aldridge, Alan, (ed). *The Beatles Illustrated Lyrics,* Dell, 1969.
Colourful and imaginative illustrations of more than 100 songs by various artists.

Carr, Roy; and Tyler, Tony. *The Beatles Illustrated Record,* Harmony Books, 1975.
This large, visually stimulating book gives perceptive critiques of every Beatles single and album.

Davies, Hunter. *The Beatles: The Authorised Biography,* revised, McGraw-Hill 1978
A best-selling, well-researched book that nevertheless omits some important, unflattering truths.

Fawcett, Anthony. *John Lennon: One Day At A Time,* Grove Press, 1976.
A beautifully illustrated book written by an assistant of John and Yoko. It focuses on their artistic and peace efforts.

Friede, Goldie; Titone, Robin; and Weiner, Sue. *The Beatles A to Z,* Metheun, New York 1980.
A well-researched, easy-to-use Beatles encyclopedia.

Harry, Bill. *Paperback Writers: The History Of The Beatles In Print,* Virgin Books, 1984.
A very helpful, illustrated bibliography of hundreds of books and magazines devoted to the Beatles. The content of each publication presented is summarized and given a rating from one to five.

King, William. *Beatlefan,* The Goody Press.
A gold mine of opinions, news items, facts, reviews and Beatles merchandise.

Martin, George. *All You Need Is Ears.* St Martin's Press, 1979.
This book, by the Beatles' producer, contains several chapters that provide a fascinating insight into the creative process of making a Beatles recording.

Meises, Charles. *The Beatles Reader.* Pierian Press, 1984.
A collection of 20 articles from major magazines and newspapers. Contains valuable lists of supplementary readings.
Norman, Philip. *Shout! The Beatles In Their Generation,* Warner Books, 1981.
A best-selling, carefully researched, well-written biography. Absorbing, but not gossipy.
Schaffner, Nicholas. *The Beatles Forever.* Cameron House, 1977.
The best illustrated, most enjoyable book ever written about the Beatles.
Schaumberg, Ron. *Growing Up With The Beatles,* Pyramid Books, 1976.
An exceptionally well-illustrated tribute in which the author describes how the Beatles influenced his life over the years.
Shotton, Peter; and Schaffner, Nicholas. *John Lennon: In My Life.* Stein and Day, 1983 (Also published under the title *The Beatles, Lennon and Me.*)
A book filled with personal anecdotes by Lennon's best friend.

Professor Gallian also runs an occasional weekend one-credit course entitled 'The Music and Lives of the Beatles'. He first presented this workshop at Vermilion Community College and the fee for the course was $24.50. The workshop covered the spectrum of the Beatles history: musical roots, musical innovations, Beatlemania, the Beatles' influence on youth, the drug culture, fashion, and transcendental meditation. It included films, pop, art, videos and readings and concluded with a discussion of the present-day cultural impact of the Beatles.

Henry Cwiazda, Professor of Music at Moorhead State University, Moorhead, Minnesota 56560, also teaches a credit course on the Beatles.

THE AESTHETICS OF JOHN LENNON

James Sauceda PhD, 488H South Chatham Circle, Anaheim, California 92806

Dr Sauceda is author of *The Literary Lennon,* the first study of all the major and minor writings of John Lennon. He is also a playwright and songwriter. He received his PhD in communication Arts and Sciences from the University of Southern California. In addition to current writing projects Dr Sauceda develops and teaches courses at USC and at California State University, Long Beach.

The Literary Lennon was first published by Pierian Press in January 1984. In Sauceda's judgement, John Lennon's accomplishment as a writer rivals his widely recognised contribution as a major musician/lyricist. Lennon's writing is noteworthy for its consistent quality, its sophisticated use of puns, and its complex verbal inventiveness strongly reminiscent of James Joyce.

Works of literary criticism and appreciation often provide an enhancement of our enjoyment of original works and this book is no exception. It was originally developed as research for one section of a course which Dr Sauceda created called 'The Aesthetics of John Lennon.' This was a six week seminar which he first taught between 9 September and 28 October 1981 at the College of Continuing Education at the University of Southern California. Sauceda has since taken the seminar to other universities including the University of California and Santa Barbara.

Dr Sauceda wrote to me, explaining: "'The Aesthetics of John Lennon' is an intensive seminar exploring the works of John Lennon as composer, performer, author and graphic artist. The course moves in three stages: part one: Beatle John:

1956-1969; part two: Literary Lennon: 1947-1979; part three: Solo John: John and Yoko: 1967-1980.

"The entire course consists almost exlusively of rare material – unreleased songs, demos, out-takes, alternate versions, as well as uncollected short stories, poetry and drawings; the *complete* Beatle performances on *The Ed Sullivan Show* 1964-1967 (prepared from the masters by Sullivan Productions specifically for the class); the unedited, colour, original version of *The Beatles at Shea Stadium* (direct from the masters at Sullivan Productions); the uncredited final interview with John Lennon just five hours before the tragedy (from Laurie Kaze, the woman who conducted the interviews) and much more.

"Before I ran the first class in September 1981, I sent a 20-page annotated syllabus to Yoko Ono. (Actually, Elliot Mintz had the syllabus specially couriered into her hands at the Dakota). Elliot simply stated that she found the course 'interesting' and had no objections to the educational nature of the class. I was, of course, very concerned that Yoko be aware of the serious study we were conducting in 'The Aesthetics of John Lennon' and was gratified to get a positive response (I never wanted my course to get confused with the fluffy 'Beatle Festival' type classes going around!)

"At the moment, I will run the course at any local University (USC or USSB for instance) only when *real* interest is shown by students. The best way for that interest to be established would be to write directly to Terry Shannon, 'The Aesthetics of John Lennon', Evening College, University of Southern California, University Park, Los Angeles, California 90007.

"I am now turning the material into a full length book called *The Unknown Beatles: Everything You've Never Been Told About The World's Most Talked About Group* (wherein I cover 13 albums worth of rare and unreleased Beatle material – some 178 songs)."

The Aesthetics of John Lennon

JOEL GLAZIER.
40th Street, Wilmington, Delaware 19802

Joel, a schoolteacher in Wilmington and one of the best-known Beatle fans around, runs a lecture course on the Beatles at Delaware University.

He is a noted authority on one area in particular, being the world's expert on the 'Paul Is Dead' theme. He has written a book on the subject, called *Here's Another Clue for You,* which he hopes soon to get published. Joel also has a very entertaining lecture show, well illustrated with slides, on the topic, which he has presented at several conventions.

He originally became a staunch Beatle fan when the Fab Four hit the States in 1964 and has, in his time, met each member of the group personally. He has been a guest at numerous conventions and is often a welcome addition to the panels of experts to be found at such events.

As the American promoter of the John Lennon Peace Forest (see Memorials) he also issues buttons inscribed with the words 'I Planted A Tree. John Lennon Peace Forest'.

ENTERTAINMENTS

Under this umbrella heading I have gathered together items of Beatles interest that do not fit happily anywhere else. They include a play, a radio show and a company that organises custom-designed Beatles tours. Although disparate, they can all be 'hired'.

STU

O'Well Productions, 23 Kimbolton Close, Lee, London SE12 0JH

This one-man show was originally presented in September 1983 at Bromley Little Theatre, Bromley, Kent and then at Beatle City, Liverpool, in April 1984. It will also have been shown at various venues in London during 1985 and plans are underway for an American tour in 1986. Those interested in booking the show should contact O'Well Productions at the above address.

Stu was written by Jeremy Stockwell and Hugh O'Neill. Jeremy came to see me early in 1983 to glean some background information about my days at art college with Stuart Sutcliffe. I then arranged for him to visit Stu's mother, Millie Sutcliffe, and he and Hugh spent six hours at her home in Sevenoaks, Kent, taping her memories.

I was unable to attend the première at Bromley Little Theatre, but Millie Sutcliffe was there and she phoned me the next day. She had obviously greatly enjoyed this tribute to her son.

The part of Stu was acted by 21-year-old Paul Almond, a graduate from Bristol University and Millie commented: "He bore a slight resemblance to Stuart – he was superb. Sadly, Millie Sutcliffe died a few months later, at the age of 76, but it gave me great pleasure to know that this play had made her happy. She had spent almost 20 years struggling to preserve the memory of her son as a pioneer of fifties youth culture.

Jeremy and Hugh have this to say about the play: "*Stu* is an attempt to portray the complex nature of a unique individual and a highly original artist who, despite his tragically early death, also informed much of popular culture since the sixties through his relationship with, and impact on, its foremost innovators. Sutcliffe's life and death embodies many of the Romantic notions of art and the artist which still persist in popular mythology, while the genuinely tragic nature of the wasted talent and unfulfilled potential that his death signifies transcends commonplace cliché to become a tangible and poignant reality." Jeremy goes on to say: "Sutcliffe was a brilliant talent and really was the first link between rock'n'roll and art. He had this aura about him. He had the kind of style that summed up a generation, really. His story is a fascinating, if not a sad one, that's why we wrote the play."

The hour-long production is split into 12 separate scenes, each preceded by slides indicating the locale of the scene. There are also slides of Stu's work from each period.

Scene 1 Hamburg, April 1962, just before his death.
Scene 2 Liverpool, early in 1959. Stu and I are sitting in Ye Cracke pub and are joined by John Lennon.
Scene 3 Ye Cracke a few months later; John asks Stu to join his group.

Scene 4 Hamburg, June 1961. Stu is painting and is joined by his fiancée Astrid Kirchherr.
Scene 5 Liverpool, 1959. Stu has sold a painting at the John Moore's Exhibition and buys a guitar.
Scene 6 Hamburg, April 1961. Stu is once again at his easel, telling Astrid about the Beatles.
Scene 7 Liverpool, June 1960. Stu returns home with a head injury and tells his mother how he has been attacked.
Scene 8 Hamburg, December 1961. Stu is tired, has constant headaches, but confides to Astrid that he is looking forward to returning to Liverpool at Christmas to see his mother and sisters.
Scene 9 Hamburg, September 1960. Stu is in a club with Astrid and Klaus Voorman, watching the Beatles perform.
Scene 10 April 1962. Stu tells both his mother and the audience of his experiences, and of his hopes and aspirations.
Scene 11 April 1961. Stu finishes playing 'Love Me Tender' in Germany, has a row with Paul, takes his guitar and leaves.
Scene 12 Hamburg, April 1962. Stu talks to Astrid as he sketches; he listens to the imaginary voice of John reading a letter Stu has sent to him discussing Hamburg and the career of the Beatles: "Today, Litherland Town Hall, tomorrow the world!" He gives a shout of pain and the play ends to the sound of the Hamburg version of the Beatles performing 'Twist And Shout'.

Paul Almond, Hugh O'Neill and Jeremy Stockwell

ROCK APPLE TOURS
PO Box 586, Lexington Massachusetts 02173

Rock Apple Tours is an American company which organises tours to places of Beatle interest in Britain and Germany. Details vary from year to year, as the tours are often arranged to tie in with a British convention or other event of interest to American Beatle fans. 1984 for instance, offered a major 'Jubilee Tour' covering Liverpool and London, a special Hamburg trip and a *Help!* tour. The company's description of the latter reads: "This 14-day tour begins on the ski slopes of Austria on 27 December on one of the prime locations depicted in the movie *Help!*. On 30 December, a short flight takes us to Manchester, England, and on to our Liverpool hotel from where

S
T
U
1940–
1962
ROMLEY
ITTLE
HEATRE
ORTH ST., BROMLEY
SEPT.
21st–24th
O'WELL PRODUCTIONS
present STU – scenes from
the life of Stuart Sutcliffe
A new play by Jeremy Stockwell
and Hugh O'Neill.
With Paul Almond as Stu.

we'll tour all Liverpool's Beatles sights, ending with a gala New Year's Mersey 'Knees Up' to bring in 1985. On 2 January 1985, we'll head for London for two days' shopping and sightseeing and on 5 January we'll fly directly to Nassau in the Bahamas for five days relaxing 'on location', returning to New York on 9 January."

The Jubilee Tour was Rock Apple's most ambitious project for 1984, comprising 12 days and 11 nights in Liverpool and London for $986.00. After an overnight flight from New York to Liverpool, the tourists were given an evening reception at their hotel. The next morning included a tour of Liverpool and a pre-convention party. The next three days were spent at the Mersey Beatle Extravaganza, Liz and Jim Hughes's last. This was followed by a free day in Liverpool before moving on to London where the first evening was spent on a pub crawl around the King's Road, Chelsea. The rest of the London itinerary was taken up by a mixed Beatles traditional tour of the capital, a walking tour, the Sotheby's Rock'n'Roll Auction, a free day and an evening farewell gala event.

An optional trip to Hamburg could be taken in the middle of the UK trip. It included an evening tour of Hamburg clubs a walking tour of the city and free time for shopping and independent sightseeing before returning to London to join the main group.

Places visited in Liverpool, apart from the convention, included Penny Lane, Strawberry Fields, Quarry Bank High School, Cavern Mecca Museum, Cavern Walks, Beatle City, the Liverpool Insitute, the Beatles garden and the former homes of the Beatles. Apart from the Sotheby's auction, the London trip included visits to Abbey Road, the Royal Albert Hall, Buckingham Palace, and the former London homes of the Beatles.

All the UK transfers were aboard luxury motor coaches equipped with Beatle music. The hotels used were the Atlantic Tower in Chapel Street, Liverpool, and the Forum Hotel in Cromwell Road, London.

The company's brochure also adds: "In addition to Rock Apple's scheduled tours, we are happy to make our specialised rock music travel service available to groups of 20 people or more. Rock Apple Tours offers your group custom-designed rock tours to the UK. Contact us for your group's individual itinerary!"

SCOTT MUNI'S TICKET TO RIDE,
14 Ardmore Avenue, Ardmore, Pennsylvania 19003

A weekly American radio tribute to the Beatles. Programme co-ordinator Kevin Gunn tells me: "Our show airs in over 95 markets throughout the US, and features educational, but offbeat angles, Beatle trivia, a weekly cover song, as well as the usual interviews, wrapped around music.

"We've found that the show appeals to the nostalgia of the 25-40 age group. We are also finding a new teen generation just getting turned on to the Beatles. Approaching these two audiences makes the show a lot of fun to do." The prorgramme's host is Scott Muni and the executive producer is Denny Somach, who should be contacted for details of how to hire the show.

PUBLICATIONS

GENESIS PUBLICATIONS LTD

Lynwood House, 51 Lynwood, Guildford, Surrey GU2 5NY

Two of the most remarkable books in the Beatles bibliography came out of Genesis Publications, a company set up in 1975, by a young British publisher, Brian Roylance, to produce facsimiles of important historical manuscripts and documents in handbound limited editions. His first book, William Bligh's *Log of HMS Bounty,* appeared in 1976 in a limited edition of 500 and has been out of print for a number of years. A number of successful limited editions followed, with forewords contributed by Lord Mountbatten, the Prince of Wales and Prince Philip.

The idea for *I Me Mine,* the facsimile of George Harrison's collected lyrics, was hatched at a meeting between Brian Roylance and Derek Taylor (who had spent many years in the Beatles' employ) in 1976. George agreed to work on the project and the three of them spent three years preparing it for publication in 1980. In his foreword to the book George gives a humorous account of how he got involved: "Ever since the war I have thought about gathering the bits of paper with my song lyrics scattered around and about. Two drunkards cornered me in a hotel room near Heathrow Airport in July 1977 and showed me that if I did find the lyrics, they could be bound into a nice book. They brought with them a copy of Captain Bligh's *Log of HMS Bounty.*"

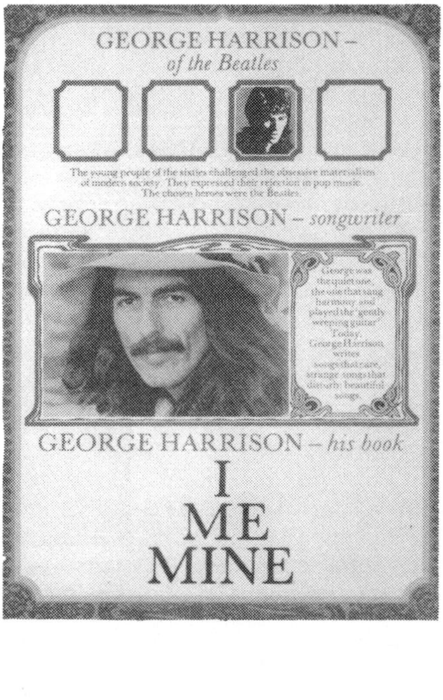

The book, which was originally to have been called *The Big Leather Job,* was limited to an edition of 2,000 copies signed by George and hand-numbered by the publisher as orders were received, so the first copies ordered were inscribed with the lowest numbers. In an exquisitely produced brochure advertising the book, Genesis wrote: "*I Me Mine* is, without doubt, a fine investment for the discerning collector." The stunning publication was favourably reviewed throughout the world, with an American fan magazine, *The Write Thing,* putting it most succinctly: "No one who buys this book is going to be sorry in the years to come." The edition was snapped up by subscribers in 45 countries and was out of print within several months of its publication. In 1984 a copy was auctioned at Sotheby's and fetched almost three times its original publication price.

I Me Mine was master printed in 28 colours. Its 450 pages, including plates, were hand-bound in goatskin with gilt tooling. It had an inlaid front cover and matching slip-case. In addition to the colour plates, there were 20 illustrations by Roy Williams which accompanied the first part of the book, a short autobiography by George with additional comments by Derek. Roy's engravings were meticulously detailed, the excellent draughtsmanship and distinct style creating a very individual atmosphere, particularly in his portrayal of blue suburban skies. From the initial scene of the barrage balloons above the Liver Buildings in wartime Merseyside, the illustrations follow George's life in Liverpool via a series of locations – his birthplace, Arnold Grove; his school, Liverpool Institute; Blackler's, the store where he had his first job and so on. There are also 50 photographs fleshing out the background to his life. The highlight of the book, however, are the facsimiles of George's song lyrics. Written on envelopes, hotel notepaper, anything to hand, embellished now and then by chord changes and the occasional doodle, they form a fascinating insight into their creator's mind. In addition to his comments on each song – why it was written and what he was trying to get across – George gives us his thoughts on, among other things, Eastern religions and the pressures of life.

There are 85 songs covered in this way and presented in chronological order. George's first song 'Don't Bother Me' appeared on *With The Beatles*. There followed three songs ('Taxman', 'Love You To' and 'I Want To Tell You') on *Revolver* in 1966, 'Within You, Without You' on the 1967 *Sgt. Pepper's Lonely Hearts Club Band* and 'Something' and 'Here Comes The Sun' on *Abbey Road*. 'Within You, Without You' and 'The Inner Light' (the first of his songs to appear on a single) marked George's ever-growing interest in the East, his explorations into Indian music and philosophy ("Let's face it, I was getting a bit out of it as far as Western popular music goes"). Now his musical ideas were gathering momentum. He made two experimental albums, *Wonderwall* (Apple 1968) and *Electric Sounds* (Apple 1969), and followed them with the greatly acclaimed classic, *All Things Must Pass* (Apple, 1970). This was the album that established George as a sole performer and dramatically elevated his status as a songwriter. He spent a long time preparing this album – he knew it was important – and employed the best musicians: Eric Clapton, Dave Mason, Ringo Starr, Billy Preston. The words and music underscored his growing absorption in spirituality and Eastern themes: conviction of an alternative way, reincarnation, the seeking of a simple, caring solution to the eternal complexities of personal relationships.

Included in the songs was 'My Sweet Lord', which had been released earlier as a single. A subtly simple and strangely haunting pop hymn, 'My Sweet Lord' had swept to the top of the charts in Britain and the US ("It was different. I stuck my neck out on the line, and committed myself, because nobody else in popular music was coming out and saying it").

In 1972, George's concern led him to organise a concert to raise money for the relief of Bangla Desh. He persuaded Ringo Starr and Eric Clapton, among others, to appear – and even wheedled Bob Dylan out of semi-retirement. ("Once you *do* something, then lots of people want to help, but not many will start it on their own. They all need a kick in the behind.").

The Bangla Desh Concert, held in Madison Square Garden, New York, was an enormous success. ("The album was not a patch on how it was in the room that night in Madison Square. The love and high energy was incredible!").

Living In The Material World (Apple), a natural progression in George's journey of self-discovery, was released in 1973. Referring to the title song, George says: "No matter how hard you try, if you turn into a yogi or a monk or a nun, in order to become God or Christ-conscious, OK – that can help a lot. But still, in the end, if we don't have the 'grace' then we can't 'make it' " .

The album *Dark Horse* (Apple) came out in 1974, the year in which George launched his own label, Dark Horse Records. The exploratory work goes on as he returns to a favourite theme: "It's like throwing a pebble into a clear lake. Those ripples keep going, so every thought, word, action or deed that we formulate is like sending a ripple out across the universe – and it comes back. Whatever you do comes right back to you."

Extra Texture (Read All About It) (Apple, 1975) was acclaimed by the critics as an upswing in form, but it was nevertheless soon overshadowed by the blatant cheerfulness of *Thirty Three & ⅓* (Dark Horse, 1976). This album symbolised the cultural and social optimism that had characterized the Beatles in their heyday: a hope amply fulfilled by George.

Fifty Years Adrift, Genesis' next Beatles-related venture, on which George, Derek and Brian again worked together, proved to be even more ambitious than *I Me Mine*. It was the second, adventure-crammed autobiography of Derek Taylor (the first, *As Time Goes By*, had been published by Souvenir Press in 1974).

Brian Roylance told me: "I asked Derek to do it fairly soon after *I Me Mine*. Then, as he often does, he got cold feet and changed his mind. Then he changed his mind again and agreed to go ahead, saying that this would be the last word he'd ever write on the Beatles. The definitive book. He took about two years to write it, finishing in 1984. Derek and I did the paste-up, checked all the galley proofs – it was quite a task. There was so much memorabilia. Derek had arranged for boxes of his material to be sent from Warners, both in LA and London. Letters from John and Paul, documents, masses of papers, so it ended up with just Derek and I picking up pages in chronological order, trying to put each facsimile in the right place. There was such a lot of stuff, it was a matter of what we had to leave out. Derek had written over 400,000 words all together. Kay Williams edited it down to around 250,000. George was very good too, reading the manuscript, offering his advice to Derek on what he found tedious or boring and what he thought was good."

Genesis keeps its subscribers informed of its publishing projects via a quarterly publication called *Origo*, available by private subscription. During the preparation of *Fifty Years Adrift*, there were various special issues giving updates on the progress of the book. In one of them, George wrote: "It has long been known by those who continually thirst for any scrap of a reason to be reminded of the sixties that Derek Taylor was in a remarkable position, witnessing, indulging and being a vital part of that bygone age. That we know.

"So much already said; yet so many continue to write about it, re-enact it, reappraise it, exaggerate it and flatulate, and try desperately to know it all or make a profit from it – or just casually throw a bit more dust onto the mirror.

"Derek is always being invited to 'tell the real story' and live the rest of his life at a Beatlefest. He could tell you a few amazing stories that would win Oscars and set the darkness on fire.

"As I am editing this book, however, I thought you should also know more about the Derek I know – the Derek we love, the Derek with a song in his heart – and how he managed to exist Fifty Years Adrift in an open-necked shirt."

Genesis also published a detailed background to the book in an outline of Derek's life: "*Fifty Years Adrift* spans a world that has changed beyond recognition. It tells of a half-century containing, somewhere near the middle, the astonishing sixties, an era which altered the entire course of the author's life and the lives of many millions of other people in dozens of countries. The sixties are therefore examined with a close attention that remains both amused. But the book is also about the author's life: about a time way, way back – long before 'flower power' and Sergeant Pepper – and about now; about living one day at a time, right up to tomorrow, as we all dig in for the deepening mysteries of the edgy eighties."

"You shoulda been there", John Lennon said of the sixties. Derek Taylor *was* there. As personal assistant to Brian Epstein, as press officer to the Beatles, as Man of Monterey and of Apple, he was part of the psychedelic tapestry that formed a backcloth to the swinging sixties; and his thorough training in journalism, on weekly, evening and daily newspapers, was to serve him well as he recorded, on train, boat or plane trips, or in his offices or at home, the stresses and tensions, joys and dreams of that not untroubled era. He wrote incessantly, sometimes in tears and often in drink. It all stands, even if, in retrospect, some of it leans perilously towards madness.

Winter 1982/3 Origo Special Issue Number 2 Copy Number:

More News on FIFTY YEARS ADRIFT

Derek Taylor and George Harrison recently visited Liverpool to undertake some research for FIFTY YEARS ADRIFT. George was photographed seated at a desk in his old school, The Liverpool Institute.

A little later Derek Taylor was asked to write an article about the work on FIFTY YEARS ADRIFT for his old newspaper, The Liverpool Echo. This is reprinted below.

Autumn 1982 Copy Number:

Origo Special Issue

News on I ME MINE and FIFTY YEARS ADRIFT from Genesis

Fifty Years Adrift: orders are flooding in

NO OTHER EDITIONS WILL BE AVAILABLE

EDITOR, AUTHOR AND ILLUSTRATOR EXAMINING THE FIRST PIECES OF ARTWORK

We are happy to report a tremendous response to our mailing of the prospectus for our forthcoming hand-made signed, limited edition of FIFTY YEARS ADRIFT written by Derek Taylor and edited by George Harrison. Subscribers to I ME MINE are seizing the opportunity to reserve the same numbered copy of this companion volume at the special pre-publication price. We are also delighted to find that many people who did not have the opportunity to purchase the limited edition of I ME MINE are ordering copies of FIFTY YEARS ADRIFT.

An order form is enclosed with this newsletter. If you have not yet ordered your copy please do so without delay in order to avoid disappointment. In the top right-hand corner of this sheet you will find your personal subscriber number.

If you have ordered your copy but have not yet received an acknowledgement we would kindly ask you to be patient as we are recording all orders as quickly as possible.

In *Fifty Years Adrift*, Derek Taylor offers an exceptional view, in close-up, of the sixties. Recounted with compassion, easy familiarity and idiosyncratic humour, his tale stands as testimony to, and sometimes indictment of, the days when all we seemed to need was love, a joint and a brandy; of the days when all the troubles of all the worlds – East, West and Third – would be solved as soon as We, the young, replaced Them, the ageing.

Sober now, but far from glum, he puts all of this into perspective as he takes us back to his childhood in the thirties, Hitler's rise to power, the New Deal, Auntie Ethel, World War II; to the fifties and his army service as a sergeant-instructor; to life on newspapers in the industrial north of England; to far-off places with the Beatles, and to the seventies and eighties. Through a kaleidoscope of careers, through his moment-by-moment involvement as husband of Joan and father of their three sons and three daughters, he tells an enriching tale, a story that offers great hope and encouragement, and sometimes flashes of brilliance.

Derek Taylor was born in Liverpool in 1932 and brought up in the seaside town of West Kirby, across the Mersey by ferry, road or rail. He did well at school at first ("shows great promise") and then not so well (long world war, hiding under the stairs from Hitler); and then well enough again, the war over and the family reunited, to leave school and become a newspaper reporter in the forties and fifties.

In May 1963, as theatre critic and columnist for the northern edition of the

London Daily Express, he went with his wife, Joan, to the Odeon Cinema in Manchester to see a hot 'new' group called the Beatles, then sharing a bill with Roy Orbison. Things were not to be the same again.

Within months, he had been signed up as personal assistant to Brian Epstein, had ghosted the late, great man's slim autobiography *A Cellarful Of Noise*, had joined the Beatles as press officer, and had been round the world with them on their first grand tour. In 1964 a brass plate in Hollywood announced that he had set himself up as a press agent. He moved on at a rate of knots to represent and befriend most of the fascinating pop stars in the great post-Beatle American explosion: the Beach Boys in their 'Pet Sounds'/'Good Vibrations' period, the Mamas and Papas at the height of *that* mania; the Byrds before, during and after 'Mr Tambourine Man', 'Turn Turn Turn', and 'Eight Miles High'; Sir Douglas Quintet, Chad and Jeremy, Captain Beefheart, Paul Revere and the Raiders for years, the Doors for about ten minutes, Van Dyke Parks; and then Phil Ochs, Herb Alpert, Procol Harum, Sergio Mendes, Tommy Boyce and Bobby Hart, Burt Bacharach and all the glittering A&M roster of artists in the late sixties, after the cascading power of the 1967 Monterey Pop Festival had changed things around once again.

Derek Taylor was publicist and one of the founders of that festival; when it was all over, and Apple Corps was being set up in England for the brave new world of the post-touring Beatles, Derek and his family sailed out of New York on a liner to Bermuda and thence to Liverpool, drove to London and started another life. Apple lived its dream for three years and then it was all over, bar the counting; but while it breathed, Derek Taylor was there at its heart, mixing metaphors, popping pills, spinning a great number of plates and dropping quite a few – and though they did break, and some people were hurt, some of it was fun while it lasted. Nobody died of 'Apple'.

Done with that he went to Warner Brothers as they honourably assumed the cloak of the new 'respect for artists as people' movement. His special gift for dealing with people was given a title: Director of Special Projects. In this loose-fitting garment, he dealt with Alice Cooper, James Taylor, America, the Grateful Dead, Rod McKuen, Jimmy Webb, Bonnie Rait, Fanny, Sparks, Rob Weir, the Faces, Judy Collins, Neil Young, Stephen Stills and on and on, from 'School's Out' to 'The Game's Up', and all with his usual élan.

His elusive memoir, *As Time Goes By*, became a cult item of some rarity. During the transition from the US to Apple, Derek Taylor became friendly with Harry Nilsson, whom he introduced to the Beatles, with all of whom Harry himself in turn became very friendly. In Taylor's view, Harry was at one with the Liverpool team in terms of originality, class, style, talent, fun and sense of the absurd. He could also drink all of them, except Taylor, under the table and established a reputation of being the only creature in the world – not including the giraffe – who could go into any bar at any time and say with complete confidence: "Tonight, the highballs are on me."

So the seventies lurched on and our hero was sometimes up with events and sometimes almost trampled by them. He was appearing on television in various guises – agitator, pundit – and was much preoccupied with cramming the rest of his life into the next hour or so. He promoted the great British jazzman, hero of all the arts, George Melly, whose stay with Warners resulted in four much-prized mainstream-jazz albums. Then, in 1975, Derek Taylor put on a tie for a few moments, put the last cork in the last bottle and was made boss of Warner Bros Records in the United Kingdom; he signed a few nice acts, including Deaf School, and then, while at a conference in Hawaii, was persuaded to return to the US, this time as Vice President of Warner Bros USA in charge of Creative Services: another of those titles which hide a multiplicity of political functions and territorial imperatives. As he was to learn . . .

To accommodate this elevation to the boardroom, the entire family emigrated again; but corporate structure was not what was needed at this time in Taylor's life, nor in that of his disorientated family, rudderless in Middle America. He fled from

Warner's colourful and generous umbrella into the English rain, finding to his relief that there was an Indian summer in the late autumn of 1978. He and Joan decided that they would be much happier if he didn't ever have a regular job again; and although he worked for Handmade Films for a year (seven days a month), and became involved with Terry Gilliam and Michael Palin, as publicity consultant on *Time Bandits*, he had to face the reality that he could no longer cut it as employee.

He had become a quiet countryman. He and his family now stay close to their watermill in the East Anglian farm country near the North Sea, and Derek now makes a kind of living doing a kind of writing. After George Harrison's *I Me Mine*, he wrote *The Making of Raiders of the Lost Ark* (commissioned by George Lucas), and then Brian Roylance invited him to thrash out his own memories.

I Me Mine was published in a cheap edition by Comet Books in London and Simon & Schuster in the States. The same will not happen with *Fifty Years Adrift*. Once the 2,000 numbered copies are sold, no other editions will become available. George Harrison has edited the book and there is a picture gallery of photographs highlighting the past half-century's events great and small, including many personal photographs previously unpublished. George also contributed an introduction, and Legs Larry Smith acted as art director on the publication. The vast amount of facsimile reproductions of memorabilia include the earliest school reports with stunning predictions, messages from King George VI and Gracie Fields, many postcards and letters – from Brian Epstein, Pete Best, John Lennon, Paul McCartney and George Harrison, and a Christmas card from Ringo – spanning a decade and a half, plus drawings by Lennon and McCartney, a watercolour by Captain Beefheart, another by Joan Taylor, all previously unpublished. There are many illustrations in colour and artist Roy Williams has also contributed more than 100 illustrations in his own inimitable style. During his editing stint, George added over 15,000 words of his own. The book is in hand-bound leather and master printed on antique-laid paper.

THE LIVERPOOL ECHO
PO Box No 48, Old Hall Street, Liverpool L69 3EB.

Merseyside's premier newspaper, the *Liverpool Echo* is the sole survivor of two evening newspapers published in Liverpool. The other, the *Evening Express* was tabloid, similar in style and layout to London's *Standard,* and folded during the fifties. The *Echo* has a companion morning paper, the *Daily Post*, on which Derek Taylor, former personal assistant to Brian Epstein, and Ray Connolly, author of *John Lennon 1940-1980* and *That'll Be The Day*, were both journalists, during the fifties and sixties respectively.

The *Echo* was never interested in the early Mersey rock bands and not only refused them editorial space, but proved very restrictive in the advertising columns. All groups and venues advertised in the classified section were placed under the heading 'Jazz' and, despite complaints and protests from advertisers, the policy was maintained for several years, even when every band and venue related to the local Beat scene. Whenever a local promoter inserted the words 'for further details, read *Mersey Beat*', the information was deleted as the *Echo* refused to allow any mention of *Mersey Beat*, even in the paid classified columns.

There was a small records review section penned by 'Disker', otherwise Tony Barrow, a Merseysider who lived in London and worked for Decca writing sleeve notes. When Brian Epstein took over management of the Beatles, he wrote to 'Disker' in an attempt to get a mention of the Beatles in the prestigious local publication. Tony pointed out that he couldn't mention the group in his column until a record had been released, but managed to put a word in with some contacts at Decca which ultimately led to the group being given a Decca recording audition. Tony later became PR for the Beatles and Nems Enterprises.

The *Liverpool* Echo continued to ignore the local scene until the Beatles' first major successes of 1963, when George Harrison (no relation!), one of the paper's senior journalists who wrote a column called 'Under The Mersey Wall', was seconded to chronicle the group's travels. From then on the *Echo* gave quite respectable coverage to the emergent Merseyside bands and also published several pop supplements over the years, including the 32-page *Around the World with the Beatles* which had a text by Harrison accompanied by lots of photographs, and was issued in December 1964.

Among recent supplements there has been a series of six celebrating the group's twentieth anniversary, one issue coming out every day from 13-18 September 1982. Each of these supplements comprised four pages of text and photographs. The first included a special feature by me called 'In The Beginning' and a photograph of me presenting the Beatles with their first-ever award, the *Mersey Beat* shield. Peter Trollope, the *Echo's* current music correspondent, wrote the next four, which were about Paul, George, Ringo and John respectively. The sixth and final issue was called *Beatlemania* and was written by former journalist George Harrison, who by now had retired and moved to the south of England.

Peter Trollope has worked for the newspaper for some years and his excellently written articles still encourage and give much-needed publicity to local bands.

The *Echo*, which went tabloid in 1983, has continued to provide Beatle fans with souvenir issues that quickly become quite rare and collectable items as they are only published locally. In 1984, after John's tragic death, an excellent collection of *Liverpool Echo* material about him was published and given national distribution. Entitled *Lennon*, the 48-page publication contained numerous photographs and a selection of articles from 1963 onwards. The frontispiece contains a photo of John as a schoolboy, a section of a Quarry Bank school photo featuring John, and the school's tie and badge with its motto *Ex Hoc Metallo Urtutem*. There are news stories on the Beatles' performances at the Palladium and the Royal Variety Show, reports of John's first book, details of when he passed his driving test, when he bought a Rolls-Royce and so on. There are reports on the initial trip to America, the *Ed Sullivan Show* and the Shea Stadium concert. Maureen Cleave contributes 'Life With Cynthia', an interview she did with John in 1966. There is also a series of articles by John's Aunt Mimi. The entire book is a marvellous compilation and a rare souvenir. Copies can be obtained by sending cheques or postal orders for £1.99 (including post and packing), made payable to the *Liverpool Echo* and crossed 'A/c Payee', to Dept M, Liverpool Echo, at the above address.

Numerous other supplements came out during 1984, the most eventful year on Merseyside since the birth of Beatlemania, what with the International Flower Festival and other festivities. The last was a special pictorial souvenir, published on Tuesday, 18 December and entitled *'84. Year Of The Scouser*. Its cover featured a picture of a tall ship passing the Liver Buildings, with small inset photographs of the Queen opening the flower festival and Paul McCartney receiving his Freedom of the City Award. Among the many items inside are photographs of the Yellow Submarine display at the International Flower Festival, the opening of Cavern Walks, Mike McCartney with the Doubleday Beatles statue, Gerry Marsden and Noel Edmunds at the Albert Docks and a full page feature on Yoko and Sean Ono's trip to Liverpool. There is also a double-page spread on the Paul McCartney presentation under the heading 'How Liverpool Gave Its Regards To Its Favourite Son', and a double-page spread on Frankie Goes To Hollywood.

Also available by mail order from the *Echo* was *Liverpool – The 60s, A Photographic Celebration*, published in 1983 by Brunning Advertising & Marketing (Liverpool) Ltd. Unfortunately now out of print, this was a book of photographs taken during the sixties, showing the cobbled streets and terraced slums (many of which were torn down during a massive rebuilding programme); the Grand National; girls in mini skirts; soccer highlights and so on. Music-related pictues include singer Billy Fury at Aintree; a mini-skirted Cilla Black; a gathering of dozens of Beat groups outside St George's Hall; Billy J Kramer and Gerry Marsden kissing Cilla Black on the cheeks, each of them holding a silver disc; Gerry Marsden with the Searchers and Sandie Shaw at a Granada TV pop promotion; the original Cavern; hordes of fans greeting the Beatles at Speke Airport; Brian Epstein at Gerry Marsden's wedding; the Scaffold; Joe Henderson, Frankie Vaughan, Ken Dodd, Jimmy Tarbuck and Gerry Marsden at a bowling rink; the Spinners; Adrian Henri; and George and Ringo.

The *Echo* more or less monopolised the local newspaper scene throughout the late sixties and seventies. One or two other modest publications started up, such as the *Mersey Mirror*, but their low circulations ensured that they didn't last. Then, in the eighties, *Merseymart*, a 'free' newspaper delivered once a week to homes throughout Merseyside, appeared.

'Free' newspapers flourished in Britain in the seventies and proved a major competition to established provincial newspapers. *Merseymart*, with a circulation of 150,000 a week, like most other free newspapers carries more advertising than editorial. The editorial material includes several regular columns – one which explores local history, another on pop music in general, with a leaning towards local bands, written by Barbara Mann, a jazz column by Alan Graham, who was an original Cavern staffer in the club's heyday, and most importantly for Beatle fans, the 'Mersey Beatle' column by Bob Wooler, the DJ who introduced the Beatles on stage more times than any other person. He contributed articles to *Mersey Beat* throughout 1961, the most memorable being the piece in which he declard that the Beatles were one of the most exciting new entries on to the music scene in years. His 'Mersey Beatle' column is mainly concerned with local Beatle associations. *Merseymart*'s main office is at No 6 Allerton Road, Liverpool 18.

Another free weekly is the *Liverpool Express*, which first appeared in September 1984. As with *Merseymart,* 150,000 copies are delivered around the Merseyside area free of charge. Published from 102 Duke Street, Liverpool L1 5AG, it is more like a traditional newspaper than *Merseymart* and originally featured two of my Beatle cartoon strips, 'The Beatle File', each week. Coverage of local bands is provided in 'Tracks', a column by John McCready. Shortly after the *Liverpool Express* was launched, the *Liverpool Echo* started a rival, the *Liverpool Star,* published from Tower Buildings, Water Street, Liverpool. This has a similar style and layout to the *Liverpool Express* and a pop column called 'Sounds Around'.

Next 14 (so called because it originally came out fortnightly, although it is now a monthly) also made its debut in 1984, on 27 April. Published from 31 School Lane, Liverpool 1, it is basically a guide to what's on in Merseyside, very similar in approach and layout to London's *Time Out,* with extensive coverage of the contemporary local rock scene.

Over the years since the demise of *Mersey Beat,* there have been various attempts to launch another local music paper. Two such publications were *Night Out* (which folded in the late seventies) and *Mersey Sound,* the later a very promising paper which folded in 1983 but has happily been resurrected in 1985. The most durable publication appears to be *Breakout,* which was launched in the early eighties by Neil Tilly who handles a local agency/management company. *Breakout* has developed from a fanzine into a newspaper and in January 1985 increased its print run to 25,000. The paper's office is at 6 Imperial Chambers, 62 Dale Street, Liverpool L2 5SX. Another regular publication featuring contemporary Liverpool bands is *The End,* a fanzine published by Phil Jones, of 16 Steerscroft, Cantril Farm, Liverpool L2.

PIERIAN PRESS
PO Box 1808 Ann Arbor, Michigan 48106

Pierian Press is a unique publishing organisation whose books can only be obtained by direct mail order. The full background story to Pierian, which has published more Beatles titles than any other publisher, is to be found in my own *Paperback Writers: The History Of The Beatles In Print.* The books currently available from the company are:

All Together Now: The First Complete Beatles Discography, 1961-1975, by Harry Castleman and Walter J. Podrazik. A complete chronological discography of all the records the Beatles were associated with as performers, writers and producers. An alphabetical listing of all the albums and songs released by the Beatles both individually and as a group. An examination of the musical heritage upon which the Beatles based their own music. Institutions: $20.00. Individuals: $14.95.

The Beatles Again?, by Harry Castleman and Walter J. Podrazik. Supplements and updates information contained in *All Together Now.* Includes a complete Beatles' touring schedule. Contains an index which covers both volumes. Sorts out myths, legends, facts and fiction surrounding the Beatles. Institutions: $15.95. Individuals: $11.95.

A Day in the Life: The Beatles Day-by-Day, 1960-1970, compiled and edited by Thomas Schultheiss. This fascinating chronological account of the Beatles in their heyday, the sixties, is drawn from more than 60 sources, representing a synthesis of published material on the Beatles. It compares, contrasts and organises everyone else's history or biography of the group. It reveals errors, discrepancies, and contradictions. It provides a groundwork for all future writing about John, Paul, George and Ringo. It includes an index of over 6,000 page references. Institutions: $15.95. Individuals: $11.95.

Things We Said Today: The Complete Lyrics and Concordance to the Beatles' Songs, 1960-1970, by Colin Campbell and Allan Murphy. This book is at once an encyclopedia of the Beatles' lyrics and a documentary of their musical development. It features full lyrics of 189 songs written and recorded by the group (lyrics represent those actually sung on the Beatles' recordings, including background vocals); the huge lyrics concordance (a word index, arranged by key word); word frequency lists; fifteen photographs of the original handwritten lyrics of songs like 'I'm Only Sleeping', 'Eleanor Rigby' and 'Yellow Submarine. Institutions $35.00. Individuals $27.50.

You Can't Do That! Beatles Bootlegs and Novelty Records, 1963-1980, by Charles Reinhart. An exhaustive compilation of non-original Beatles records, featuring details of nearly 900 Beatles bootlegs and counterfeit records; a novelty section containing a discography of 400 records about, or somehow associated with, the Beatles; an impressive set of indexes to the above sections, including a Personal Name Index, a Song and Album Title Index, a Record Label Index and a Topical Index. Institutions: $17.95.Individuals: $14.95.

Collecting the Beatles, by Barb Fenick. An introductory guide to collecting for neophyte fans and novice collectors, as well as a quick reference handbook for more practised collectors and all others who deal in Beatles memorabilia; tips on telling counterfeit collectables from the genuine article; how and where to buy Beatles collectables – shopping, bidding and making the final purchase; a price guide listing over 800 items; and an exlusive appendix of nearly 100 merchandising licences granted during the 1963-64 era. Individuals: $15.95. Institutions: $19.95.

As I Write This Letter: An American Generation Remembers the Beatles, by Marc A Catone. Over 160 letters and 70 drawings from and by fans combine to form the delightful memoirs of an American generation – Beatle fans now largely in their late twenties and early thirties. The striking illustrations are enhanced by the book's bold layout and design. Letters are candid, articulate, poignant, perceptive, funny and sad. They evoke the harmony and the conflict, the turbulence and the sheer exuberance of those bittersweet years. Institutions: $24.95. Individuals: $17.50.

The Literary Lennon: A Comedy of Letters, by James Sauceda. The first study of all the major and minor writings of John Lennon provides an in-depth analysis of Lennon's very significant literary legacy. He was an accomplished writer, comfortable with a variety of styles and genres, and his writing is noteworthy for its consistently high quality, the insight into Beatlemania it affords the reader, and its complex verbal inventiveness strongly reminiscent of James Joyce. Institutions: $17.95. Individuals $14.95.

The Beatles at the Beeb: The Story of Their Radio Career, 1962-1965. A comprehensive history of the group's radio career and a general survey of Beatles' history and music. *The Beatles At The Beeb* chronicles their frequent appearances on the radio and traces their musical development and progression to stardom between March 1962 and June 1965. It includes commentaries on the 88 songs they performed on the airwaves and information on 36 songs that never appeared on Beatles' records, as well as a date chart and numerous photos of the group. Institutions: $15.95. Individuals: $12.95.

The Longest Cocktail Party: An Insider's Diary of the Beatles, by Richard di Lello. A fascinating first person account of the Beatles' Apple years, 1968-1970, by a member of the Apple press office. It describes the day-to-day excitement of Apple in London – from the optimism and naive enthusiasm that launched the venture to the bitter wrangling that tore it apart. Institutions: $22.95. Individuals: $17.95.

As Time Goes By: Living in the Sixties, by Derek Taylor. An intimate look at the Beatles and others, including Mae West, Brian Wilson, the Byrds, Brian Epstein and the Beach Boys, by the Beatles Press Officer and confidant. Provides a fascinating look at these stars from an insiders's point of view. *As Time Goes By* contains many photographs and has been given a new index which adds to its usefulness. Institutions: $17.95. Individuals: $14.95.

A Cellarful of Noise, by Brian Epstein. A memoir by 'the fifth Beatle', the personal and business manager of the Beatles from 1961 until his death in 1967; reprints the original 1964 British edition, with a new index and a new foreword by Clive Epstein, the author's brother. Institutions: $17.95. Individuals: $14.95.

The Beatles Reader: A Selection of Contemporary Views, News and Reviews of the Beatles in Their Heyday, by Charles P Neises. A collection of over twenty classic articles from magazines and newspapers spanning the Beatles' career, here anthologized for the first time. Grouped in sections, with recommendations for further reading. A perfect 'sampler'. Institutions: $17.95. Individuals: $14.95.

The End of the Beatles, by Harry Castleman and Walter J Podrazik. The third in a series of definitive discographic volumes (following *All Together Now* and *The Beatles Again?*) which together span the Beatles' recording careers from 1961-1982. *The End Of The Beatles* is divided into five sections: 'The Magical Mystery Tour Rolls On' continues the year-by-year chronological discography, picking up the story from 1977's *Love Songs* album and carrying it through to 31 December 1983, adding nearly 200 items on the way; 'Pandemonium Shadow Ballet' provides background on records connected to the Beatles in other ways: spoken word packages and releases by such performers as Yoko Ono and Harry Nilsson; 'All Sales Final' examines bootleg records; 'You Can't Say We Never Told You' offers eight in-depth essays on such topics as studio out-takes, audiophile discs, and publications devoted to the group. Finally, the 'Indexes and Instructions' section serves as a guide to using the book and the 15 indexes. Institutions: $39.50. Individuals $29.50.

Fab Four Twenty-Year Calendar for 1985. This unique calendar features daily events in the lives of the Beatles from 1964 – the year of their first momentous concert tour of the US. With original drawings by Susan K Park and text by Tom Schultheiss, author of *A Day in the Life,* the calendar provides a year-long feast of events in the public and private lives of the Beatles. $7.50. The 1983 and 1984 calendars are still available at $6.50, and others will be publised annually.

Unfortunately, the calendars, *The Beatles at the Beeb, Things We Said Today* and *A Cellarful of Noise* are not for sale to customers ordering from outside the US and Canada.

A 20 per cent discount is offered for offers of a special package containing *All Together Now, As I Write This Letter, As Time Goes By, The Beatles Again?, The Beatles at the Beeb, Collecting The Beatles, A Day in the Life, The Literary Lennon, The Longest Cocktail Party, Things We Said Today* and *You Can't Do That!* The offer also includes a free calendar and the price to institutions is $191.00 and to individuals $152.00.

THE SCOUSE PRESS

4 Windermere Terrace, Liverpool L8 3SB

Liverpool has long been famous for its 'Scouse' sense of humour, that peculiar brand of deadpan wit that is manifested by so many Liverpudlian comedians today. As 'Scousers' the Beatles had plenty of this; it quickly endeared them to the world and was a breath of fresh air to jaded journalists, who had not been fed such a feast of readable copy since the days of Sam Goldwyn's and Marilyn Monroe's one-liners. Their Scouse accents and the introduction of phrases such as 'fab', 'wack', 'the gear' and 'grotty', which suddenly became 'in' words, added to the charm.

When George Martin asked them to listen to a playback and commented: "...and tell me if there's anything you don't like", quick as a snake, George Harrison quipped "Well, I don't like your tie for a start." This incident is credited with melting the ice between Martin and his new recording act.

Ringo's explanation for wearing so many rings was, "Because I can't fit them through my nose." When asked what they did when they were cooped up in hotel rooms, George said "We ice skate." On arriving in the States, Ringo was asked how he found America and replied, "We went to Greenland and made a left turn."

There is also a sort of surrealism in their humour, most pronounced in John Lennon's writings, but evident in some of the group's interviews. Paul, for instance, told a press confernece: "I once knew a fellow in the Dingle who had two dads. He used to call them number one dad and number two dad. Now apparently number one dad wasn't nice. He used to throw the boy on the fire – which can develop a lot of complexes in a young lad."

One of the most popular quotes came from John during the Royal Command Performance. He told the audience: "Would those in the cheap seats clap their hands. The rest of you can rattle your jewellery." At another prestigious variety appearance, Paul referred to the plump American star Sophie Tucker as one of his favourite groups.

Anyone wishing to delve further into the world of Scouse will find a veritable treasure chest of books at the Scouse Press which has published a series of three booklets on Scouse. My favourite is *Lern Yerself Scouse, Volume I* by Frank Shaw, Stan Kelly and Fritz Spiegl. It's the best introduction to Scouse I've come across. The other two are *Lern Yerself Scouse, Vol II – The ABZ of Scouse* by Linacre Lane, edited by Fritz Spiegl, and *Lern Yerself Scouse, Vol III: Merseyside Words and Phrases* by Brian Minard.

Spiegl is a Merseyside humorist, musician and writer who in 1964, recorded the EP 'Eine Kleine Beatlemusik', a semi-classical interpretation of 'She Loves You', 'A Hard Day's Night', 'All My Loving, 'Please Please Me, 'I Want To Hold Your Hand and 'I'll Get You'. In a detailed foreword to *The ABZ of Scouse* he sketches the background to Scouse, and perhaps betrays a certain weariness at the attention which the Beatles receive in post-sixties references to Liverpool. He writes: "What is the first shrine at which the visitor to Liverpool now worships? Allerton Hall, where William Roscoe fought for the abolition of slavery? Jesse Hartley's Albert Dock, that breath-taking, unique example of early Victorian dock architecture? Wood & Wyatt's Town Hall or the exquisite Queen Anne symmetry of the old Blue Coat School? None of these. Be he a dollar-spending tourist or publicity-seeking politician, the first place he makes for is a dank, sweaty, underground warehouse where 'The Liverpool Sound' was born – probably the most successful mass bamboozle since the virgin birth."

In the book, sexual intercourse is referred to as 'bayonet practice', toilet rolls are 'carnival ribbons' a bathing costume is a 'cozzy', absent-minded people are described in such terms as 'he'd forget his arse if it wasn't riveted on' and harmonicas are known as 'gob organs'. The mild coarseness of such phrases is an essential ingredient of Scouse humour.

In his story 'Liddypool', which first appeared in *Mersey Beat* and later in the book *In His Own Write*, John Lennon refers to many actual Liverpool places by names other than their official ones. This is another Liverpool trait, as you will find in the Scouse books. The new space-age Cathedral is known as 'Paddy's wigwam' or the 'Pope's launching pad'. The overhead railway, now dismantled, used to be called the 'dockers' umbrella' because the dockers used it to shelter from the rain, and the 'cazzy' refers to the Cast Iron Shore.

The Scouse books present the pronunciation of words phonetically, which might give the reader some idea of the Scouse accent. For instance, 'fairies' is pronounced 'furries', 'fur' is 'fir', 'where is' becomes 'wirse', 'got to' is 'gorra' and so on. The third book, by Brian Minard, subtitled *How to Talk Proper in Liverpool* is not so satisfying, not so much because the author has been living in New York since the late sixties, as because a lot of the words aren't really Scouse. When he refers to eyes as 'mince pies', the chin as 'Vera Lynn' and the feet as 'plates of meat', I think immediately of Cockney rhyming slang, not Scouse. Still, there are numerous phrases which capture the flavour of Scouse humour. Without writing them phonetically, I'll present just a few samples, which are given with their translation into 'proper English'! "She's got a personality like an open grave": she's a rather dreary girl; "I've seen more blood in a banana": he's rather pale; "She's got legs like knotty pine": she has terrible legs; "She can eat an apple through a tennis racket": she has prominent teeth; and

"She could sing a duet on her own": she's rather plump! Incidentally, Scouse humour is a touch chauvinist.

There are common Scouse phrases like 'this avvy': this afternoon; 'a bevvy': an alcoholic drink, and so on. They are all presented in an entertaining way in the Scouse books.

The Scouse Press has other books for readers interested in Liverpool itself. A series called *Liverpool Packets* contains maps, plans, prints, views, photographs and documents relating to all aspects of Mersey history from prehistoric to modern times. There are four titles in print and others in preparation. The available 'packets' are *Liverpool Street Songs and Ballads, The Growth of a City in Maps and Plans, Liverpool Transport Through the Ages* and *The Liverpool-Manchester Railway, 1830.*

Other titles from Scouse Press include: *Offbeat Liverpool* by Alan Brack; *Literary Liverpool* by William Amos; *From My Sporting Wife* by David Prole, *English As She Is Written* by Carolino/Spiegl; *Up The Reds/Up The Blues* by Bill Tidy; *The Everton Story* by Gladys Street; *Andrew Stephen's Diary* by Don Smith; *A Small Book of Grave Humour* by Fritz Spiegl and Jane Knight and *What the Papers Didn't Mean to Say, More of What the Papers Didn't Mean to Say, The Black on White Misprint Show* and *The Ugly Face Clubb Of Leverpoole,* all by Fritz Spiegl.

One of the most recent additions to the list is *An Everyday History of Liverpool,* described as 'a concise chronicle of everyday events on Merseyside from the earliest days to the end of the nineteenth century in facsimile reprint from Gore's directory, 1895: designed for stimulating a greater interest in local history and for futher study in school and colleges'.

UNDER AN ASSUMED NAME

John Squire, F12-13 Marcel Avenue, Clovelly, 2031 New South Wales

John Squire's book, *Under an Assumed Name: The Beatles Secret Reunion,* has never found a publisher, but Squire has produced a booklet about it, which he advertises in fanzines: "In 1973 did the Beatles secretly reform under the assumed name of Klaatu? My six years of investigation clearly suggests/proves they did. A limited edition of Klaatu photo and newsletter folios is now available for only A$3.50 or A$6.00 for both, postage free." The edition might well be sold out by now, but it is possible that he has undertaken a reprint.

The book concerns what Beatle fans know as the 'Klaatu Konspiracy'. On 3 August 1976 Capitol issued an album in the US by a group called Klaatu. The eponymous album contained the tracks 'Calling Occupants Of Interplanetary Craft', 'California Jam', 'Anus Of Uranus', 'Sub Rosa Subway', 'True Life Hero', 'Doctor Marvello', 'Sir Bodsworth Rugglesby III' and 'Little Mevtrino'.

Klaatu remained relatively unknown until an article by Steve Smith appeared in a newspaper in Providence, Rhode Island, claiming that Klaatu were the Beatles. As is the case of the 'Paul Is Dead' episode, numerous 'facts' were trotted out to prove the case. In a detailed article in issue 13 of *Beatles Unlimited,* Ian Ballon listed a number of the alleged 150 clues linking Klaatu with the Beatles: "At the University of Miami, voice prints of Klaatu and a recent McCartney album were made – and found to be the same. . . . In Australia a disc jockey said that Klaatu was a missing Beatles album called Sun . . . one of the tracks from the album, 'Sub Rosa Subway', was played backwards at different speeds, using a vera-speed low-frequency oscillator, and the vocals were sharpened with a set of filters. This message was found: 'It's us, it's the Beeeeeeatles!' " Other newspapers and DJs took up the cause and within an eight-week period over 300,000 copies of *Klaatu* were sold.

In their book, *The Beatles Again?* Harry Castleman and Walter J Podrazik identify the members of Klaatu as John Woloschuk, L M Carpenter, Chip Dale, Terry Draper, David Long and Dino Tome.

In spite of this apparently concrete proof that the band was not the Beatles, the fascination with Klaatu continued; further 'clues' ferreted out by Squires are: "A song on the album, 'Sir Bodsworth Rugglesby III' is misspelled on the back album cover so that it says 'Rubblesby'. Defining 'bods, 'worth' 'rubbles', and 'by' Bodsworth Rubblesby could mean 'persons of importance, born of quarrying.' The Beatles were first known as the Quarrymen!"

Squire's book is full of items of this nature, collated over six and a half years of investigations. The sample booklet he has been advertising comprises 34 pages of excerpts, with illustrative material. John was originally born in Yorkshire in 1949, moving to Australia with his family in 1956. He played in a number of bands and also became involved in the psychic scene.

I do not for a moment believe any of the Klaatu Konspiracy, but it's certainly an entertaining subject, and John Squire has exhaustively analysed texts and illustrations to prove his theory. He reproduces the original design for the *Goodnight Vienna* album. It shows Ringo Starr as the Klaatu figure from the film *The Day the Earth Stood Still* and is entitled: 'Don't Forget: Klaatu Borada Nikto.' He reproduces the 'sun' symbol on Klaatu's first album and contrasts it with the 'sun' symbols on a number of George Harrison recordings. Some of the 'clues' he offers stretch the imagination a little too much: for instance, in an attempt to make a connection between Klaatu's third album *Sir Army Suit* and the fact that John Lennon appeared in the film *How I Won The War* he asks: "Could *Sir Army Suit* be a reference to this film?"

To strengthen his case he continues "Could *Sir Army Suit* also be a reference to the Beatles album *Sgt. Pepper,* which featured cut-outs of a person dressed in ARMY clothing? . . . George Harrison's first performance with the Beatles took place in a Salvation ARMY hall in Liverpool . . . When the Beatles gave their first live concert performances in America they were all dressed in ARMY JACKETS of an off-white colour . . . In both the Beatle films *Help!* and *Magical Mystery Tour* all four Beatles can be seen wearing full-dress ARMY CLOTHING or ARMY SUITS . . .In the Beatles film *Yellow Submarine* the Fab Four can be observed wearing ARMY SUITS. I guess it's just another one of those coincidences?"

And if that weren't enough, he points out that: John Lennon was originally going to title his first solo album *SERGEANT LENNON* but later decided on the title *Mother;* there may have been a connection between all the Beatles awarded their MBEs and their titles 'Sir John Lennon', 'Sir Paul McCartney', 'Sir George Harrison', 'Sir Richard Starkey' and the title of Klaatu's album *Sir Army Suit;* in the Beatles song 'A Day In The Life', Lennon can be heard singing the line *'The English army had just won the war',* whilst Lennon's solo album *Imagine* contains a song title 'I Don't Wanna Be A Soldier'; in McCartney's song 'Jet', Paul can be heard singing *'Jet was your father, as bold as the Sergeant Major';* between the years of 1968 to 1971, John and Yoko were often photographed wearing part or full ARMY DRESS clothing.

The above 'clues' are not only tenuous to say the least, but a number of them are plainly inaccurate. The first track on John's first solo album was 'Mother', but the album's title was *John Lennon/Plastic Ono Band.* The Beatles indeed received MBEs, but these have nothing to do with knighthoods. The Beatles were certainly not dubbed 'Sir' when they received their awards from the Queen.

Klaatu have issued five albums altogether, all of which have been deleted. John Squire has amassed mountains of detail about each one. He is currently seeking an enterprising publisher for his completed project.

Books and Magazines

Details of hundreds of Beatles books and magazines can be found in my book *Paperback Writers: The History Of The Beatles In Print,* published by Virgin Books. Unfortunately, the majority of them are now out of print. Collectors can find out-of-print books at conventions, jumble sales and charity bookshops. A number of publishers still have Beatle books on their lists and I outline a brief guide to some sources:

ROCKPOST (PO Box 13819, Wauwatosa, Wisconsin 53213) has a large collection of Lennon, McCartney and Beatles music books available by mail order. Write, enclosing a self-addressed and stamped envelope for a full list of titles. The company concentrates on music books and their stock includes: *The John Lennon Collection; Lennon: The Solo Years; Paul McCartney Anthology for Easy Guitar; Paul McCartney: Composer/Artist; Wings at the Speed of Sound Songbook; The Best of McCartney for Piano; The Songs of Paul McCartney; Songs of Lennon and McCartney; The Beat of The Beatles; Beatles Greatest Hits; Wings Band on the Run Songbook* and many others.

GOLDMINE is an American magazine aimed at the record collector and has contained many features on the Beatles. It also has a regular column on Beatles records by Charles Reinhart and hundreds of advertisements relating to records and memorabilia for sale. A six-month subscription of 12 issues, together with one extra issue, costs $22 from Goldmine, the Circulation Department, 700 E. State Street, Iola, Wisconsin 54990.

VERMILION BOOKS is an imprint of the Hutchinson Publishing Group, and published Spencer Leigh's *Let's Go Down the Cavern* in 1984. Its addresses are 17-21 Conway Street, London W1P 6JD; PO Box 496, 16-22 Church Street, Hawthorn, Melbourne, Victoria 3122, Australia; PO Box 151, Broadway, New South Wales 2007, Australia; 32-34 View Road, PO Box 40-086, Glenfield, Auckland 10, New Zealand; PO Box 337, Bergvlei 2012, South Africa.

AURUM PRESS (33 Museum Street, London WC1A 1LD) has published two books of mine: *The Beatles Who's Who* and *The Book of Lennon.*

HAMISH HAMILTON published the 1983 biography *Paul McCartney* by Alan Hamilton, part of a series by the children's book division, entitled 'Profiles'. Their address is Garden House, 57-59 Long Acre, London WC2E 9JZ.

KOZMIK PRESS (49a Astonville Street, London SW18 5AL) published *John Lennon's Secret* by David Stuart Ryan. The book is 256 pages long, includes a free full colour poster, 32 full pages of photographs, a full discography and a full bibliography.

SIMON & SCHUSTER (Rockefeller Center, 1230 Avenue of the Americans, New York, NY 10020) published, on their 'Fireside Book' imprint, *The Beatles on Record,* a detailed illustrated discography by well-respected Beatles researcher and enthusiast Mark Wallgren.

BIG EYE PUBLICATIONS (1861 Middlebrook Road, Bound Brook, New Jersey 08805) is the publisher of *The Music of the Beatles* by Martin E Horn. This illustrated, 8½" x 11" paperback is another in-depth Beatles recording book with reviews of every Beatles album and single. Details include recording dates; original labels and release dates; chart positions; who wrote each song; who sings on each song; who plays which instruments; a description of the music; production techniques; technical data and special effects; historical background; and what each song means; a critical analysis of each song and original album covers and inserts.

WILD & WOOLLEY PRESS (PO Box 41, Glebe, New South Wales 2037, Australia) is the publisher of Glenn A Baker's *The Beatles Down Under.*

PAVILION BOOKS (196 Shaftesbury Avenue, London WC2H 8JL) is the publisher of *Give My Regards to Broad Street* (text by Andrew Harvey); *Paul McCartney: Composer/Artist* and *Photographs* by Linda McCartney.

PROTEUS BOOKS (Bremar House, Sale Place, London W2 1PT or 9 West 57th Street, Suite 4503, New York, NY 10019) is the publisher of Chris Welch's *Paul McCartney: The Definitive Biography;* Bob Woffinden's *The Beatles Apart* and *A Tribute to John Lennon.*

MULLER, BLOND AND WHITE LTD (55-57 Great Ormond Street, London WC1) published Mike Evans' *The Art of the Beatles.*

BLANDFORD PRESS (Link House, West Street, Poole, Dorset BH15 1LL) published Jeff Russell's 1982 book *The Beatles Album File and Complete Discography,* Carol Bedford's 1984 *Waiting for the Beatles;* 1985's *Fab! The Sounds of the Sixties* by Tony Jasper – and later the same year, under their Javelin Books paperback imprint, my own *The Book of Beatles Lists* and *Ask Me Why: The Beatles Quizbook.* Their American associate is Sterling Publishing Co. Inc, 2 Park Avenue, New York, NY 10016.

BEAT PUBLICATIONS (45 St Mary's Road, Ealing, London W5 5RQ) publishes *Beatles Monthly.* Annual subscriptions are £14.00 in the UK, IR £16 in the Irish Republic and £15.00 in Europe, inclusive of postage and packing; $33.00 in the US, Canada and South Africa; $38.00 in Australia and New Zealand and 35,000 eruzeiros in Brazil. All rates outside of Europe are for airmail postage. A companion magazine, *Record Collector,* is available from the same address for £1.15 per copy.

COMET BOOKS (44 Hill Street, London W1X 8LB) published the paperback edition of George Harrison's *I Me Mine* and John Green's *Dakota Days.*

HODDER & STOUGHTON (Mill Road, Dunton Green, Sevenoaks, Kent TN13 2YJ) published Richard Wootton's *John Lennon: An Illustrated Biography.*

HAMLYN BOOKS (Astronaut House, Feltham, Middlesex) is the publisher of Jeremy Pascall's *Paul McCartney & Wings,* Fred Dellar's *NME Guide to Rock Cinema* and John Blake's *All You Needed Was Love.*

NEW ENGLISH LIBRARY (47 Bedford Square, London WC1) are the publishers of Roy Carr and Tony Tyler's *The Beatles Illustrated Record,* Mark Shipper's *Paperback Writer,* Anthony Fawcett's *One Day at a Time* and a paperback edition of Brian Epstein's *A Cellarful of Noise,* and *The Playboy Interviews with John Lennon and Yoko Ono* by David Sheff.

BBC PUBLICATIONS (35 Marylebone High Street, London W1M 4AA) is the publishers of *The John Lennon Tapes* by Andy Peebles and *The Beatles at the Beeb* by Kevin Howlett.

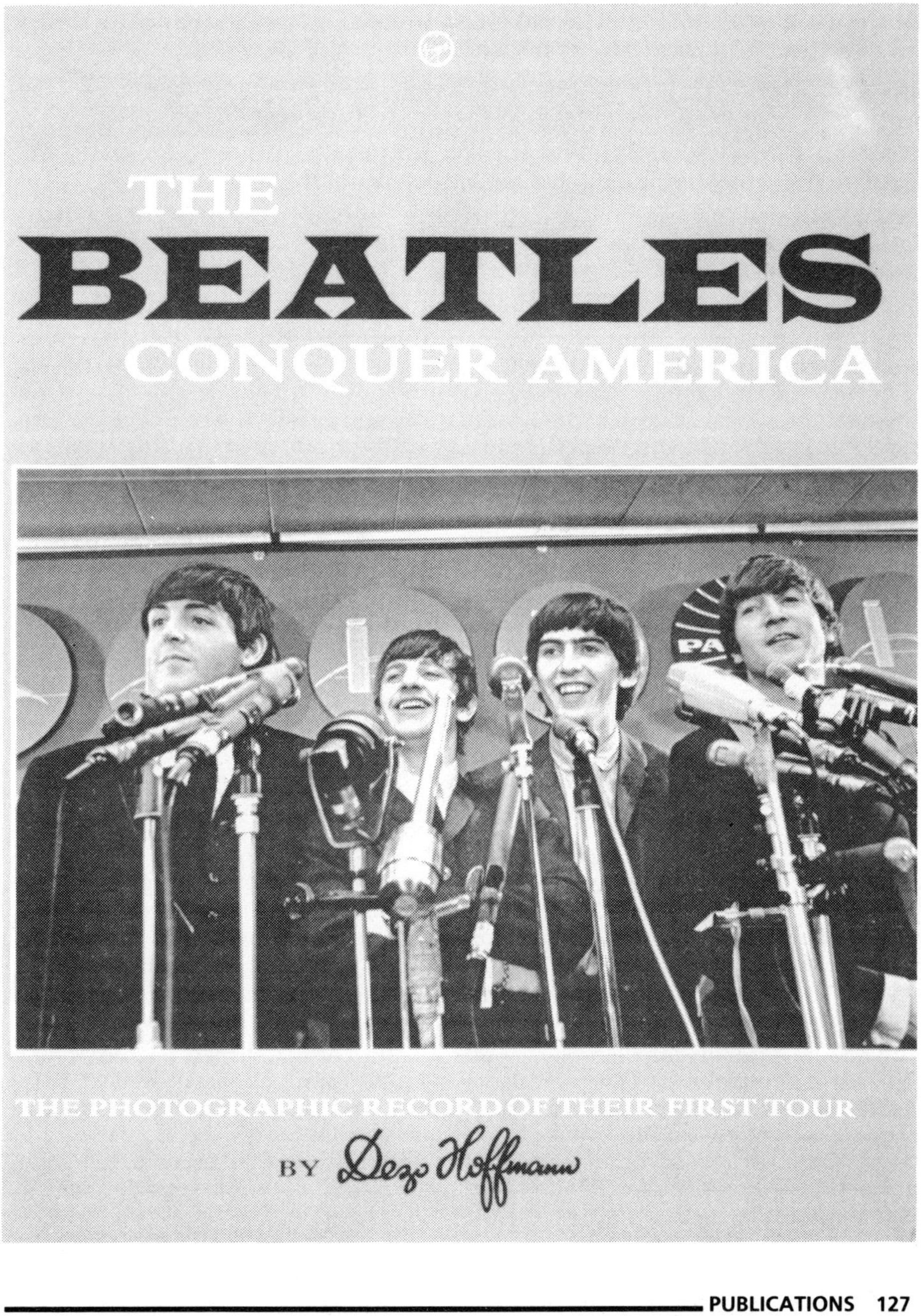

THE BEATLES ENGLAND was originally published in 1982 by 910 Press, PO Box 22361, San Francisco, California 94122 and in the UK by Columbus Books, 24 Red Lion Square, London WC1

EYRE METHUEN LTD (11 New Fetter Lane, London EC4P 4EE) published *Up Against It: A Screenplay for the Beatles* by Joe Orton and *The Beatles A to Z* by Goldie Friede, Robin Titone and Sue Weiner.

WEIDENFELD & NICHOLSON (91 Clapham High Street, London SW4) is the publishers of *Yesterday* by Robert Freeman.

DEANS INTERNATIONAL PUBLISHING (52-54 Southwark Street, London SE1 1UA) is the publisher of *The Beatles* by John Tobler.

COLOUR LIBRARY INTERNATIONAL (80-82 Coombe Road, New Malden, Surrey) is the publishers of *The Beatles Forever* by Helen Spence, also published as *The Beatles*

STAFFORD PEMBERTON PUBLISHING LTD (Ruskin Chambers, Drury Lane, Knutsford, Cheshire WA16 6HA) is the publishers of *The Beatles for the Record.*

PAN BOOKS (Cavaye Place, London SW10 9PG) is the publisher of George Martin's *Making Music* and the British paperback edition of Peter Brown and Stephen Gains' *The Love You Make.*

VIRGIN BOOKS (328 Kensal Road, London W10 5XJ) England has been publishing a series of Beatle reference books, of which this present volume is the fifth. The others are *The Long and Winding Road* by Neville Stannard, *Working Class Heroes* by Neville Stannard and John Tobler and *Paperback Writers: A History of the Beatles in Print* and *Beatlemania: A History of the Beatles on Screen* by me. The company has also published Dezo Hoffmann's superb collection of photographs of the 1964 American tour in *The Beatles Conquer America.*

MUSIC SALES (78 Newman Street, London W1P 3LA) had published over 40 different Beatle titles by 1983. These were mainly music books, but the company also issues other Beatle volumes, including Dezo Hoffmann's *With The Beatles; Beatles in Their Own Words,* compiled by Miles; *Paul McCartney; In His Own Words* by Paul Gambaccini; *George Harrison* by Ross Michaels; *A Day in the Life* by Tom Schulltheiss; *John Lennon in His Own Words,* compiled by Miles; and my own *Mersey Beat: The Beginnings of the Beatles.*

An example of their music books is *The Beatles Complete,* which contains the full, original lyrics to all the Beatles songs. It is the first music book to publish the words of every Beatles' song recorded and, apart from the 213 Beatles numbers, includes for the first time those by George Harrison and Ringo Starr. All the music has been freshly arranged in the actual keys of the original Beatles records, and each song crisply re-engraved. The cover features a gold embossed commemorative medallion, specially engraved from a portrait by artist John Holder and there is a unique collection of portrait photographs, most published for the first time, together with a special introduction by Ray Connolly. The book is available in two versions. The guitar/vocal edition includes guitar chord-box diagrams on all songs. The piano/organ/vocal edition contains an organ registration guide for use with each composition.

JHS Music-Video, 39 Main Street, Garforth, Leeds, England.
The retail division of John Hornby Skewes & Co Ltd has published a series of nine keyboard compilations. Of immediate interest is the *Family Organ Book: 40 Popular Beatles Songs,* specially edited for single manual 49-key and 61-key automatic organs, with guitar chords, presented on a single stave with chord symbols and lyrics. The book can be obtained from the above address by sending a cheque, postal order, or international money order for £5.25 for each book, which covers cost and postage.

VIDEOS

Although there is a considerable amount of video material of the Beatles, not much of it is available in high street stores. What follows is a short selection of companies which have put out Beatles material on general release. Further information on Beatles films, TV appearances and videos can be found in my companion volume in the Virgin series, *Beatlemania: A History of the Beatles on Screen.* Some fan clubs and memorabilia dealers also have video material for sale.

GLASS ONION PO Box 892, Ridgfield, New Jersey 07657.

Details of this Beatles Video Club are available free. The stock includes *The John Lennon Video Album,* which is a 30-minute collection of nine John Lennon numbers, available on VHS and Beta. Comes in a specially designed case, $35.00 postpaid.

MUSIC FILM COLLECTIONS Nicolas Beetslann 168, 2273 RG Voorburg, The Netherlands.

This company is the European Agency for the Fenno Werkmann collection of films. Fenno has the world's largest collection of Beatles material on film, in excess of 600 hours of items which fill a 58-page catalogue.

Fenno has been collecting Beatles film material since the early sixties and his work as a film archivist has preserved many items which would have been lost or destroyed. For several years he has been providing the film and video material for Beatle conventions in Europe and America and more recently has supplied material, once clearance has been arranged, for a number of video and television companies. He was able to come up with material for Abbey Road's *Cavern Beat* programme and CCTV's *The Story of Mersey Beat* (to be issued in September 1985 in both Britain and America under the title of my first book *Mersey Beat: The Beginnings of the Beatles.)*

PALACE VIDEO 8 Poland Street, London W1.

The Rutles is available on both VHS and Beta in a package with a 30-minute documentary on David Bowie and the making of his film *Merry Christmas Mr. Lawrence.* Rather unfortunately for Palace the BBC screened *The Rutles* once again in January 1985.

PICTURE MUSIC INTERNATIONAL c/o EMI Records, 20 Manchester Square, London W1

The Beatles product from PMI has been issued mainly in conjunction with Dave Clark International. Dave Clark, the drummer whose group was to rival the Beatles in

America in the mid-sixties, bought the rights to most of the music products of the former London television station, Rediffusion. These included the recordings of *Ready, Steady, Go!*, the *Around The Beatles* TV special and *Beat City*, a documentary about Liverpool by the late Charlie Squires, an award winning director. I was programme assistant on this film, which was originally screened in 1963. It was shown again in Britain on Channel 4 on 31 January 1984, but it has yet to be released as a retail video.

A number of *Ready, Steady, Go!* tapes have been issued. *Volume One*, released in November 1983, features the Beatles performing 'You Can't Do That' and 'Can't Buy Me Love' and includes an interview with the group. *Ready, Steady, Go! Volume Two* came out on 14 May 1984 and features the Beatles performing 'Twist And Shout' and 'She Loves You'.

On 29 April 1985, PMI issued *The Beatles – Live*, for a retail price of £14.99. The information blurb reads: "This 20-minute video features footage from a TV special entitled *Around The Beatles* originally recorded at Wembley TV studios in front of a specially invited audience in April 1964. The video also includes an exclusive performance of 'Shout'.

"The Beatles, then at the height of their poularity, are shown performing 'Twist And Shout, 'Roll Over Beethoven', 'I Wanna Be Your Man' and 'Long Tall Sally'. Paul then introduces a medley of their first hit singles – 'Love Me Do', 'Please Please Me', 'From Me To You', 'She Loves You', 'I Want To Hold Your Hand' and 'Can't Buy Me Love'.

"The video ends with John bidding us a fond farewell and credits roll to the added strains of 'All You Need Is Love' – the song that captured the mood of the entire Beatles era."

There is no explanation as to why the company didn't issue the entire *Around The Beatles* show on video. All PMI videos are available on VHS and Beta.

THORN EMI VIDEO Thorn House, Upper St. Martin's Lane, London WC2H.

Paul McCartney's 102-minute movie *Rockshow* and George Harrison's 95-minute *Concert For Bangla Desh* are available, both on VHS and Beta.

VIDEO DISCOVERIES Suite 614, 80 Wall Street, NYC, New York 10005.

A selection of Beatles videos and a free list are available.

VIDEOFORM Brunswick Industrial Park, New Southgate, London N11.

This company has issued *The Magic Christian* in which Ringo co-starred with Peter Sellers, and the three-hour long *Princess Daisy*, in which he appeared with his wife Barbara Bach. Also available from Videoform Music Yoko Ono's *Then And Now*, a 56-minute film costing £24.95. All videos on VHS and Beta.

VIDEO PROGRAMME DISTRIBUTORS Building No. 1, GEC Estate, East Lane, Wembley, Middlesex.

VPD has issued *Sextette*, starring Mae West and Ringo Starr on its Media label.

VINTAGE IMAGES 1101 Post Oak Boulevard, Suite 9-657, Houston, Texas 77056.

A free list of Beatles films, which include vintage live concert footage, is available.

WARNER HOME VIDEO PO Box 59, Alperton Lane, Wembley, Middlesex HA0 1SJ.

Unlike most of the other companies, Warner prefers only to rent their titles and does not offer them for sale. These include Ringo's *Caveman*, which was issued on 8 July 1983, *Rock 'n' Roll High School*, featuring the Ramones. Paul McCartney's number, 'Did We Meet Somewhere Before' which he originally wrote for *Heaven Can Wait*, at last found a home in this movie. Available on VHS and Beta.

COMPUTER GAMES

BEATLE QUEST

Number 9 Software, 47 St George's Avenue West, Wolstanton, Newcastle-Under-Lyme, Staffordshire

This computer adventure game based on the Beatles lyrics is the first of its kind and was devised by Garry Marsh. A lot of care, attention and enthusiasm has gone into this 32k program which is currently only available for the Commodore 64, although there will soon be versions for the Spectrum 48k and Amstrad.

Garry, a Beatle enthusiast, has come up with an intriguing adventure game and a complex text with over 150 locations, 200 messages and 60 objects all based on Beatles lyrics. Wherever possible, the 'story-lines' of the songs have been followed. Permission to use material from Lennon & McCartney compositions was given by Northern Songs Ltd, and the large wrap-around cover is a full colour reproduction of the Alan Aldridge illustration that contains 13 hidden song titles.

Beatle Quest will take you weeks, even months, to solve. The booklet that accompanies the cassette outlines the initial adventure:

"Life on space station nine, in the year 2953, is sedate and peaceful. It is also very boring. Gone are the worries of everyday life; all your needs are catered for by the supreme machine, Sel-taeb 4.

"The last pioneers left for Betelgeuse over two centuries ago. There is nothing left to do but wait, as you circle the worn out Mother Earth far below. Wait, and it may be you and your generation that receives the news that New Earth has been found.

"As 'Keeper-of-the Archives', a treasure house of all the remnants of Earth's history, it will be your responsibility to ensure that New Earth has access to its past, ancestral beginnings. Your work, at present, is concerned with pre-Dark Times mythology, particularly research into the ballads of the so-called 'New' Renaissance Minstrels.

"You hear, in wonder, of places long ago, peopled by exotic characters, in the reign of the 'Four Kings of EMI'; you listen in awe to the sound of cultural battles with 'their Satanic Majesties'.

"Your imagination is caught by the vivid descriptions of the colourful lands described in the ballads. You long for excitement; to return to the magical lands of EMI; to tour the mysteries that lay there. All you need is . . . love, emotion, experience and maybe even death itself. So you steal into the 'dome-of-pleasure', where you feed all known information about the 'Four Kings' into the data-banks.

"Time travel is still not an assured reality, but within the pleasure-dome, fantasies become reality. You may even find something of interest or value to return with.

"The lights dim as you lie on the couch and a voice booms out, above the strains of 'Yesterday', 'Welcome'. . ."

The game is available from the above address at the following prices:
UK £9.95 (including p&p); US $15 ($2 extra for air mail); Europe $15 (including p&p); elsewhere as for US.

Beatle Quest is Part One of a trilogy concerning the Beatles. The next two games, A Day In The Life and Across The Universe, will be available in 1986.

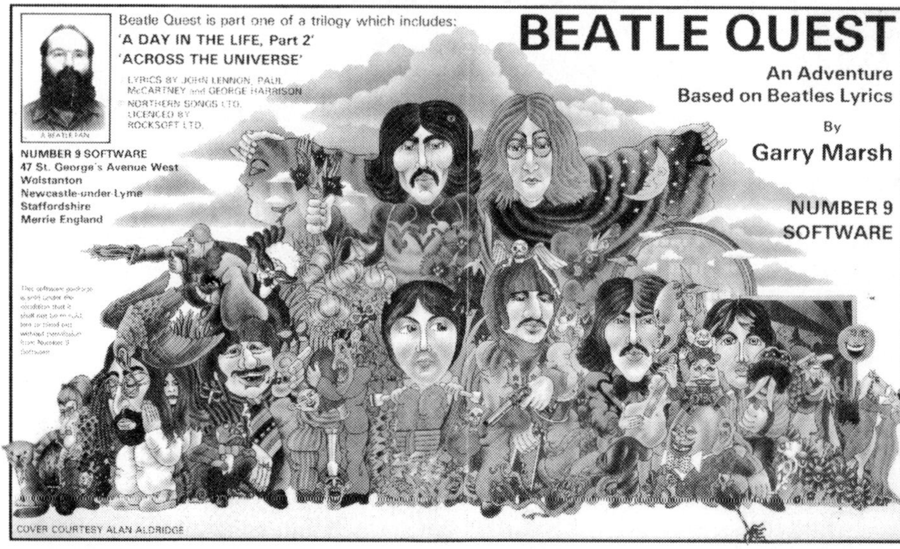

GIVE MY REGARDS TO BROAD STREET

Argus Press Software Ltd, Liberty House, 222 Regent Street, London W1R 7DB

Centred on Paul McCartney's film, this computer game (In Argus's 'Mind Games' series), was also based on an idea by Paul. The actual program was devised by the Merseyside firm Concept Software and took five people ten weeks to complete. Paul Clansey, a member of the Concept team, comments: "The program contains the biggest map to go into a computer of this size and the program used virtually the entire memory of the Commodore 64. Synchronising music and pictures required a lot of 'interrupts' – a TV picture is updated every fiftieth of a second and we had to do the same."

The game is available for the Commodore 64 and Spectrum 48k computers.

The large wrap-around cover features the film artwork and inside the package is a large full colour map of London showing famous landmarks, tube stations and other information, together with biographies and colour pictures of Paul, Linda, Ringo and other stars of the film who are included in the game. There is also a free colour poster containing actual stills from the movie.

The 'Mind Games' blurb on the packet reads: "Seven busy characters, ten lost chords, 15 hours, 48 traffic wardens, 95 London tube stations, 125,720 square miles of London, seven million Londoners. . .943 action filled screens.

"The new single is missing and the band have gone home for the weekend – leaving you just 15 hours to re-create the missing tune.

"Driving around a full scrolling map of London and knowing their lifestyles you must find each member of the band and get to the studio on time. Remember the musicians only move around on the Underground. To help you in your search your car computer is linked to the London Transport master computer.

"Watch out for meanies, wardens and Rath."

Full loading instructions and gameplay appear in English, French, German and Spanish.

FAN CLUBS AND FANZINES

A selection of current fan magazines was given in my book *Paperback Writers: The History of the Beatles in Print*. Some of the magazines mentioned there have since folded: *Dark Horse,* the George Harrison fanzine, has been incorporated into *Good Day Sunshine; Cavern Mecca; Ringo* and *Ram On* are all no more. However, new 'zines have sprung up in their wake.

Most fan clubs and magazines have offers available. Apart from the usual books, magazines, T-shirts and memorabilia, they are a good source of original photographs, particularly those clubs devoted to individual members of the ex-Beatles. Whenever writing to fanzine editors, it is always a good idea to enclose a stamped, addressed envelope or an IRC (International Reply Coupon available from Post Offices) as many of them are non-profit making organisation and cannot answer letters which don't include return postage.

THE HARRISON ALLIANCE. Patti Murawski, 67 Cypress Street, Bristol, Connecticut 06010.

Current subscription rates for this George Harrison fan magazine and details of back issues available can be obtained from the above address (remember to enclose SAE or IRC). The magazine also has an incredible stock of several hundred George Harrison photographs. A list of all available pictures can be obtained from Patti and to give you some idea of the range, type and price of the photos, I shall describe a few:

439. Colour, set of two; March 1983, George at Long Beach Grand Prix in pits with friends. In one photo he's talking seriously, in the other he has his head thrown back, laughing (cute photo!). In both photo's he's wearing sunglasses, pale yellow shirt jeans, black jacket, is clean shaven and has a short haircut. Taken by Jennie Swenton. $1.20 set.

442e. Colour, 5″ × 7″ only: March, 1983, gorgeous close-up of George, semi-profile, with a delightfully huge smile on his face. George is wearing sunglasses, a black jacket, and pale yellow and blue palm tree print shirt. He's clean shaven and has short hair. Exceptional photo. Taken by Patti Murawski. $3.50 plus two stamps or IRCs to the value of 20c (prices differ slightly for overseas orders).

A56. Colour: Summer 1970, George and Mal Evans in EMI Parking lot. George is signing autographs and looking into the camera. He has long, long hair and beard, is wearing an orange shirt and huge round sunglasses and carrying a jacket and a copy of *Autobiography of a Yogi.* Taken by S Dufresne. 50c.

MY SWEET LADY JANE. Penny Lane, PO Box 1399, Campbell, California 95008.

This Jane Asher fanzine is published four times a year in January, April, July and October. Penny also offers a photographic service. She has the world's larget collection of Jane Asher photographs for sale, with over 100 black-and-white shots for 40c each and colour pics for 50c each. She also has a series of special shots at various prices. Penny has a nine-page list of her available shots which will be sent on receipt of 25c plus two stamps or IRCs.

WELCOME BEATLES. Conatella Rossi Lennon, L.go, Leopardi 12a, 00185 Roma, Italy.

A 40-page fanzine covering the Beatles associations with Italy. Further details from the above address.

THE BEATLES ADMIRATION ALLIANCE. Penny and Kate, 26 Glebelands Road, Knutsford, Cheshire WA16 9DZ.

A new club. Further details from the above address.

THE McCARTNEY OBSERVER. Doylene Kindsvater, 220E 12th Street LaCrosse, Kansas 6754; Marie Lacey of 537 W 6th Street, Plainfield, New Jersey 07060, and Susan Di Lorenzo, 3307 S 133rd Street, Omaha, Nebraska 68137.

Doylene and Marie are co-editors, assisted by Susan of this quarterly magazine. Fees are $6.00 per annum in US and Canada, plus eight 20c stamps (Canadian members may send $7.60.) Back issues are available at $2.00 plus two 20c stamps. There are also two double issues (15/16 and 24/25) available at $3.50 plus three 20c stamps or IRCs. Foreign members should write for details of postal rates to their own countries.

The *McCartney Observer* always has a selection of photos of Paul available, and provides a special list with each issue. The photo's measure 5″ × 7″, cost $3.50 each and can be ordered from Doylene, who also requires an appropriately sized SAE (two stamps for the first photo, one extra stamp for each additional three).

BEATLES NOW. Roger Akehurst, PO Box 307, Walthamstow, London E17 G11.

Roger publishes and edits this glossy colour magazine every two months. Annual subscription rates for the six issues are £5.95 inland, ($12.00 and $15.00 to the US surface mail and airmail) and £7.10 elsewhere. The classified advertisements of this particular magazine always include some interesting Beatles items for sale, such as the latest limited editions from Unique Posters, special offers from David J Smith and special editions of Beatle art products made by fans.

YOKO ONLY. Brian Hendel, 61Middle Drive, Toms River, New Jesey 08753.

This is a relatively new fanzine devoted to Yoko, with articles, photographs and members contributions. Annual subscriptions are $9.00 for six issues (US) and $12.50 (overseas). Yoko herself is pleased with the publication and wrote to them saying: "I'm just watching it grow. It's great."

INSTANT KARMA. Marsha Ewing, PO Box 256, Sault Ste, Mre, Michigan 49783.

This is a long established 'zine devoted to John and Yoko. Regular correspondents include Tony Gorse in England, John O'Meade in Ireland and Chris Devos in Belgium. Six issues are available annually, for $9.50 in the US and $13.00 overseas, with cheques payable to Marsha. Yoko is pleased with this 'zine too and she regularly drops a personal line to the mag. At the end of October, 1984 she wrote: "It's really fun to read your letters in the magazine. Many of you amaze me for your understanding and knowledge of us, all of you teach me something through your interpretation of what we are, and I keep feeling warm love for you regardless of your opinions, as you are my extended family. Thank you for being."

BEATLES MAGAZINE. PO Box 29113, River Station, Rochester, New York 14626.

This contains more than 26 pages packed with up-to-date Beatle news, information on Beatles' instruments, video and record reviews, plus in-depth articles. Annual subscription rates are $12.00 for six issues (US and Canada), $19.00 elsewhere (airmail).

FROM ME TO YOU. Peter Schuster, Postfach 555, 6430 Bad Hersfeld, West Germany.

Peter has been running this glossy magazine since 1978. It contains an English language section.

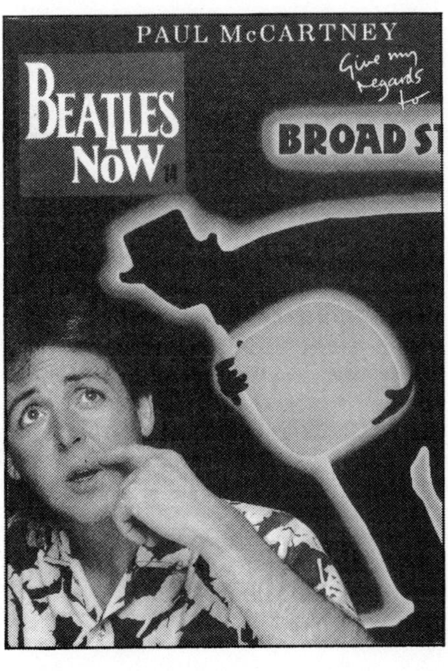

BEATLES UNLIMITED. PO Box 602, 3430 ap Niewegein, The Netherlands.

A year's subscription covering six issues for Europe is f30 (£7.50 or $12.00); for North and Central America, Africa and the Middle East, f32.50 (£8.00 or $13.00); for South American, Asia and Australia, f35 (£9.00 or $14.00). The 'zine is sent airmail outside Europe, except for Canada, New Zealand and Australia, where it is sent by surface mail. All back issues are still available at f5 (£1.20 or $2.00) each. Evert Vermeer is editor-in-chief, Rene van Haarlem is overall co-ordinator and Jos Remmerswaal is assistant editor. For collectors, the 'zine also has special binders in red and blue with the words 'Beatles Unlimited' in gold lettering on the spine. Each binder can hold 13 issues. These can be inserted by means of a rubber band system which means the magazines will not be damaged. The club also organises Beatle conventions in Holland.

BEATLEFAN. William King, Goody Press, PO Box 33515, Decatur, Georgia 30033.

Annual subscriptions for six issues are $8.00 in the US ($12.00 for express delivery by first class mail); $12.00 in Canada and Mexico; $15.00 in Britain, Europe and Latin America; and $17.00 elsewhere. Sample copies are available for $1.50. The magazine also puts out glossy reprints of articles from out-of-print issues of *Beatlefan:* the Badfinger three-part interview and an album review from 1979 is $2.50 postpaid; the story of the Beatles Cartoons series by King Features (complete with cover art and comic strip based on the original) is $2.50 postpaid. A special offer includes both reprints for $4.00.

REVOLVER. Gwyn Jenkins, 37 Hare Hill Close, Pyrford, Woking, Surrey GU22 8UH.

An annual subscription for six issues costs £3.00, inclusive of postage and packing. Back issues are available as follows: Nos. 1-6, 40p each; No. 7, 45p; No. 8, 35p; No. 9, 50p; Nos. 10 and 11, 65p each; and Nos. 12-15, 80p each. A bumper back-issue package can be obtained for £7.50.

THE FAB FOUR. Jacques Volcouve, Club Des 4 De Liverpool, 43 bis, Boulevad Henri-IV, 75004, Paris.

This magazine is in French, is lavisly illustrated and crammed with information. Jacques also runs a Beatles information service.

THE BEATLES VIDEO NEWSLETTER. John Dobrydnio Jr, 184 Emerson Street, Springfield, Massachusetts 01118.

A newsletter dedicated to the collection and trading of Beatles videos. Annual subscritpion rates for six issues are $7.00 inland and $10.00 outside the US.

HOW DO YOU DO IT. Ray Schweighardt, PO Box 504, Elmwood Park, New Jersey 07407.

This new Beatles fanzine specialises in information about unreleased Beatles music. Ray will provide details about the magazine on receipt of an SAE.

MAXWELL'S SILVER HAMMER. Allison Villone, 15 Rock Ridge Road, Larchmont, New York 10538.

Annual subscription rates for this fanzine, published every two months, are $7.80 (US, Canada and Mexico), $13.80 (Europe, Central and South America), and $14.80 (Australia, Japan and Asia). For further details and/or a sample issue ($1.00) send an SAE or IRC to the above address.

CLUB SANDWICH. Wings Fun Club, PO Box 4UP, London W1A 4UP.

For details on how to join the club and receive its official magazine write to the above address.

Beatlefan
Vol. 4
P.O. Box 33515, Decatur, GA 30033
No. 2
Paul McCartney:
Remember Him?
Album News & Tributes Inside
Cynthia Lennon Interview
Mike McCartney Interview
New Guide To Collectibles
Design/Artwork by Jaime Sustaita

Beatlefan
Vol. 3
Box 33515, Decatur, GA 30033
No. 3
RICHARD STARKEY
"Caveman": Ringo's Back!
A Guide To Beatlesque Recordings
Wally Podrazik's Mystery Of The Missing Beatles Song
"Shout!" The Controversial New Beatles Biography

'Give My Regards To Broad Street'

Beatlefan
NOW IN DOLBY STEREOPHONIC SOUND!
BEATLES
A HARD DAY'S NIG
WILFRID BRAMBELL
The Man Behind The Beatles Films

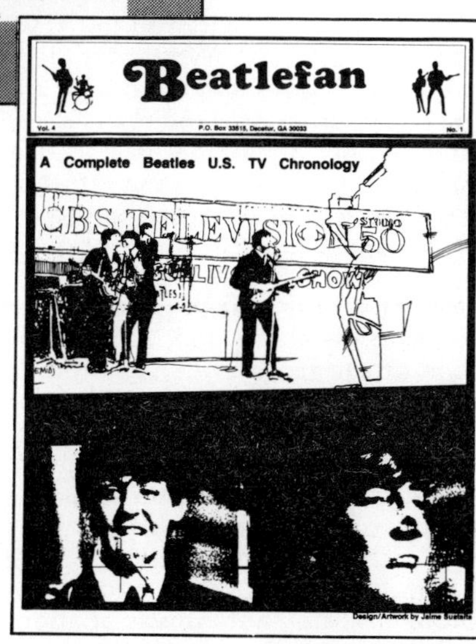
Beatlefan
A Complete Beatles U.S. TV Chronology
CBS TELEVISION
Design/Artwork by Jaime Sustaita

WORKING CLASS HERO. Barb Whatmough, 3311 Niagara Street, Pittsburg, Pennsylvania 15213.

Of the two publication's using this title, Barb's is the longer established. For details send an SAE to the above address.

WORKING CLASS HERO. Patty Owens Rycyk, Star Route 2, Jefferson City, Missouri 65101.

Patty's publication was still in preparation at the time of writing, its first issue due out later in 1985. However, in a full-page advertisement in *Beatleads,* she has decribed her forthcoming 'zine as "a new creative publication dedicated to John Lennon, his ideas, his philosophies. It will feature stories, poems, articles, artwork, news clippings, a pen-pal listing and free advertising for other Beatle-orientated material. Each issue will be 50-100 pages long, offset printed on high-quality paper and will feature a silk-screened colour cover." Some of the proposed items for the first issue are 'Dreams Are Never Over', a 'hard-hitting' story by Sandra Necchi about a college student, politics and Lennon's assassination; a first-hand account of Patricia Connerley's thrill at receiving two handwritten letters from John when she was fourteen; and a special communication from a 'twenty-third century John Lennon fan' who would apparently find his philosophies quite 'logical'!

BEATLEMANIA MAGAZINE. Royce Hurt, 702 South Main Street, Ripley, Mississippi 38663.

Royce suspended his former publication, *Beatle Beat,* and kept in touch with members by newsletter while he prepared this new fanzine. He told me: "The first issue of *Beatlemania* will be printed on glossy paper and will have a colour photo cover. It is going to be a full size magazine at 8½" × 11". We will be printing four issues a year and sending out newsletters in between them – we are a fan club as well."

ALL TOGETHER NOW. Vlasta Paul, 240 W Lincoln Avenue, No. 4 Escondido, California 95008.

Contact the above address for details.

APPLE'S KIN. Leanne Clarke, Route 2, Box 194, Vashon, Washington 98070.

This organisation of kindred spirits whose common interest is a love of the Beatles describes itself thus: "What is Apple's Kin? Apple's Kin is whoever joins it. Meaning that where it goes and what kind of personality the group has will be very much dependent upon how members contribute. Apple's Kin is a group of people with common (though not identical) concerns. Most basic is a compassion for the world, coupled with a desire to help effect change that will steer us towards humaneness. The five statements that are 'basically' agreed upon by group members are these: 1) We are one people in one world – boundaries mean nothing when it comes to human need. 2) Respect has to be extended to all living things – not just humans. 3) Don't let society take form without questioning the shape it takes or by blindly accepting the status quo; as individuals we must take some responsibility for the shape of society, even when others have turned their head. 4) Anger can be an important weapon, but it is better directed towards issues, not people. 5) We have to believe the world can improve and we should not trust in 'fate' to make it better – it is up to all of us to make changes.

"Apple's Kin membership originates among Beatle fans. We began in 1982 as a network of letter writers who shared information and distributed our 'information sheets' through an organised pen-pal system in which each person had the responsibility of copying and passing information to two assigned people. In October '83 this system was abandoned in favour of subscription to allow more efficient distribution as well as longer newsletters. Why Beatle fans? First, a number of us were already in communication via letters, clubs, magazines and conventions – we were (and are) a resource for ourselves just waiting to be tapped. But secondly, and most importantly, we were (and are) an *inspired* resource – made up of people influenced by the music and lives of four people whom we saw searching their own lives and asking questions of the world, who were examples of positive, independent thinkers, and who together wove the kind of magic that aroused and changed the imaginations of millions of people. The spark which ignited was not just political – it was cultural, and of the spirit, individual and yet communal. We have been sparked. We should not waste the fire. So that's why Beatle fans. But this is not a Beatles club, and anyone wanting to join is most welcome. Sparks come from many sources.

"The objective with Apple's Kin is just to provide another avenue for people to express themselves and to work together. We wish to create a supportive group of people who can share resources and learn from one another. We have people of various ages, interests, and experience levels. Five committees (each with a contact person) currently exist: *Gun Control*, Celeste Sabatini, 1875 19th Avenue, Moline, Illinois 61265; *We Are World*, Haley Land, c/o Apple's Kin; *Nuclear Disarm*, Janet Vasil, 330 Kent Avenue, Bridgeport, Connecticut 06610 (the three topics that Apple's Kin members determined to be most pertinent to the group); *Lennon International Peace Day* and *Strawberry Fields In Central Park*, Bonnie Keny, 18425 Halsted Street, No. 16, Northbridge, California 91325. We write letters together, spread petitions, ideas, and share friendship.

Members also address and report on many other issues including animal rights, world hunger, women's rights, political prisoners, refugees, magic, music, poetry – you name it. Everyone has their chance.

All information sheets (currently five pages) consist of members' reports, current legislation news, members' editorials, essays, poems – whatever – and come out about eight times a year. The subscription rate is $4.00 (cheques made out to Leanne Clarke).

BEATLEADS. PO Box 3423, Springfield, Illinois 62798.

First generation fan Katie Collard, took up the reins of this fanzine (published every two months) when original editor and founder Tim Anderson decided to shut up shop. Katie told me: "I asked him if I could take it up and keep it going. He gave me his permission and the rest is history. For me, anyway!

"I like the idea of providing the collectors of Beatle memorabilia with a marketplace to sell and buy their wares and I include news, reviews, photos, fan artworks and writings and profiles.

"The subscription price stands at $8 a year for the US and $10 for overseas. That is for six issues. The ads are relatively inexpensive as well: $1.50 for 50 words and under; $3.50 for half a page and $5 for a full page – and subscribers get their ads at half these prices! I'm also planning on having one issue per year with unlimited free ads for subscribers."

The 'zine also carries competitions with prizes of particular interest to collectors – such as Beatle Tie Tacs on their original cards. There are ads for records, magazines, fanzines, books, films, videos, pen-friends and memorabilia.

An example of one of the rare items is the ad for a Wings souvenir: "*OFFICIAL WINGS*; Vickie and Roger Francis carved the ivory Wings that Paul and Linda wore during their '76 tour. Roger made up 100 gold replicas, each numbered with a certificate of authenticity. The 'Wings' replica is 14k gold and about the size of a half-dollar. What makes these 'Wings' so valuable is that Roger wrote to Paul's attorney asking permission to cast these pieces. No word was heard for a long time so Roger went ahead and cast them. Then the answer came; it was 'No'. The few that were sold are collectors items ($600.00, or best offer). The Wings number is 13 and it is one of a limited collection."

Another interesting ad was the full page taken in issue 10 by Patty Owens Rycyk of Star Studio (see Working Class Hero). Patty, a professional artist, was offering 'Paul 1965', a drawing she originally did in 1965. She recently had it hand-carved in imported linoleum and hand-printed on Rives 100 per cent museum-quality rag paper (made from cloth pulp, not wood pulp), and issued it in a limited edition of 30. It measured 11″ × 14″ with an actual image size of 8″ × 10″. Copies, ready to frame, were available at $25 postpaid.

THE BEATLE ROOM CLUB. Anthony White, Swirrell Edge, Church Road, Rotherfield, East Sussex TN6 3LA.

For an annual membership of this Beatles fan club send £3.25 (overseas £4.00) to Anthony White at the above address, and you will also receive a club magazine called *Mersey Beatles Magazine*, published quarterly in March, June, September and December and sent to readers in England, Scotland, Wales, Italy, Australia, America, Spain, Germany, Peru, Poland and Canada. Produced in black-and-white (although there are plans to include colour in future issues), the publication now has around 30 pages per issue and contains various articles, competitions and photographs. The December 1984 issue, for example, ran a cover pic of Times Square in New York in 1969 with a 'War Is Over' advert and a photograph of the Fab Four on the back cover. There was an editorial, the 'Barrett Column', fanzine reviews section, a review of *Valotte*, the story behind an Australian Beatles compilation album, an article on Julian Lennon and a competition.

Members also receive: a pen-pal list, issued twice yearly in January and July; a 'Help' service – "If a member can't answer a question, we will. If we can't, we will give the peron asking the question a prize"; a poster shop – "We sell specially reproduced posters from the sixties and some new ones"; money reductions – club members receive a 10 per cent discount from the shops Beatles Bazaar and Impressions; a membership card; gifts – *Faraway Stars* book, poster and other items if available; T-shirt – club T-shirt for sale; competitions, one in each issue of the club magazine; and a Christmas cassette – plans are underway to produce a cassette for Christmas 1985.

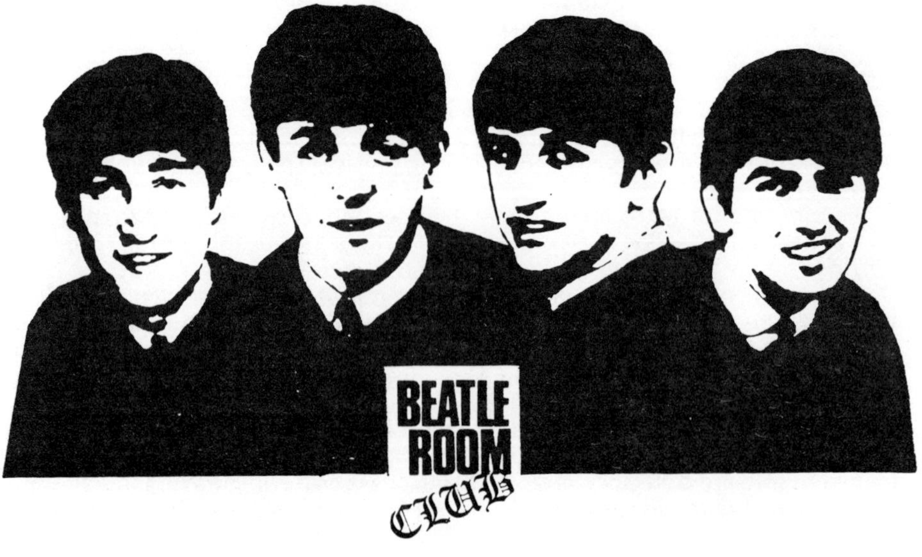

Here is an outline of what members have received over the five years the club has been in existence, as given to me by Anthony:

November '80: All members were sent a membership card.
October '83: A set of Liverpool leaflets.
March '84: Three postcards and a club badge.
June '84: Beatle City deal – members could get into Beatle City for a 15 per cent reduction during a two-week period.
September '84: Two large posters were given free to members.
October '84: Second design of membership card sent out.
November '84: Beatles leaflets, stickers etc.
December '84: Special Beatles Christmas cassette produced for members.
January '85: Welcome Beatles black-and-white poster and a special club pack of club information, press release etc.
February '85: New membership card sent out.
March '85: Free extra magazine and badge, and Beatle Holiday leaflet.

Anthony also provided me with this potted history of the club:

November '80: After joining a Beatle pen-pal club, which was a rip-off, he decided to start his own pen-pal club for Beatle fans from around the world. Membership was £1.50 and for that they received two lists of pen-pals.
October '83: After a few years of running the club he decided it would be much better to have a newsletter which he could send to members of the club with their pen-pal lists.
March '84: The first newsletter/magazine was published and contained some recent news. We called it the *Mersey Beatles Magazine* after the *Mersey Beat* newspaper.
April '84: One of the club members wrote to him saying, "Let's have some articles in the mag", so he asked her to write some. She's Susan Barrett who lives in London.
June '84: Issue No.2 of the magazine was published containing articles by Susan, a news section, and information on the specially reproduced posters that members could buy.
July '84: Issue No. 3 was published in the new A5 format. There were two versions of the magazine, a Liverpool issue and an international one.
November '84: The club's pen-pal service was merged with Sgt. Pepper's Lonely Hearts Club.
December '84: Issue No. 4 came out, with the 'Help' service.
March '85: Issue No. 5 came out, together with a special magazine called *Faraway Stars.* The extra magazine was about a new Beatle-style pop group.

CHARLES F. ROSENAY!!! Executive Producer, Liverpool Productions, 397 Edgewood Avenue, New Haven, Connecticut 06511.

Charles (and he always includes those three exclamation marks after his name) is one of those fortunate fans who has used his entrepreneurial skills to his best advantage: he is engaged in Beatles activities on a full-time basis as fan club organiser, fanzine editor, promoter of numerous Beatle conventions and dealer in merchandise.

His fan club Good Day Sunshine produces its own fan magazine (every two months) and also has many goods on offer. The fanzine itself has absorbed two other fan magazines: *Dark Horse* and *Here, There and Everywhere.* Membership to the fan club, which includes a year's subscription to the magazine, is $5.00 plus fifteen 20c stamps in the US; $10.50 for Canada and $13.00 for elsewhere in the world. Apart from the magazine, members each receive a membership card. A sample issue of the magazine can be obtained for $2.00 and Charles has a selection of back issues available.

The fanzine has regular competitions with interesting Beatle items as prizes. There are news and reviews pages, readers' letters, video news, convention reports and various articles in each issue.

Via the Club Sales Department, Good Day Sunshine has various special offers available for members. A series of paperback book titles, including many rare items, a number of which are priced below the original cover prices, is unfortuntely available only to members in North America. The club also offers original and reissue copies of the *Beatles Monthly* books.

On the merchandising side, there is a Good Day Sunshine Official T-shirt, costing only $6.00 each (please specify size). With black lettering on a yellow background, these were designed by GDS member Caroline Harrison and printed by Daron Enterprises. A limited number of four-colour sweatshirts (small and medium sizes only) from the 1982 American Beatles Convention, which was held in Tokyo, Japan, are also available, at $12.50 each.

GDS has also decided to present a series of videotape offers, the first of which was the Japanese TV special *The Beatles Best Hit 20.* This is how the club's information sheet describes it: "Offered to readers of *Good Day Sunshine* only, this one-hour special is from Japanese network television. All commercials have been edited, but every other aspect of this unique all-Beatles programme is intact. Imagine Casey Kasem doing an exhaustive American Top Ten countdown using rare clips, promos, concert footage, interviews and performances while counting down the country's viewers' favourite songs. Then add rare material and some specially-produced bits and you're getting close to what's on this videotape. It's the ideal tape for the new video collector or the old pro! On the videotape you'll see documentary footage of Brian Epstein, the boys meeting the Queen, arriving at Kennedy Airport, the MBE awards and interview in Sweden with Jimmy Nicol. You'll see excerpts from their Shea Stadium concert, Washington DC show, and feature films. You'll see interviews with Japanese Beatle fans (finding out their favourite songs) and performances by Japan's No. 1 Beatles band, Lady Bug, captured live in the Tokyo nightspot, the Cavern Club. You'll see group and solo promos from *Revolution* to *Woman.* You'll see the Japanese station's tour of Liverpool to all the famous Beatle sights. But probably best of all is the 'home-grown' material: The Beatles' Tokyo interview, fans filing into the Budokan for the concerts, a look at the warm-up bands who preceded the Budokan performances and, of course, the Beatles' black suit concert (with the red shirts) in the very best full colour quality you've ever seen. They are shown playing 'Rock and Roll Music', 'Nowhere Man', 'Paperback Writer' and 'Yesterday'. The only thing we won't tell you is what song was voted No. 1!

"For your own copy of *The Beatles Best Hit 20* send $60.00 (we pay postage and insurance), and indicate format (VHS or Beta). Make cheque or money order payable to Charles F. Rosenay!!! (address above). No orders outside of North America. Please allow four to six weeks for delivery. (VHS orders filled a bit sooner)."

Since the late seventies, Charles has also been co-presenting an Annual New England Beatles Convention. The conventions are three-day affairs. An example of these is the Fifth Annual New England Beatles Convention Weekend which took place from 25-27 November 1983 at the Park Plaza Hotel, New Haven, Connecticut. Special guests included May Pang, Lou O'Neill, Sam Leach and Brant Mewborn and the groups who performed Beatles music were the Neatles, the Excerpts, Rubber Soul and Revolver. Films and TV shows included *Around the Beatles, What's Happening in the USA*, the *Washington DC Concert, The Beatles in Tokyo, Let It Be, Beatles at Hollywood Bowl, Magical Mystery Tour* and the *Ed Sullivan Shows*. There were dress contests, look-alike contests and lots of dealers' tables.

Charles also organised a convention with the radio station WAXY FM to celebrate the Beatles twentieth Anniversary. Entitled Beatles Expo, the convention took place at Omni International, Miami, from 7-12 February 1984. This event was unique at the time in that admission was free; and it proved such an overwhelming success that Charles decided to make it a regular occurrence. The second Beatles Expo took place at the Omni International from 7-10 February 1985, and once again admission was free. Entertainments included a Beatles look-and-sound alike band, The Mahoney Brothers, who performed a daily musical tribute, celebrating three different eras of Beatles fame; a Beatles memorabilia trade fair; an exciting collection of newspaper and magazine articles depicting the Fab Four's history in print, and some original Beatles merchandise manufactured since 1964 and licensed by Seltaeb, the company authorised by Brian Epstein in 1964 to license Beatles material; rare Beatles films and videos; and special guests who included Allan Williams and Sam Leach.

Charles points out: "This annual event is made possible through the co-operation of many organisations such as Capitol Records; *Good Day Sunshine* magazine; Liverpool Productions; Eastern Airlines; WAXY FM; the RKO Radio Network; the Omni Association and many others. It is free to the general public and is organised for the fans to relive the memory of the Beatles and relove the music that brought us so much joy over the years!"

The Omni Complex houses two hotels, movie theatres, 21 restaurants, an amusement centre and 165 stores and can be found at 1601 Biscayne Boulevard, Miami, Florida 33132.

Featured above is Charles F. Rosenay !!! the executive producer of Liverpool Productions and the publisher / editor of "Good Day Sunshine", the Beatles fan publication in the United States, holding a few of the tens of thousands of Beatles memorabilia items for the Beatles Expo.

THE DUTCH BEATLES FAN CLUB. PO Box 1464, 1000 BL, Amsterdam, The Netherlands.

The club claims to be the longest-running Beatles fan club in existence, having first been launched in November 1963. It has its own magazine, *Beatles Visie*, published quarterly. Current fan club President Johnny te Lintelo says: "We also publish many fan club papers such as membership cards, posters, calendars, special magazines etc. We've sold all kinds of rare items at low prices to enable young members to buy them. Any profits made are put back into the fan club. We've appeared on Dutch radio about 125 times and about five times on Dutch TV."

Johnny provided me with a brief history of the world's oldest extant Official Beatles Fan Club. It's history starts in December 1962, when Har van Fulpen launched a new Dutch pop magazine that ran the hit parades of several countries. Aimed at young people, the magazine was called *Hitparade* and was produced on a mimeograph. A few months later, in March 1963, the Beatles were mentioned in *Hitparade* for the first time when their second single 'Please Please Me' reached No. 4 in the English charts: Har predicted that there would soon be an invasion of new vocal groups.

Soon after this, Har wrote to the Official English Fan Club asking if he could begin an Official Beatles Fan Club in Holland. He received a positive reply and founded the club on 10 November 1963. He also received permission from EMI-Holland. Har was interviewed about the fan club on Dutch radio on 26 December 1963; several Beatles recordings were played, including their first Christmas single.

When the Beatles came to Holland, on 5 and 6 June 1964, to play two concerts and appear on a TV show, EMI invited Har to welcome them at Schiphol Airport. During their two-day visit he spoke to the Beatles on several occasions, and on 12 June he put out a special edition of *Hitparade* featuring a report on the occasion. Around this time, Dutch radio DJ Cees van Zijtveld began presenting weekly advertisements for the fan club on the radio.

In November 1964, Har had to do his military service, and publication of *Hitparade* was temporarily suspended; but the fan club continued in conjunction with the new music magazine, the monthly *Beatbox*. Har contributed to the publication until August 1966, when he completed his military service. Once out of the army, he immediately relaunched a magazine for the fan club, this time calling it *Chains*, after the song recorded by the Beatles. From February 1967 until February 1970, it featured a Beatles Top 50, which during the last two years of that period became a Top 100.

In December 1967 Radio Veronica started a weekly Beatles show in conjunction with the fan club.

In March 1969 the fan club moved from Leiden (where Har lived) to Pharus 74, in Zaandam, and its new address was printed on the backcover of the 'Hey Jude' single. That same month, from 21-28, John Lennon and Yoko Ono staged their 'Bed-In for Peace' at the Amsterdam Hilton. The fan club was invited to meet them on 23 March. John answered every question about the Beatles in a way which always brought the subject around to peace. He also signed some fan club magazines and was featured on the front cover of the new issue.

From September 1969 until January 1970, Radio Veronica presented a weekly Beatles Show, hosted by Dutch DJ Adje Bouman and Har van Fulpen.

On 24 April 1970, the fan club presented two showings of *Magical Mystery Tour* in a Zaandam cinema, managing to get hold of the only existing 16mm film of it.

In September 1970, the magazine *Chains* mentioned 'bootleg' for the first time. Between then and July 1982, more than 800 bootlegs were made of Beatles and solo Beatles recordings.

On 25 September 1970, the first of the news bulletins, *Nota Beatles*, appeared; it filled the gaps between issues of *Chains* which came out every two months. By February 1971, there had been 28 issues of *Nota Beatles*.

On 11 September 1971, the fan club organised its first Beatles convention in

Leiden. The one-day affair was a big success, attracting 2,000 visitors.

In January 1972 the Official English and American Beatle Fan Clubs ceased operating, but the Dutch club continued.

On 29 February, 1972, Dutch radio presented 'Veronica's Beatles Day', setting a world record with 20 hours of Beatles music. The event was held in conjunction with the fan club and also included music by solo Beatles, interviews with famous Dutch artists and rare recordings from the fan club archives. In the week following the event, 20,000 Beatles records were sold in Holland.

In May 1972, the fan club interviewed Ringo Starr and featured the article in *Nota Beatles*. The same year, on 25 and 26 July, it helped Radio Veronica DJ Lex Harding to present a two-day John Lennon special featuring the album *Some Time In New York City* and the bootleg *Telecasts*. On 30 July, *Nota Beatles* mentioned that the fan club had succeeded in obtaining tickets for the Dutch concerts by Paul McCartney and Wings which were to be held from August 17-21, respectively in Rotterdam, in Groningen, at the Concertgebouw in Amsterdam (mentioned in the song 'Rockshow' from the *Venus And Mars* LP) and in The Hague (where 'The Mess', the B-side of 'My Love, was recorded live). Before the concert in Groningen the fan club interviewed all five Wings members, Paul, Linda, Denny Laine, Henry McCullough and Denny Seiwell, for *Nota Beatles.*

Also in 1972, on 22 November, Radio Veronica began a weekly half-hour spot, 'The Beatles Story', with co-operation from the fan club, which also provided a full page each week for Veronica's radio/TV magazine.

In 1974 the fan club organised a trip to England, which included two Wings' concerts at the Odeon Hammersmith, and a visit to McCartney Productions Ltd. The fan club reported the concerts for *Nota Beatles* and the Dutch pop magazine *Oor*.

In September 1975, the fan club produced the first of a series of books called *Beatles Playback;* the same month fan club members compiled a Beatles Top 30 which was broadcast on Radio Mi Amigo's *Flashback Show* from Joop Verhoof.

In October 1975, the fan club wrote a lengthy Beatles story for *Oor*, and on the fourth of that month organised a Beatles evening in the famous Paradiso concert hall in Amsterdam. The event was a sell-out, with over 1,400 people attending. The programme included film shows (some of them 8mm), a playback game, a Beatles quiz, community singing, a swap-shop, a fan club information centre and the presentation of the famous book, *The Beatles: the Complete Records Story.*

On the weekend of 17 January 1976, a new Dutch record was set when two DJs played 50 hours of non-stop Beatles music. On the twenty-sixth Dutch television presented a Beatles programme and interviewed Har van Fulpen. Two months later fan club members around Amsterdam received a news bulletin prepared jointly by the fan club and EMI-Holland detailing the arrival on 24 March of Paul McCartney and Wings at the Amstelhotel in Amsterdam. They were given a big welcome and the next evening appeared at a concert in Rotterdam, followed by a concert in Paris the next day. Reports of both concerts were featured in *Nota Beatles*, issue 101, which became a magazine from that issue.

The fan club's third Beatles Convention took place on 25 September in Utrecht. On the programme were films, videos, a Beatles Top 100, a dance contest with a weekend for two in London as the prize, a picture show, an exhibition from the fan club archives, a Beatles market and swap-shop.

In December 1976, the fan club organised another trip to London to attend a major Convention with guests who included Allan Williams and Bob Wooler.

On 3 February 1977, George Harrison visited Holland for a day to promote his album *Thirty Three & ⅓*. The fan club interviewed him for 30 minutes – in the very same room in the Amsterdam Hilton in which John and Yoko had stayed in March 1969!

On 11 April 1977, the fan club visited Allan Williams in Liverpool and interviewed the people behind the album *The Beatles Live at the Star Club in Hamburg, 1962.*

On 12 February 1978, the fan club organised the fourth Convention in The Hague, with a market, films, an exhibition and a DJ.

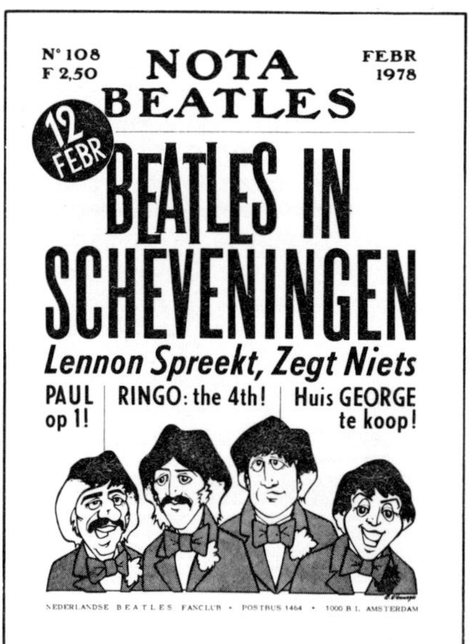

1979 proved to be a dramatic year for the Dutch fan club. Its fifth Convention took place on 7 April in Nieuwegein and was the usual success, with films, videos, a large market, a swap-shop and an exhibition. There was also a live group, The Bootles, and Allan Williams was guest speaker. But, when interviewed on the TV show *Countdown*, which had filmed parts of the Convention, Har confirmed an announcement that he had made a month earlier – that the fan club would cease to exist at the end of the year, as he felt that there was a lack of interest. After 15½ years crammed with Beatles-related activities, this came as quite a blow to the fans.

Undeterred, four fan club workers started a video section in June, intended as an archive of Beatles films of both group and solo performances from all over the world. Other workers at the fan club joined them and it was decided to keep the club going. In August Har helped them produce issue 111 of *Nota Beatles*, which carried an advertisement requesting help in this venture. On 10 October the decision to keep the fan club going was announced during a two-hour radio show on Beatlemania.

The club was saved by a whisker, and in March 1980 it announced that a new quarterly publication, *Beatles Visie*, would replace *Nota Beatles*.

On Monday, 8 December 1980, John Lennon was killed in New York. The fan club was deeply shocked and sent a condolence telegram to Yoko Ono. It contributed to a Dutch radio memorial programme on John, and was also represented on Friday evening, 12 December, during the torchlight walk for John Lennon from the Doelenhotel (where the Beatles stayed in June 1964) to the Hilton Hotel (where John and Yoko stayed in March 1969). On Sunday, 14 December, the fan club respected Yoko's wishes and held a ten-minute wake before the Hilton Hotel.

In conjunction with the fan club, Har van Fulpen wrote a memorial book about John. All the profits were used to reprint the 'War Is Over – If You Want It' posters, which were then spread all over Amsterdam, just as they had been in 1969.

On 3 January 1981 the fan club was present at the opening of the world's first Beatles Museum, Cavern Mecca in Liverpool.

In 1981 the magazine *Beatles Visie* was voted into first place in the Dutch magazine *Muziekparade's* Fan Club Top 10.

In October 1981 and April 1982, Henry Scheepers tried to break the European record of playing Beatles and solo-Beatles music non-stop. He broke his own record the following April, with 63 hours.

In April 1982, Har van Fulpen's book *Beatles Dagboek* appeared. Har was interviewed on the radio about the book and the fan club.

In October 1982, the club contributed to two programmes celebrating the twentieth anniversary of 'Love Me Do'. The first on 5 October, was an 11-hour radio show on the Beatles; the second, on the tenth, was a TV programme, *The Story of the Beatles.*

The club celebrated its own twentieth anniversary in 1983, and is still recruiting members, who receive a large poster, a four-colour membership card, four fan club magazines and occasional newsletters. Write to Johnny te Lintelo at the above address for further details.

EDINBURGH BEATLES APPRECIATION SOCIETY. Janet Rich (President), 36 Woodburn Terrace, Morningside, Edinburgh EH10 4ST.

The society is officially registered at Edinburgh University, which provides it with a modest grant and access to University facilities – halls, bars, rooms, equipment etc, at reasonable rates. However, it is not primarily a University Society as over half the active members are non-students.

Janet writes: "Membership currently stands at about 40 which may not seem very large, but I believe there is a place for this kind of society in Beatledom. We do not publish any sort of magazine or newsletter, I believe the demand for such publications is amply filled by the dozens of available circulars and magazines ranging from the highly professional to the very informal. The Society was formed in October 1983 with the sole aim of providing regular meetings on a local basis, providing members with the opportunity to meet socially, to exchange memorabilia and simply to share important news items (a new LP, a new No. 1 single etc), as most of us are living most of our lives among people who seem to find these events trivial.

"Our meetings include video shows (we have access to an excellent collection of material thanks to the generosity of one of our members), quiz nights, sixties dances, guest speakers etc. Victor Spinetti was kind enough to share some of his memories with us when he was in Edinburgh appearing in a play.

"We spent a year collecting money to purchase a memorial bench which is dedicated to John Lennon and stands in Princes Street Gardens next to the Scott Monument. The dedication of the bench took place on 9 December 1984 and it was officially unveiled by Ray Coleman. The inscribed plaque read: 'John Lennon 1940-1980. Dr Winston O' Boogie, Bless You, Wherever You Are.'

"We also keep a library of cassettes and books for the use of members. The society is run by volunteers and finances itself through subscriptions (students £1.50, non-students £3.00), raffles and social events, plus the small grant already mentioned."

EVERY LITTLE THING. Sally Smallwood, No. 711, 176 The Esplanade, Toronto, Ontario M5A 4H2.

Sally tells me: "The fanzine is a joint effort by myself and my good friend and long-time Beatle fan, Craig Rowland. We are both 19 and own quite extensive collections of Beatle books, records, mags and memorabilia. We also both love to write. Every issue has regular features: 'Read All About It' (for George); 'Beaucoups Of News' (for Ringo); 'On Ono' (Yoko); 'All Paul' (Paul); 'Just Julian' (Julian); 'Who Goes There' (Beatle news); 'Think For Yourself' (Beatlequiz) plus 'Name And Address', 'There's A Place' and 'The Word (Search)'."

The 'Name And Address' section includes information on Beatle memorabilia shops, with comments about their wares. In issue No. 2, two such outlets are covered: Pakra of Box 224, Brooklyn, New York, and Queen's Comics And Memorabilia of 1962 Queen Street East, Toronto, Ontario. Commenting on Pakra's catalogue, Sally says: "This Beatles catalogue is without doubt one of the best around. It's crammed with original memorabilia, records, books and mags. The prices are a nice surprise too: they're very reasonable on average. A set of four blow-up 'cartoon' Beatle dolls sold for £150.00 at Sotheby's two years ago, while the same thing with wrapper was selling for $45.00 in Pakra! Another bonus: after *buying* the first catalogue, when you order something you will be sent the next one free of charge."

On Queen's Comics, she says: "This store is probably the only one of its kind left in Toronto. It sells old and new Beatle memorabilia and some books and records. Annette Lawrence, who owns the store, holds the bi-annual Toronto rock 'n' roll conventions at the Lakeshore Inn. Annette herself has been a Beatle fan for many years and owns an extensive collection of Beatles paraphernalia."

Advice about dealers and conventions is given in the same issue and Sally and Craig discussed the TO Rock And Roll Convention in Toronto: "All conventions have huge selections of singles. They come as picture discs, or with or without picture bags. I bought seven, all originals with picture bags, including three George Dark Horse singles, one George Harrison Apple, plus three US 45s by Paul, John and the Fabs. Gary Brongo from Rochester had the best selection of domestic and foreign 45s at the convention.

They add a warning note: "TAG Distribution had a stall selling a 'butcher' cover for $250.00. Its cover was either very carefully steamed off, or it had been an original. Also at this table were gold singles (for 'Hey Jude' and 'Let It Be'), one gold EP (for 'The Beatles' Million Sellers') and one gold album (for 'The Beatles'), selling for between $150.00 and $350.00. These were almost certainly fakes. The RIAA must certify its authenticity on the award, and this certification was absent on all four of the above mentioned discs. Therefore, we would strongly suggest you check out such awards for their authenticity before you shell out a lot of money for a piece of worthless rubbish."

And finally, a critical observation: "Among the dealers who did not show up at this convention was the Beatles Boutique. In past conventions they have displayed a hardcover US copy of Yoko's *Grapefruit* (second edition) with a ripped and stained dustjacket, for $25.00! Other examples include a sealed US copy of *The Whale* by John Tavener for $60.00 (worth $15) and a sealed US copy of *Unfinished Music No. 2: Life with the Lions* for $125. However, the memorabilia that the Beatles Boutique sells is even more shocking in price: they had the Beatles 'flasher' ring set for $12.00 at one convention. You can buy these rings from Pakra for $2.00 for all four."

Every Little Thing is published every two months and annual subscriptions are $6.00 in Canada, $8 in the US and overseas.

THE JOHN LENNON WORLDWIDE MEMORIAL CLUB. 23 Mathew Street, Liverpool 1.

The gathering place for Beatle fans on Merseyside is situated next door to the Grapes pub, where the Beatles used to go in the early sixties when they appeared at the Cavern, and was formerly called the Left Bank Bistro. The entrance sports an oil painting by a local artist called *Imagine* and on the club's white walls and black wooden beams are hung many photographs of John and Yoko, togehter with a large John Lennon collage and drawings and paintings of John by local artists.

The premises are owned by Frank Sharrock, but as it is a private members' club it is actually run by a committee led by secretary Eddie Porter. John's uncle, Charlie Lennon, is President and Yoko Ono is an Honorary Member. Other members include Father Tom McKenzie, Victor Spinetti, Bob Wooler, Allan Williams and a host of local Beatle fans. The membership list has passed the 2,000 mark.

Membership costs £2.50 per year and an applicant must be proposed and seconded by a member. A member is allowed to sign in two guests. The club committee is currently seeking special permission from the police to exempt tourists from the 48-hour waiting period which, by law, must elapse before membership is taken up.

The club has seating for 100 people, but its full capacity is 150 persons. It has the approval of Cynthia Lennon, and Eddie Porter tells me its atmosphere is pleasant and friendly. Bands such as Mojo Filter, who play Beatle-style music, are presented every Wednesday evening and on weekend afternoons. There is a jukebox which has sixties music and Beatle-related records from the sixties to the present. There is also a guitar behind the bar and anyone who feels like it can have a sing-song. The club is particularly popular with foreign visitors who are looking for a taste of the Mersey Beat scene, as it is frequented by many former members of Mersey bands such as Faron of Faron's Flamingos and Paddy Chambers of the Big Three.

LIVERPOOL BEATLES APPRECIATION SOCIETY. c/o John Chambers, 19 Ashbank Road, West Derby, Liverpool L12.

This organisation promotes the Beatles name and lobbies for various positive actions to be taken to honour the group. It was the Liverpool Beatles Appreciation Society which helped to promote the idea of Beatle street names in Liverpool, of having a statue of the Fab Four in the city centre and several other campaigns. One of their current proposals to Liverpool City Council is to have the music of the Beatles included in Merseyside Schools' curricula. The three main figures behind the society are John Chambers, Gene Grimes and Leslie Priestley.

The campaign for a Beatles statue in the city actually began in January 1977, when John and Gene launched The Beatles Monument Campaign. Within two years they had each spent £3,000 of their own money on the project and in 1978 the cost of a statue was estimated at about £40,000.

To give you some idea of the dedication of the society, I will outline the background to the Monument Campaign. John originally came up with the idea of having a Beatles statue in Liverpool in 1965. Once the campaign was launched in 1977 he wrote to the City Council's press officer David Marlowe, who replied that he was not particularly interested and considered the Arthur Dooley madonna sculpture in Mathew Street a sufficient tribute.

During the next year, John was involved in a lively correspondence with various public figures in his efforts to attract support and financing for the venture. But the council continued to reject the idea. Councillor Roy Stoddart commented: "It is my opinion that they are not worthy of a place in our history", and another councillor, Tony McVeigh, added: "The Beatles could not sing for toffee. They ended up taking drugs and bringing tremendous discredit to our city. They have turned down requests to appear in the city on official functions and the Queen awarded them medals and they sent them back."

Even Paul McCartney was not impressed with the idea of the statue and said: "Personally, I'm not into being commemorated. That's something for dead people and I'm very much alive."

John would not accept the initial thumbs-down and wrote to the Lord Mayor, the Queen, the Prime Minister, MPs and other public figures. He roused public opinion in the press and on the radio and finally saw his efforts rewarded when the Council said they would agree to the erection of a statue because of "The musical achievements of the Beatles and the world-wide fame that has accrued to Liverpool as a result of their talent."

The City Council's General Services Committee had agreed to view models by various sculptors on 15 February 1978 and to make a firm decision. At the meeting the Committee favoured a sculpture by Brian Burgess, sponsored by Allan Williams and Bob Wooler and recommended this to the Liverpool City Council. Burgess has now completed a model-scale of his statue and funds are still being raised for the full-scale version.

At the time in 1978 John wrote to me: "Although Messrs Williams and Wooler are the official sponsors of the statue, they are a separate entity to Gene and myself. However, I am still continuing with the campaign as I want the siting of the statue to be changed from Williamson Square to Church Street. Church Street is the main pedestrian shopping area and I feel, as do many supporters, that if located there, it would receive maximum public exposure. The BMC will not cease until it has achieved its objective, which is to have a commemorative monument of the Beatles in Liverpool City Centre, preferably Church Street." Even in 1985, Chambers is fighting to have the site of the statue moved.

THE O'NO REVUE. Vickie Woods-Lovett, 13043 Meandering Way, No. 269, Dallas, Texas 75240.

This is a fan magazine devoted to Yoko, edited by Vickie (former co-editor of *Yoko Only*) with the help of associate editor Katie Collard, and originally called *The Yoko O'No Foundation.* Vickie told me: "I started this 'zine out of admiration and respect for the woman that John Lennon loved and the world hated. I think I understand her and her art. She's a neat lady." Describing the magazine, Vickie writes: "*The O'No Revue* is that club that goes a step beyond conventional 'fan clubs' and really takes in hand the events of Yoko Ono – her creative and unique style – and ponders as well what to do to make this world a better place. We don't judge, but present a showcase of peace and hopes. Ms Ono has acknowledged us and supports us with great enthusiasm through letters to the members of the *Revue* and is aware of all our doings.

"We do many events in her art style. Recently we were part of the 'Peace Days' events and sent Yoko roses. In turn she sent each participant a personally autographed 'Milk And Honey' poster and rare 'Every Man' sweatshirt."

Annual US subscription rates for the magazine are $12.50 for six issues. Also accepted are half payments of $6.25 with the balance payable on receipt of the third issue. The rate for Canada and elsewhere is $19.00, acceptable in US money order only.

There is also a series of items available by mail order for members only, including Yoko with Sean/Yoko/Sean badges, $2.50 each (specify choice); 'Honk If You Love Yoko' bumperstickers, black with white letters (vinyl), black with orange letters, or dark blue with white letters (vinyl) $3.75 each; *O'No Revue* bumperstickers, $3.50 each; memorabilia poster, $5.00 each; and 'Every Man Has A Woman' poster, $3.50 each. All prices include postage.

SGT. PEPPER'S LONELY HEARTS CLUB. 2 Birch Hill Avenue, Wakefield, Massachusetts 01880.
Tom McDonald, who runs this club, dropped me a line to say: "I've sent you our club package . . . it has taken me over seven years to complete it and I'm very proud of it. I've worked really hard on this project and kept the cost down for all the lonely people . . . PS We're also working on a pen-pal list to include in our package."

Tom's package included a large full colour badge of 'Sgt Pepper's Lonely Hearts Club Band'; a smaller lapel button in blue with the Beatles silhouettes and the words 'I believe in yesterday'; an Official Membership Card, which is a two-colour item, similar to a visiting card, with the club's address and the design from the club's bumpersticker; a bumpersticker with the word 'I', followed by a large red heart and a silhouette of the Beatles; and 'Club Foot Notes', which is a fold-out sheet with cuttings on both sides relating to various fanzines and Beatles memorabilia shops.

For further details of newsletters and fees write to the above address.

THE WRITE THING. Barb Fenick, 3310 Roosevelt Court, Minneapolis, Minnesota 55418.

An international Beatles fan club with a quarterly magazine, The Write Thing celebrated it's tenth anniversary in 1984. In her editorial in the anniversary issue of the newsletter, Barb wrote: "In January of 1974, The Write Thing started up with a few loyal friends and some former members of Beatles Rule (my first Beatles fan club 1967-71) . . . some of you who have been with the club since the beginning will remember the pages run off on a high school mimeo, and then a cheap Sears special. When I started The Write Thing I was in college and having Insty Prints do it a little more grandly (and legibly) on these larger pages. After leaving college I gave the club my full attention for many years. The whole idea in the beginning was to have a place to collect all the news and happenings, collate them and send them back out to be shared by everybody, so no one would feel left out of things and isolated."

In the club's promotional leaflet, Barb writes: "The Write Thing is the oldest and largest Beatles fan club in the world today – with over 2,000 members world-wide. Our newsletters are approximately 30 pages long – fully illustrated. All the current news and pictures from all over the world, plus many unpublished photos, printed here first! Regular features also include: collectors' column (tips on what is rare, where to buy and current values); question and answer pages; video reviews and news; record and book reviews; free pen-pal listings, and stories by fans who have met the Beatles. We also present several pages of want ads and display ads for trading-buying-selling. The Write Thing also sells many hard-to-find Beatles items: rare records, promos, imports, books from other countries, magazines, old collectables, gum cards, T-shirts, photos and more. A sales list is included with every newsletter and an additional quarterly sales list is sent out between issues.

"Annual subscription rates are: US/Canada/Mexico – $10.00 Europe/South America – $15.00 airmail; Asia/Australia – $18.00 airmail.

"The Write Thing also produces its own special Beatles T-shirt with a white design on aqua blue or raspberry. The T-shirts are 50 per cent cotton, 50 per cent polyester and come in sizes small (34-36), medium (38-40), large (42-44) and X-large (46-48). A limited stock of black sleeveless sweatshirts is also available. Details and prices can be obtained from the above address.

#42
The Write Thing
the Beatles in America
1964~1984
20c
usa
S. LONG 83

"As has been mentioned, The Write Thing has a large selection of Beatles merchandise for sale. Of particular interest to collectors might be the gum cards, some numbers available from all series. Send list of numbers needed. We'll pull out what we can and bill you. Cost $1.00 each, plus post. We are also running a one-off video sale. Over 30 titles, one of each, Beta format, from my own private collection, and selling out. Send SAE for xerox list. Rare opportunity to get Beatles films, promos, TV specials, interviews, programmes otherwise not for sale. First come, first served, till they are gone."

WITH A LITTLE HELP FROM MY FRIENDS. Pat Simmons, 10290 Pleasant Lake Blvd, F-21, Cleveland, Ohio 44130, and Joy Kilblane, 16430 Holland Road, Cleveland, Ohio 44142.

Pat and Joy believe small is beautiful and keep their club within manageable bounds. Pat wrote to tell me: "We started off over 12 years ago with only 70 members and even now we stay with an average of 400. We only advertise in other newsletters that trade ads with us: we can't afford advertising in magazines, which is about the only way to have a really large club. Frankly, we *prefer* being small, anyway. When a club has thousands of members, it can't possibly give them all personal attention. When I was a member of the New York City Club, before I became its area secretary, it always drove me crazy writing to them with questions and never getting a reply. But it's just impossible to answer every letter when your club is so large. And clubs that big become more like corporations where each member is a number, not a fellow fan, and to me that takes away from what fan clubs are all about. We make no profit from our club the way so many others do (some of them make so much that they employ full-time staff); I'd feel *guilty* if we made money from it. Again, to us, that isn't what a fan club is *for*. We exist simply to share things with other fans – printing foreign articles some fans may not have access to, for example. Our club is not a business, it's just for fun and for sharing. Both Joy and I each have our own full-time jobs aside from this club (and even though it's small, it's like having a second full-time job anyway!)."

With A Little Help From My Friends began in Florida in 1972 as a chapter of the Official Beatles Fan Club in New York City. When the New York club disbanded, the chapter continued independently but its organiser soon had to give it up for financial reasons. Joy, who had been a member and had helped administratively on many occasions, took it over, brought in Pat, gave it its present name and started putting out newsletters. Today, it is an international club for all four Beatles, with members in 18 different countries, who receive quarterly newsletters (February, May, August and November). Each issue is 32-38 pages long and is crammed with pictures and news from magazines and newsletters from all over the world, sent in by members. Pat and Joy admit to being suckers for the 'good old days', so each issue has a large nostalgic section – reprints of interviews, articles and pictures from sixties magazines – in addition to current news and pictures. There are also articles contributed by members who have met the Beatles or been to a Beatles or solo concert.

The club also sells Beatles photographs, from the sixties to the present – pictures from magazines worldwide, London press shots, concert photos and photos by fans, including some by Pat and Joy themselves. Each issue of the newsletter features two full pages of new photo offers, with the previous issue's offers being added to the stock list which is now over 40 pages long and which includes every photograph sold since the club's inception in 1972. A copy of the list can be obtained for six stamps in the US, six IRCs in Canada and Mexico, and ten IRCs in any other country.

Xeroxes of interviews (old and new) from magazines and newspapers worldwide, and tape cassettes of Beatles concerts in many different countries, some quite rare, are also available. For Xeroxes and/or tape lists, send an additional two stamps per list (two IRCs Canada and Mexico, four IRCs overseas). All lists must be ordered from Pat, who will also advise on prices for non-members.

Each issue of the newsletter also offers auctions of old and new books and mags and other material from different countries; there is also an occasional stationery offer.

Annual subscription rates are as follows; US, $7.00 plus eighteen 20c stamps; Canada/Mexico, $11.00; airmail to Japan/Australia/New Zealand; $16.00; airmail to any other country (receive issues in 7-10 days), $15.00; surface mail to all overseas countries (receive issues in 6-8 weeks), $10.00. Individual sample issues can be bought for $1.50 and four stamps in the US; $2.25 Canada/Mexico; $3.50 overseas airmail. All profit goes towards printing and postage costs.

THE BEATLES CINE CLUB. PO Box 115, Shibuya Post Office, Tokyo, Japan.

The Beatles Cine Club was originally established by Tetsuo Hamada in July 1966. The club was given its authorization by Toshiba EMI Records, licensee of the Beatles' records in Japan. As of June 1983, membership to the club stood at 48,000.

The club's objectives are: to let new generations know, in a variety of ways, how wonderful the Beatles were; to carry out studies aimed at understanding the Beatles more deeply and comprehensively; and to enhance communications between all those who love the Beatles.

The club is so called because in the early days it was dedicated to showing Beatles films. Today, it is involved in many more activities besides, some of which are listed below:

1. Publishing *The Beatles*, a 34-page glossy monthly magazine, containing the latest information, study reports, essays, photographs, subscriber's corner etc. About one third of its material each month comes from *Beatles Monthly*, on which it is based, with the permission of Sean O'Mahoney of Beat Publications. The other two thirds originates in Japan.

2. Staging regular Beatles Festivals; these are held three times annually (winter, spring and summer) in 12-14 cities throughout Japan. Each festival includes a presentation of Beatles films, record concerts, merchandise relating to the Beatles, an information corner, question and answer games, etc. About 20,000 Beatles fans gather at these occasions.

3. Collecting and studying information on the Beatles. The results of the studies are published in the form of extra issues of *The Beatles*, with special themes.

4. Carrying out public relations aimed at giving the younger generation a better understanding of the Beatles. This is done through the provision of information and news on the Beatles to newspapers, TV and other media and the holding of Beatles exhibitions at college festivals, in department stores and halls, etc.

5. Publishing professionally produced books of high quality, usually printed on coated paper to produce a rather lavish look and to enhance photographic reproduction. The club's *Beatles Forever*, for instance, sold 60,000 copies. All the books are in Japanese. They include:

Beatles Album. Comparison of English, American and Japanese version of Beatles and solo-Beatles recordings.

Early Beatles and Liverpool. Studies of the Beatles before their debut, from six viewpoints. It includes an index of articles from the *Mersey Beat* newspaper, the first of its kind in Japan.

John Lennon Memorial Issue. This includes John's personal history, general information, chronological chart, etc.

Beatles Bibliography. List and description of all books and publications on the Beatles, centring on those published so far in England, the US and Japan.

The Beatles Forever. The first half of this publication is a Japanese translation of the Colour Library International book of that name, with all the high-quality photographs. There is an additional encyclopedia of the Beatles which includes a chronological chart, personal histories, a discography and so on.

MERCHANDISING
THE SELLING OF THE BEATLES

The Beatles had found success before any of the Liverpool firms realised the value of obtaining licences for merchandising. I realised this when Thorpe & McCann, a firm of plastic engineers from Sefton Park, approached me at *Mersey Beat* for suggestions regarding a series of plastic masks of local artists which they wanted to produce. They had approached Brian Epstein, but he had rejected the idea of the Beatles being involved. This was a pity as there would have been some unique masks of the boys, taken directly from their faces, which would have undoubtedly become very collectable items. Brian, at the time, was very particular about what merchandise he would grant licences for. Thorpe & McCann produced what they called 'Starplaks', three-dimensional life-size sculptured faces of Liverpool singers, costing 9/11d (approximately 50p). A mould was taken of a singer's face and the resulting gold-coloured, three-dimensional 'plak' jutting from a square frame was realistic and impressive. Unfortunately, the demand wasn't high and masks of Mark Peters and Sonny Webb were the only ones produced before the series was discontinued.

A deal which Brian did agree to was for the confectionary firm Sayers to produce party-size Beatle cakes in the shape of a guitar with real photographs of each member of the Beatles on them, costing 5/6d (approximately 27p). There were also smaller sized cakes with individual pics of the Fab Four at 5d each (2p). Within 12 hours of the cakes being advertised in *Mersey Beat,* 25,000 had been sold. It was no

longer a case of someone asking for two cream buns and a custard, it was 'Two Ringo's and a George, please'!

Another firm which obtained permission to use the Beatles in their advertising campaign was Lybro Jeans. Their account was handled by Millican Advertising which produced some very effective advertising images with black-and-white artwork.

In February 1964, in issue No.67 of *Mersey Beat* I wrote an article about the Beatles merchandise on sale in Britain. The piece, appearing opposite a half-page advert for Vox amps which featured the group ('Vox go the Beatles?' was the selling line), was called 'Beatles Buys' and was headed by pics of two girls wearing Beatle caps. It read in part: "Beatle wigs, boots stockings, talcum powder, sweaters, chewing gum, are only some of the many, many Beatle buys on the market. . .

"[There are also] the Beatle Caps produced by Kangol, a fashion trend which could catch on. The caps are available in 11 different colours, and two of the models are pictured above.

"There is an incredible demand for Beatle wallpaper, which is produced by a photogravure process from actual colour photographs of the group. There's Ringo with his drums at the back, John singing into the microphone and holding his rhythm guitar, while George, in the middle of the largest group, plays lead guitar, and Paul, on the left, bass. The design was produced by arrangement with Nems Enterprises and even includes the boy's signatures."

The sale of Beatles merchandising was actually an amazing phenomenon which must have generated almost $100 million in sales during 1964 alone, yet the story behind it all was one of greed, cock-ups, drama and law suits. The details were not to emerge until more than a decade had passed, when researchers delving into Beatles history came across the incredible tale of Seltaeb. The extremely complicated saga has been explored in a number of books such as McCabe and Shaumberg's *Apple to the Core,* Philip Norman's *Shout!* and Peter Brown's *The Love You Make.*

Basically, Brian Epstein wanted to maintain a standard of taste with the merchandising bearing the name of his boys. At first, when the first enquiries began to seep in, he was able to control the flow (at one time, at a slightly later date, he was asked to endorse a licence for a Beatles sanitary towel!), but as the flow turned into a flood, his office at Nems just couldn't cope with the enquiries. He was advised to consult a fasionable show-business lawyer, David Jacobs, which he did, passing the responsibility over to him and giving him authority to sign merchandising deals on behalf of Nems.

Jacobs initially had one of his assistants coping with the enquiries, but realised that the task needed a different approach. He felt it should be all dealt with by someone acting as agent for the merchandising and he decided to ask Nicholas Byrne, a young man who moved in the same social circles as himself. Jacobs had met Byrne at a few parties and surmised he was ambitious and young enough to be able to cope with such a task. Byrne decided to go into partnership with five of his friends: Lord Peregrine Eliot, Simon Miller-Munday, Mark Warman, John Fenton and Malcolm Evans. Byrne took over the title of President of the company and asked each of his friends to invest £1,000, for which they were to receive 20 per cent of the shares. They called the British end of their company STRAMSCACT and the American end SELTAEB (Beatles spelt backwards).

Jacobs apparently had no yardstick by which to judge the percentages arising from such a deal, but he also seemed to lack a basic common-sense understanding of haggling – that as a rule of thumb someone looking for a deal expects you to bargain them down and will always start by throwing into the ring a percentage far higher than they would anticipate getting on the presumption that it will be bargained down. Byrne said his company would take 90 per cent of the fees they received from licensees and grant Nems and the Beatles a derisory ten per cent. To Byrne's surprise, Jacobs immediately accepted.

Byrne then went to America where firms were queuing up and clamoring for a share in the Beatles market; his team of reps found hundreds of firms willing to make bids, which turned Byrne and his partners into millionaires virtually overnight. The *Wall Street Journal* estimated that Beatles merchandising would make over $50,000,000 in the States in 1964 alone, but the sales of hundreds of ranges of goods were so successful that several sources have put the estimate at twice that figure.

One company which had a licence to manufacture Beatles clothes sold over two million T-shirts in a fortnight and also had healthy profits from sales of pants, hats, beach shirts, tennis shirts and other clothing. Another firm producing Beatles wigs could hardly cope with orders of over half a million when they were going all out to produce 15,000 per day. The Reliant Shirt Corporation, which had paid Seltaeb $100,000 for a licence to manufacture Beatle T-shirts, sold more than a million in only three days. Byrne was licensing so many products – guitar-shaped brooches, cookies, Beatle nut crunch popsicles, stationery, candies, toys, alarm clocks, scrapbooks, nighties, bubblegum, buttons, trays, penny banks, bubblebaths, sneakers, plates, lunch-boxes, loose-leaf books, pillows, purses, wallets, patches, wallpaper, belts, key-rings, pencil cases, commemorative medals, coathangers, dish-clothes, dolls, play balls, scarves, toothbrushes, towels, aprons, balloons and so on – that he was living a lavish life-style in the best hotels, buying expensive cars and availing himself of an expense account on which he personally ran up a bill of over $100,000.

The first inkling Brian Epstein had of the momentous blunder his British lawyer had committed by literally giving away the merchandising rights came when Byrne visited him on his arrival in the States with the Beatles and gave him a cheque for almost $10,000

Brian realised that if Byrne could afford to give him this amount Seltaeb must have already pocketed around $90,000 – and the merchandising sales were hardly underway! In June 1964 a new agreement was reached in which Nems were to receive 45 per cent from the deal, but things continued to go wrong. Nems sued Byrne for refusing to return the agreed royalities and Byrne's partners also sued him for his profligacy in spending over $150,000 on personal expenses. Byrne discovered that Nems had begun granting licences to American firms behind his back, having the fees sent directly to the company in Britain, so he in turn sued Brian for $5 million.

There was another mix-up when an American court upheld his claim for the staggering amount because Brian Epstein had not turned up in court. He hadn't been told! American attorney Nat Weiss realised that Brian needed American representation and fixed him up with a lawyer who was able to explain the mix-up to the court and eventually arranged for Brian to make a settlement of less than $100,000.

Because of the various cases, major US firms cancelled their orders and almost $100 million was lost in potential merchandising sales (Woolworths and Penney's alone had intended placing orders valued at $78 million). Eventually, a few years later, the Beatles launched their own merchandising company, Maximum Enterprises, but it was too late – the big merchandising boom had passed its 1964 peak.

An incomplete list of the licences granted, mainly to the British firms, was discovered when merchandising rights were transferred to Apple Corps Ltd. The list is to be found in Barbara Fenick's book *Collecting The Beatles.* Some of the licences included:

Aluminium locket by Rudolf Stein of London

Artificial jewellery by Anglo American Jewellery Ltd

Bat and ball games (also shufflecock sets and coat hangers) by Raymond of London

Beatle coat hangers by Saunders Enterprises Ltd

Beatle bingo by Toy Works of Marlow

Beatle phones by Fomisa of Switzerland

Bedheads by Robert Dunn Ltd of Belfast

Blankets by Charles Early & Marriott of Oxfordshire

Booster pins by 7 Kay Enterprises of New Jersey

Bracelet by Fleetway Publications of London

Bracelet (also rings, pendants, brooches, earrings) by Lau-Kee Ltd of Dublin

Brooch by Exquisite Jewellery Ltd of Solihull

Brooch by Invicta Plastics of Leicester

Bubble bath by Sachet Productions of Rudenshaw

Busts and statuettes by Starstats of Liverpool

Calendars (and posters and murals) by Louis F.Dow of New Jersey

Candlewick bedspreads by L Hilton & Co of Ashton-under-Lyme

Chewing-gum (and trading cards, chocolate, rock, lollipops, humbugs and fondants) by ABC Chewing Gum Ltd of Essex

Children's satchels (open ring binders, schoolbags, briefcases, exercise books) by Bell Manufacturing of Canada

Cotton jockey hats (and felt and plastic hats) by Sto-Rose Toys Ltd

Compacts by Kigo Ltd of London

Comb (and plastic wig) by Lido Toys of New York

Costume jewellery by Freevy Ltd of Aylesbury

Curtain fabric by Gordon Dunn of Doncaster

Cushions and cushion covers by Unitrend Ltd of Surrey

Diary (and autograph book, telephone address book, record carrier, pencil-case, treasure-box, carry-all, secrets'n'such, notes and numbers, deskette, picnic-case, sewing-basket, dolls travelling cabin and trunk and dolls luggage) from Seagull Products of Cumberland

Dresses by Littlewoods of Liverpool

Dresses by Sharene Creations of Australia

Dolls (and pyjama dolls, hand puppets, metal badges) from Barton's Agencies of Glasgow

Drums (and guitars, tom toms, record rack and musical greeting cards) from Selcol Products of London

Earthenware plates (and mugs, saucers and dishes) by Washington Pottery of London

Female briefs by L & C Vincent Industries of New South Wales

Fob watch in shape of Beatles by Smiths Clocks and Watches of Cricklewood

Floor coverings by Centro Carpets of Old Bond Street, London

Glass tumblers by Joseph Lang of London

Gonk toy models (and socks, pyjamas, T-shirts, salt and pepper pots, hair shampoo, chocolate, sheets, pillow-cases, towels, biscuits, egg-cups, rubber toys, hair clips, hair ribbons, hair bows, lighters, mechanical toys, swimwear, cuff-links, book matches, soft drinks, watches, nylon stockings, blouses, women's suits, casual jackets, slacks, skirts, shirts and men's suits, slacks, casual jackets, ties and shirts) by Daniel Buckley Enterprises of London.

Head-and-shoulder models of the Beatles by Cavendish Exports

Hair slides by Emanuel Langsam of London

Handkerchiefs (and pennants and headsquares) by Maddocks & Dick Ltd

Hats and berets by Kangol of London

Ladies fancy garter belt with locket by Leonard Page & Co of Sussex

Lead pencils (and ball point pens) from Bailey's Agencies of London

Leather watch straps by Clarke Bros of Liverpool

Lipstick by Industrial Gifts

Magnetic drawing cards by J & L Randall of Potters Bar

Medallion by Allan & Co of Glasgow

Metal trays by the Metal Box Company of London

Money bank by Selcol Productions of London

Official Beatles sweater by R B Weldon of Peckham

Ornament in the shape of a golden disc by William Foster of St Helens

Perfume by Fancy Jewellery of London

Pendants on chain (and brooches, rings, bracelets) by A & R Cotter of London

Plastic toy mats by Meadway Manufacturing of London

Plastic wigs by Bell Toys of London

Photographic ball point pens by Cotswold Plastics of London

Photographic albums (and brief cases) by Invincible Industries of South Africa

Pocket brush by Lester Belliston of Utah

Pompom from Clapp, Lattrall & Schillings of San Francisco

Printed fabrics by N V Stoomweverij Nijvverheid of Holland

Printed table cloth by Ulster Weaving of London

PVC plastic moulded figures by Subbuteo of Tunbridge Wells

Record cabinets (and chairs, ottoman, linen baskets) by R.Slocomb & Sons of Somerset

Ringo's boots by Regis Shoes of Shoreditch

Rock (and rock novelties, plus lollipops and humbugs) by R D Blackwood & Son of Blackpool

Sculptured panels by Studio Jon Douglas of London

Silver medals by Medal Import

Stainless steel bracelets by George Wostenholm & Son of Sheffield

Table lamp by Searchlight Electric of Salford

Table mats by Proudholme Products of Brighton

Talcum powder by Sidney Margolis of London

Tiles by Dorincourt Potters of Surrey

Travelling bags by European Travel Goods of London

TV lamps by Excel Fancy Goods of Blackpool

Waist belts by Barroe, Hepburn & Gale of London

Wallpaper by Wallpaper Manufacturer's Ltd

Wall plaques and plates from Frank Ross of London

Wigs from L Rosenthal of London

Writing pad (and jigsaw puzzle, scrapbook) from Thomas Hope & Sankey Hudson of Manchester

Vinyl playballs by David Marsh of Manchester

Following the flood of merchandising in the years 1964 and 1965, the number of licences granted was reduced to a trickle and the next range of memorabilia came on to the market in 1968. This was the merchandise copyrighted to King Features Syndicate Inc of America and the novelties were all based on the theme of *The Yellow Submarine.*

Corgi Toys, owned by the Mettoy Company of New York, produced one of the most interesting items of merchandise – a miniature yellow submarine, die-cast in metal with moving periscopes and tiny plastic Beatles with moving heads.

There were several books, including *The Official Beatles Yellow Submarine Magazine* with 40 pages of photographs from the film; *The Yellow Submarine Gift Book,* a large, hardbound authorised publication from World Distributors in Manchester and *The Beatles in Yellow Submarine* by Max Wilk, published by Signet in New York and New English Library in Britain, a paperback with full colour scenes from the movie.

Golden Press Inc of New York published a large poster and International Posters issued posters, laminated book covers, paper Tiffany lamps and paper bags. Craft Master produced a 15" x 21" poster which you virtually made yourself –60 'put-ons' of characters from the movie, ranging from Old Fred to the Snapping Turks, came in a box and these you stuck on the poster. Posters, postcards and embroidered patches were produced by Poster Prints, whilst, more posters emanated from the Topps Chewing Gum Company which also issued tattoos, styrofoam gliders, trading cards and sensitive stickers.

There were wood figures, key chains, mugs and coin banks issued by Pride Creations of New York; and a *Yellow Submarine* comic book, together with wall decorations and a desk calendar from the Western Publishing Company of Wisconsin.

The Hummel Company issued figurines of each of the main characters from the film; and lunch boxes and vacuum bottles came flooding from a factory in Connecticut.

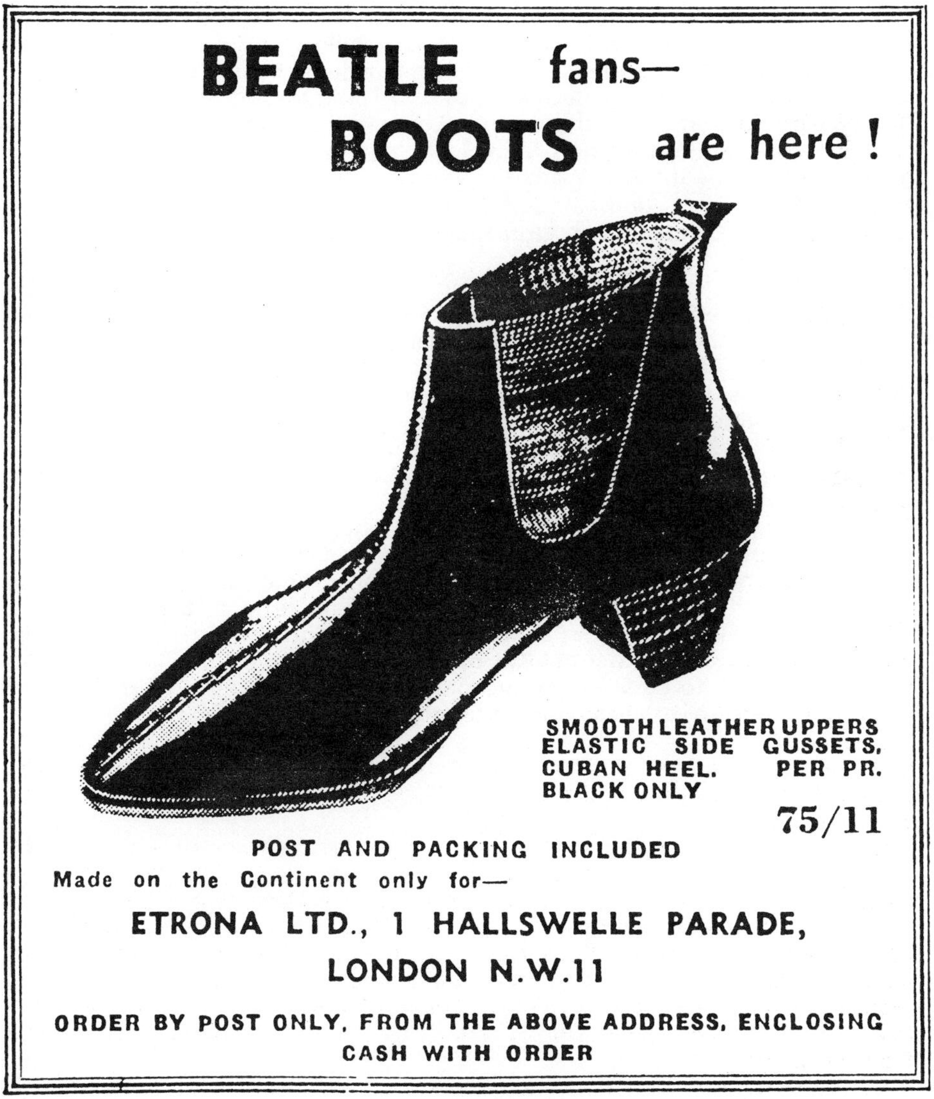

There was lots of stationery. The Sunshine Art Studios of Massachusetts produced mobiles, greetings card notes, while Unicorn Creations Inc issued paper bookmarks, cardboard bulletin boards, picture frames, posters, large paper postcards and boxed writing sets; a pen, blotter, memo pad, letter desk set, pencil cup, scrapbook, diary, address book, autograph book, buttons and a photo album were among the goodies from the A & M Leatherline Company. There were several types of bulletin boards, including a large pin-up of a Blue Meanie with the words 'Stamp Out Fan' and a set of six that consisted of one of each member of the Beatles, one cartoon of the group and one of the Yellow Submarine itself.

Hobby kits and plastic assembly kits were issued by the Model Products Corp; paint-by-numbers sets, sandpaper painting sets, mosette sets, dry transfers and paper sculpture by the Craftmaster Corporation; pencil-by-number sets, board games and poster-by-number sets by Hassenfield Bros of Rhode Island; and card games and giant trading cards by the Ed-U-Cards Manufacturing Corporation.

A company called Mass Arts lived up to its name by issuing vinyl aprons, plastic and wooden lamps, tote bags, vinyl key-rings, inflatable vinyl earrings, three-dimensional vinyl replicas and inflatable pillows. Vinyl playballs were manufactured by Barr Rubber Products, while pyjama bags, curler bags, stuffed pillows, show bags, felt wall decorations stuffed dolls and inflatable swim toys ran from the production lines of the Ideal Toy Coporation. There were sweatshirts from Varsity House, carnival hangers from Henderson-Haggard Inc, and wristwatches and clocks from the Sheffield Watch Company.

One of the most unusual items, produced by the Collegeville Flag and Manufacturing Company (whose main line was flags) were *Yellow Submarine* Halloween costumes.

There were *Yellow Submarine* ceramic 'Beatle-banks' of each member of the Beatles; coaster sets; cartoon kits; clocks by Oris; book markers shaped into characters from the film; bubble gum cards in several sets; cardboard coat hangers of each of the Beatles cartoon characters; placards; plastic model kits; photo albums; wall plaques; pop-out decoration books; jigsaw puzzles; stickers; switch plates and many other items.

The *Yellow Submarine* period ended mass merchandising available in shops. In subsequent years, posters, photographs and other items on the Beatles were available, but never on the same scale.

A new range of souvenir items was created when Apple opened its offices, but these were not for sale to the general public; most of it was merchandise produced in limited quantities for promotional purposes and included key-rings, pins, display apples, ties, dartboards and the special Apple watch made by Old England.

The rebirth of interest in the Beatles in the mid-seventies, which has continued to grow, has produced a cottage industry producing Beatles memorabilia. The original sixties material is to be found at auctions, conventions and specialist shops, but beware. . .there is a certain amount of counterfeiting.

MERCHANDISE OLD AND NEW

The largest regular source of information about Beatles merchandising is contained within the classified advertisements pages of the various fanzines. In addition to information on numerous dealers, there are details of special limited edition souvenirs and material produced by the fans themselves. The classified pages are an ideal showcase for fans wishing either to buy or sell collectable items.

What follows is a selection of dealers who have advertised in various fanzines, including *Instant Karma, The Write Thing, Beatles Now, Beatlefan, Beatles Unlimited, Beatleads, With A Little Help From My Friends* and *Good Day Sunshine.*

ABBEY ROAD RECORDS PO Box 2105, Longview, Washington 98632.
Rare Beatles records, books and memorabilia for sale. The catalogue is available for 25c.

ACROSS THE UNIVERSE Wrno Guzek, Hovedstensvej, DK2650, Huidoure, Denmark.
This booklet has details of 4,000 releases by the Beatles and solo Beatles and their labels in more than 40 countries. £3.00.

G ARCHER 4539 North Holt, Fresno, California 93705.
Archer has a collection of photographs of Beatle sites in England. The assortment of colour photos includes a selection of Abbey Road studios and of sites in and around Liverpool and London. He will send a list on receipt of an SAE.

F ASHCROFT 57 Craven Park Road, London N15
Ashcroft has a collection of Beatles memorabilia for sale, with many rare items.

JEFF AUGSBURGER 507 Normal Avenue, Normal, Illinois 61761.
Jeff buys and sells rare Beatles memorabilia. An example of his stock is the 'bobbin' head' Beatles, a mint set of 8" dolls in their original display box, available for $200.00 inclusive of postage and insurance.

STEVE BARANASKAS 335 W Main, Bloomsburg, Pennsylvania 17815.
Steve's list, available on receipt of an SAE, has a selection of Beatles posters, magazines, books and records.

BEATLES AMERICA 560 Chickadee Lane, Stratford, Connecticut 06497.
An eight-page catalogue containing hundreds of items is available on receipt of an SAE.

BEATLE BACKLIST 350-14 North Corona Avenue, Valley Stream, New York 11580.
A selection of reproductions of Beatles articles is available. A free list is obtainable on receipt of an SAE.

THE BEATLES COMPULOGUE PO Box 1020, Stanton, California 90680.
This specialises in Beatles memorabilia and has an extensive stock. A current list can be obtained by sending two 20c stamps to the above address. Items for sale include rare records, sheet music, underwear, John Lennon pillow-cases, hardback and paperback books, 45s, LPs, movie items, posters, promo items, 8-tracks and magazines.

THE BEATLES AT THE GAUMONT Val King, 14 Eskdale Rise, Allerton, Bradford, West Yorkshire BD15 7QU.
Val King has put out this booklet, which concerns the various Beatles concerts in and visits to Bradford in the sixties, in a limited edition. Val writes: "The text is compiled from actual accounts of fans at the time, including the newspaper reports and photographs published by local newspapers for the group's visits. Eyewitness accounts make it very interesting reading." Send cheque or postal order, made out to Val King for £1.00, plus 25p post and packing to the above address.

BEATLES MINI 125 W 55th, New York, New York 10019.
A set of 16 miniature (3-inch) replicas of the Beatles American album covers, each containing song lyrics and record-shaped bubblegum. Albums and lyrics are: *Rubber Soul,* 'Michelle'; *Meet The Beatles,* 'I Want To Hold Your Hand'; *Let It Be,* 'Let It Be'; *1967-1970,* 'Strawberry Fields Forever'; *1962-1966,* 'Yellow Submarine'; *Sgt. Pepper,* 'Sgt. Pepper'; *A Hard Day's Night,* 'A Hard Day's Night'; *Revolver,* 'Eleanor Rigby'; *White Album,* 'Revolution'; *Beatles '65,* 'I Feel Fine'; *Something New,* 'And I Love Her'; *Hey Jude,* 'Hey Jude'; *Abbey Road,* 'Come Together'; *Beatles VI,* 'Eight Days A Week'; *Yesterday And Today,* 'Yesterday'; and *Reel Music,* 'Can't Buy Me Love'. The bubblegum sleeves are also available from Minis of Box 3065, PP Station, Milford, Connecticut 06460, for 50c each.

BEATLES PRODUCTS LTD PO Box 29113, River Station, Rochester, New York 14627.
Various items are available, such as a series of black-and-white 8" x 10" glossies at $2.25 each; Beatle postcards at 75c each; a 14" x 18" black-and-white poster for $4.50 and a Beatle magazine for $2.00

BEATLE SONG PRINT PO Box 70, Johnston, Iowa 50131.
A limited edition of a fine art print in full colour which contains 25 hidden Beatles song titles. Suitable for framing, it is available from the above address at $4.95, plus $1.00 postage and handling charges.

B E COLLECTABLES PO Box 651, Chatsworth, California 91311.
A list of Beatles items is available on receipt of an SAE.

KENT BEESON 3702 Redwood Falls, Houston, Texas 77082.
Kent has rare imports, promos and rare magazines from the early sixties. His catalogue is available free of charge.

BETTER DAYS 11 Asquith Boulevard, Leicester.
A range of music magazines and papers from 1963-1972 with many rare and obscure Beatles items. A list is available for 25p in stamps or $1.00

DANIEL BIESEMANS Rue Beckers, 10-1040, Brussels, Belgium.
Daniel has a selection of European Beatles records for sale. A free list is available.

BLUE FLAKE PRODUCTIONS INC. Box 2666, Station B, Kitchener, Ontario N2H 6N2.
A large range of records are available, including Beatle and Apple singles from Mexico.

BLUE JAY WAY PO Box 9312, Anaheim, California 90009.
This company buys and sells Beatles memorabilia, including records, books and magazines. A catalogue of items is produced every three months and can be obtained from the above address, price $1.00

BOJO'S COLLECTABLES Box 10411, Eerie, Pennsylvania 16514.
Bojo stocks Beatles memorabilia, as well as material on Elvis, *Star Trek* etc. A catalogue is available for $1.00.

BOOK CITY COLLECTABLES 6631 Hollywood Boulevard, Hollywood, California, 90028.
Book City has over 500 original Beatles items for sale from the years 1963-1980. A catalogue is available for $1.00

LIZZIE BRAVO 992 Britton Road, North Bellmore, New York 11710.
Lizzie has the 12" Brazilian promo 'Judo Comecou' for sale, together with a number of photographs of the Beatles from the sixties. For a list of items available, send her an SAE or two IRCs. Incidentally, Lizzie is one of the two Beatles fans who sang on 'Across The Universe' in 1969.

BRAZELL PO Box 394, Desert Hot Springs, California 92240.
Numerous items of memorabilia are for sale here, including Beatles toys, dolls and games. A 16-page list is available on receipt of $1.00.

BROMOTE SOUNDS PO Box 176, Edison, New Jersey 08818.
A full list of this large selection of Beatle records on cassette (concerts, studio work, interviews and solos) is available on receipt of an SAE.

JOEL BUCKNER PO Box 1379, Conroe, Texas 77301.
Joel has a large selection of memorabilia, records, magazines, books, unique items and autographs. Examples include a portrait of Pattie Boyd drawn by Paul McCartney in 1965 for $4,500; Yellow Submarine lunch-boxes at $60.00 each; bubblegum cards at $30.00 for a set of 50. A catalogue is available at $1.00, refundable with the first order.

HENRIQUE CARBALLAL Alvarez Filho, Caixa Postal 65.095, Rio Di Janeiro. RJ, CEP 20.115, Brazil.
Henrique has many Brazilian Beatles items for sale including records, books and magazines.

NICHOLAS CAULKIN 4 Westminster Court, Handsworth Wood, Birmingham B20.
Nicholas is a Beatles fan who specialized in calligraphy. He first began to show a talent for artistic handwriting twenty years ago and has had several one-man shows of his work in the West Midlands. He has completed a full size poster on the theme of an A to Z of all the songs officially recorded by the Beatles. Full-sized copies of his poster can be obtained for £1.95, including postage and packing from the above address.

CAROLYN CHAPMAN 74 Hampton Road, Southport, Merseyside PR8 6QD.
Carolyn has Beatles records, books and memorabilia for sale. A list is available on receipt of a large SAE.

CLEAR VISIONS 423 Buckthorn, Pennsylvania 17104.
T-shirts with Beatle song-titles, printed within an apple shape, are available.

DAVID COHEN Box 548, Rockville Centre, New York 11571.
David has an extensive collection of rare Beatles tapes. There are over 100 titles of group, solo, studio, concert, soundtrack, interview and press conference records. All cassettes contain title, dates and source of recording. A catalogue is available free of charge.

THE COLLECTABLES CABIN PO Box 5429, North Hollywood, California 91616.
The Cabin has a selection of original Beatles items such as dolls, records, magazines, Yellow Submarine items, picture sleeves and other rare memorabilia. A free list is available on receipt of a postage stamp.

ED COLLINS PO Box 5922, Philadelphia, Pennsylvania 19137.
Ed has some photographs of John and Yoko taken in New York in 1980. Send $1.50 for list of photos and charges.

LEDA CONQUE PO Box 272, Abbotscord, Victoria 2067, Australia.
Leda has books, magazines, posters and memorabilia for sale.

COPPOLA'S CATALOGUE Berry Road, Derry, New Hampshire 03038.
This catalogue lists more than 100 items of Beatles memorabilia available, including scarves, postcards, playing cards, John Lennon dolls, bookcovers, self-inking stamp, tie tacks, musical watches, movie promos, pin backs, puzzles, concert promo items, etc. Send $1.00 for catalogue.

COX & COX PO Box 1917, Fort Pierce, Florida 33454.
A limited edition colour poster of the original Apple Boutique, size 23" x 34", showing the psychedelic poster by the Fool, is available.

GARY CRADEN of 2819 Dorcaster Court, St Louis, Missouri 63129.
Gary has a limited amount of *The Compleat Beatles* promo radio special on two albums. Two hours of interviews and music in authorised conjunction with the video-rock book of the same name. Only 300 were produced by Retro Rock. Copies available for $103.00 inclusive of first class postage and insurance.

DARON ENTERPRISES 184 Emerson Street, Springfield, Massachusetts 01118.
A selection of Beatle T-shirts, and ones of Paul McCartney in concert or Wings Over The World. Ask for small, medium, large or X-large and send $6.50 per shirt. With every shirt you order include the name of your favourite Beatle and you will receive a free button of him.

ROBERT E ETTINGER 350-14 North Corona Avenue, Valley Stream, New York 11580.
Robert provides a wide selection of Beatle article reprints from the sixties and seventies. A catalogue of the high-quality photocopies can be obtained by sending two IRCs to the above address.

CHRIS ECKERT 4814 Overcrest Drive, Nashville, Tennessee 37211.
Chris has a rare record and memorabilia list available on receipt of two stamps.

FOLLIES ANTIQUARIUS 135 Kings Road, London SW3.
Follies has a range of Beatles merchandising and memorabilia for sale. The shop is open from Monday to Saturday from noon until 5pm. A list is available on receipt of three first class stamps.

ALAN AND SUZANNE FRIEDMAN PO Box 402242, Miami Beach, Florida 33140.
Dealers in original Beatles memorabilia, the Friedmans will send their current catalogue on receipt of an SAE, plus 40c postage.

FAN CREATIONS PO Box 633, Bryn Mawr, California 92318.
Here is a selection of Beatle-theme craft kits, including machine appliqué; counted

cross stitch; needlepoint; embroidery; candlewicking; liquid embroidery; crewel embroidery and crayon transfers. A free catalogue is available on receipt of a large SAE.

FRYE 21 W 950, North Chesterton, Indiana 46304.
Frye has a large selection of Beatles memorabilia for sale, circa 1964/5. An illustrated catalogue is available for 50c.

STEVE FREEDMAN PO Box 2054, Central Station, East Orange, New Jersey, 07019.
Steve has a large stock of original Beatles merchandise available. Examples include: a Beatles watch which plays 'Yesterday' ($20); a 1968 Yellow Submarine Decoration Kit ($6); a John Lennon radio with Lennon doll attached ($15); and a 100-card set of 1970s Beatles story gum cards from Europe (Set $30).

FOUR THOUSAND HOLES PO Box 568, Spokane, Washington 99205.
A collection of Beatles memorabilia is for sale, including items such as John Lennon's 1969 Diary ($4.00) and *The Beatles in Italy* (318-page discography, $15.00). A free list is available.

MARK FRANCIS 7 Snowdonia Close, Felmore East, Pitsea, Basildon, Essex.
Mark has a large list of Beatles and related records for sale. List available on receipt of a large SAE.

FIXING A HOLE 2 Kingsland Cottage, Congden Coleham, Shrewsbury, Shropshire.
This is a record-finding service, specialising in the Beatles and Beatles-related items. Send your sales list (or your requests) with an SAE.

M FRIEDMAN SPECIALITY CO. Box 5777, Baltimore, Maryland 21208.
This company has a series of satin tour jackets available. The jacket for the 1964

British tour is charcoal-black satin with silver embroidery on the back, a soft nylon lining and a Byron collar. The jackets for the 1965 American tour are a limited supply of originals which were sold at the Shea Stadium concert. They have gold lettering on purple satin. Send SAE for details of prices.

RAY GALLO 41 Rolfe Street, Cranston, Rhode Island 02910.
Ray has Lennon car-plates, stickers, suitable for car, club, den or window. They have a white background with green letters.

GANG OF PRINTERS PO Box 908-B, Salem, New Hampshire 03079.
A range of quality Beatles T-shirts, in 50 per cent cotton/50 per cent polyester, and jerseys are available. T-shirts $6.50; jerseys $8.50. Designs range from one to four colours and orders over $60.00 receive a free T-shirt of their choice. Catalogues are free with orders. Designs include: No.1 – red shirt, with the words 'Beatles 10th Anniversary. 1964-1974'; No.2 – white shirt with pics of the Beatles holding instruments; No.3 – white shirt with red sleeves and a portrait of the Fab Four; No.5 – blue shirt of *A Hard Day's Night* cover; No.6 – a silver shirt of *The Beatles Rock 'n' Roll Music* cover; No.7 – a tan shirt of the Beatles *Love Songs* cover; No.9 – a white shirt of the *Revolver* cover; No.10 – a white shirt of *A Hard Day's Night* logo; No.11 – a silver shirt with four portraits; No.12 – a silver shirt with all four in full length pose; No.12 – white shirt with *The Decca Tapes* cover. There is also a Wings logo, and a selection of shirts featuring the individual members. When ordering, don't forget to state size.

JIM GEORGE 1529 Luzerne Street, Reading, Pennsylvania 19601.
Jim has on offer an original colour photograph of John Lennon taken in May 1985 at the WFIL Radio Marathon in Philadelphia. This rare 10" x 8" print is available for $8.00

WERNER GERARDS Freunder Landstra.7, 5100 Aachen-Brand, West Germany.
Werner has rare Beatles records for sale. A free list is available on receipt of an IRC.

GET BACK The Beatles Collector's Shop, I-32-3 Takadanobaba, Shinjuku, Tokyo.
A selection of goods is for sale here, including a 44-minute video, available only in Japan called *The Beatles Live in Japan.* The video features their 30 June 1966 concert, the group's arrival in Japan and news, film clips and interviews from the trip. The price, inclusive of air mail costs, is $120. The first 5,000 tapes sold will include a free colour poster from the concert and every tape includes a free six-picture postcard set.

GOOD TIME VIDEO 9903 Santa Monica Boulevard, Suite 167, Beverley Hills, California 90212.
A special VHS or Beta video of the Beatles' three 1964 *Ed Sullivan Shows,* plus a rare 1965 show, all available on the one cassette for $69.95.

TONY GORDON PO Box CM, Tujunga, California 91042.
Tony has a large Beatles memorabilia list available for $1.00. His stock includes original material such as dolls, plastic items, clothing and shoes.

JOHN GIROLAMO 279 North Broadway, Yonkers, New York 10701.
John has a free Beatle-button catalogue available. Send an SAE.

BERNE GREENE Box 140845, Portland, Oregon 97214.
Berne has a stock of over 100 different Beatle items, including gum cards, sheet music, posters and records. He has a sales list available for 50c.

JOHN GUISINGER II 69-B Taft Street, Shelby, Ohio 44875.
John has a large selection of Beatles records. His list is available on receipt of $1.00.

HAKES AMERICANA & COLLECTABLES PO Box 1444, York, Pennsylvania 17405.
Various rare Beatles items and details are to be found in this company's quarterly list, available for $2.00

HB MAC Kvarngatan 23, 5-68600, Sunne, Sweden.
This stock of rare Beatles records from Europe includes the Beatles EP and LP collections in their original sleeves and the singles collection in new printed sleeves. Prices for box sets, freight charges included, are: The Beatles Singles Collection (27 records) $55.00; The Beatles EP Collection (15) $42.00; The Beatles LP Collection (14) $90.00; The John Lennon Box (8) $58.00. A catalogue is available for $1.00.

HERITAGE ART CLASSICS 6196 Rodeo Lane, Salt Lake City, Utah 84121.
A cast bronze bust of John Lennon on a marble base is available in a limited edition of 500.

HIDDEN STUDIO Box 55, Cornish, New Hampshire 03746.
A limited edition of *John Lennon: A Real, Live Fairytale,* written and illustrated by Marcia Hyette. The text was originally written in the mid-seventies and there are 50 surrealist drawings and two colour plates. Each book is signed by the artist. Enquiries to the above address.

STEVE HOLMES 15 Ganton Walk, Dovecoates, Pendeford, West Midlands WV8 1YL.
Steve has a list available of his Beatles records, books and memorabilia on receipt of an SAE.

HOUSE OF OLDIES 35 Carmine Street, New York 10014.
A large selection of Beatle records can be found for sale here.

JOHN HUFFMAN 486 East 56th Street, Long Beach, California 90805.
John has a list of Beatles movies on VHS and Beta. A catalogue is available.

IF PRODUCTIONS Box 32005, Cincinnati, Ohio 45232.
A large selection of video cassettes on the Beatles is available in VHS and PAL. The Beatles material includes: *What's Happening* (In The US/MBE Interview/Liverpool to Sullivan/Come to Town); *Cold Cuts No.3* (Coming Attractions to Bangladesh/Beatlemania/Last Waltz/Rutles/All This and WWII and Sgt. Pepper/Silly Love Songs/My Love/Some Other Guy) and *John And Yoko No.1* (Man of the Decade/Harrison Sings Crackerbox Palace/This Song/Blow Away/True Love). The company points out that none of the Beatles films and videotapes on offer contains any songs assigned to ATV music.

IT'S ONLY ROCK 'N' ROLL 49 West 8th Street, New York.
This is a collectors' shop which has a large selection of Beatles merchandise – videotapes, books, magazines, posters, pillow-cases and rare Beatles toys.

RICK JONES Box 1095, Belleville, Illinois 62223.
Rick has 12" x 18" reproductions of drawings of Lennon and McCartney costing $7.00 plus $2.00 postage.

JUST KIDS NOSTALGIA 251 Main Street, Huntington, New York 11743.
A large range of Beatles items to choose from – magazines, jewellery, Corgi submarines (in box), cushions, notebooks, Yellow Submarine banks, lunchboxes, sneakers etc. A full list is available for $2.00

MATTHEW KILNER 3 Rushley Drive, Dore, Sheffield S17 3EL.
Matthew will send his Beatles record list on receipt of an SAE.

RAMSEY LAWRENCE ASSOCIATES LTD 68 Penkett Road, Wallasey, Merseyside L45 7QW.
Artist Ramsey Lawrence, who now lives on Merseyside, set up this company to supply original Beatles merchandising – mainly bronze casts and postcards and prints of his own work. Born in Glasgow in 1930, Ramsey studied at Glasgow School of Art, Jordanhill Training College, Accademia de Bella Arte, Rome, and Liverpool University. He later taught art at the Liverpool Polytechnic Faculty of Art & Design (the former Liverpool College of Art) and at the School of Education of Liverpool University.

Ramsey has had over a dozen major one-man exhibitions throughout Europe and his qualifications include a Diploma of Art from Glasgow, Diploma of Fine Arts (Hons) from the Accademia de Bella Arte in Rome, a Masters Degree in Education from Liverpool University and Doctor of Philosophy CNAA.

He wrote to me, commenting: "My life size head of John Lennon was commissioned by Beatle City in late 1983 and was completed in cold cast bronze early in 1984. It was exhibited in the Art of the Beatles at the Walker Art Gallery, although you will not find it in the catalogue since it was included after the catalogue had been printed. It is now on permanent exhibition at Beatle City. There is a limited edition of this of 250 which are to be sold through Beatle City Ltd. However, all the other material is available direct from me. The small heads are cast in cold cast bronze, wood finish or ivory finish resin."

The items available include cold cast bronze busts, approximately 5" high, of John (£16.50), Paul, George (both £14.50) and Ringo (£12.50) individually. Ramsey also supplies a series of individual busts in wood, marble, bronze and resin (ivory). The bronze cost £16.50 each and those in the other materials are £8.50 each.

There are cold cast bronze medallions of Ringo and George (£8.50 each) and a series of key-rings based on Ramsey's pastel drawings from the *Sgt Pepper* sleeve at 69p each. They include individual portraits of John and Paul, one of Paul and George together and one of John and Ringo together. There is also a series of postcards of Ramsey's Beatle artwork including a poster portrait of John, a drawing of Paul and the Liverpool Institute, John and the Art College, the Strawberry Fields gates, John and Paul and Penny Lane and John and Strawberry Fields.

FRANCK LEENHEER RECORDS Smidstraat 70, 2231 En Rijnsburg, Holland.
A free 16-page Beatles catalogue, available from the above address, describes Lennon, McCartney, Harrison, Starr, Apple label and related singles; EPs and LPs, new and used; collectors items, promo books, magazines, posters and memorabilia.

L'ENCAN DU DISQUE INC 509 Notre Dame, Joliette, Quebec J6E 3H6.
Here you can find the Canadian edition of the Beatles *Get Back* book from the *Let It Be* box set. It is the same quality as the British edition and contains more than 60 pages in glossy full colour and 25 pages of the original script from the movie. US$19.95, including shipping by first class mail.

LENNON MEDAL 1000 4th Street, San Rafael, California 94901.
A commemorative medal in sterling silver for $19.95 plus $2.00 shipping and handling charges, or a 22-carat gold one for $300, can be bought from this outfit.

FELIX LIPSKY Box 4154, North Hollywood, California 91607.
Felix has a collection of Beatles records, buttons, jewellery, magazines and other items available. A list is provided on receipt of an SAE.

LORD SITAR RECORDS Box 543, North Bellmore, New York 11710.
A free list of rare Beatles, Apple and Dark Horse records.

DREAMBEAT RECORDS PO Box 1505, New York 10185.
'A love That Lasts For Ever (Tribute to John Lennon)' c/w 'Just Another Dreamer' is a record on which *Rolling Stone* writer Brant Mewborn has assembled lines from songs by John and put them to his own music. Available for $5.00 cheque or money order.

LSC PUBLICATIONS 209 Indiana Avenue, Mishawaka, Indiana 46544.
This company has a limited edition of a Beatles lithograph measuring 24" x 18" for sale. Each lithograph is colour-separated and hand-etched on bonded paper and individually signed by American artist D Colburn Rouen. Details of current prices and a free brochure are available from the above address on receipt of an SAE.

LSR RECORDS PO Box 542, North Bellmore, New York 11710.
A series of rare records is for sale, including copies of a special British EMI issue of 10,000 LPs in a limited mono series. "These recordings are more than a remix of stereo versions – many cuts are distinctly different from their counterparts, and are only available in mono form. This is EMI's first mono pressing in ten years – and their last," says LSR's ad.

LYRIC ART PRODUCTIONS PO Box 3517, San Rafael, California 94912.
A series of Beatlegraphics, collections of beautifully illustrated greetings cards inspired by Beatle songs is on sale here, each 5" x 7" full-colour card combines original art with a personal message drawn from the Beatle lyric, all of which are used by permission of ATV Music Corp, Hollywood. The collections are: *Collection A:* 'Strawberry Fields Forever', 'The Long And Winding Road', 'Imagine', 'Everybody's Got Something To Hide Except Me And My Monkey', 'All You Need Is Love', 'The Fool On The Hill', 'Help!', 'I'm Looking Through You', 'A Hard Day's Night', and 'When I'm Sixty Four.' *Collection B:* 'I Am The Walrus', 'We Can Work It Out', 'Got To Get You Into My Life', 'I'm Happy Just To Dance With You', 'Eight Days A Week', 'Fixing A Hole', 'Honey Pie', 'With A Little Help From My Friends', 'Getting Better', and 'Baby, You're A Rich Man'. *Collection C:* 'Drive My Car', 'It's Only Love',

'Birthday', 'You Won't See Me', 'Golden Slumbers', 'Hello Goodbye', 'If I Fell', 'Can't Buy Me Love', 'Blackbird', and 'Why Don't We Do It In The Road'. Each ten-card collection costs $10.00 plus shipping and handling charges of $1.00. All three collections are available at the special price of $26.95. The company also produces special Beatles calendars.

MAC RECORDS PO Box 541, Bergenfield, New Jersey 07621.
A free list of Beatles records and memorabilia is available on receipt of a large SAE.

T McLOUGHLIN 94 Riversdale Road, London N5 2JZ.
McLoughlin specializes in Apple/Beatles rarities and has a sales list available on receipt of a large SAE and two IRCs.

M McNAMARA 10 Blagdon Close, Darley Dale, Matlock, Derbyshire DE4 2GW.
Golden Beatles stickers for sale at £1.25 per hundred.

MORRISON'S TRAVEL 18 Cambridge Arcade, Southport, Merseyside.
The agency produces a Beatle pack containing details of the weekend stays that it organises in Liverpool. For the full pack, which also includes details of rare records, send a large SAE and 50p to the above address.

GRAHAM MOYLE PO Box 303, Magill 5072, South Australia.
Write to Graham for a 12-page catalogue of Beatles memorabilia.

DAVE NEAGUS 27 Lockington Crescent, Dunstable, Bedfordshire LU5 4ST.
Dave has a selection of Beatles material for sale, including Revell kits, photocopies of letters, autographs, scrapbooks and paintings. He also has a Penny Lane drawing of the Beatles at £1 per photocopy.

PHILIP NEVITSKY c/o Piccadilly Plaza Exhibition Ltd, Exhibition Hall, York Street, Manchester MI 4AH.
Philip has published a set of four Beatles postcards of the *Melody Maker* caricatures by James Hall. The set of four costs £1.25, including postage in the UK, and £2 or $3.00 in the US or abroad. Philip has been organizing special Records Fairs in Manchester since 1977 and on Sunday, 30 September 1984, launched his first Beatles Day. This one-day event from 11am to 6pm took place at the Piccadilly Plaza Exhibition Hall and had stalls specializing in all Beatles items: records, books, posters, postcards, sheet music, rare Beatles collection items – and non-stop Beatles videos all day on a giant 45" screen. Philip intends to present further Beatle Days in the future.

THE NOTTINGHAM GROUP LIMITED RFDI, Box 680, Epping, New Hampshire 03042.
The group provides first edition prints of an original oil painting of the Beatles by New England portrait artist William Kelly. The portrait, of the four in Sgt. Pepper costumes, measures 22" x 28" and costs $25.00 plus $5.00 shipping and handling charge.

THE NOVELTY PRESS PO Box 236, Sea Cliff, New York 11579.
A series of original Beatles lithographs is available at $5.00 each plus $1.00 postage. These posters are exclusive to the company, which has been producing Beatles stationery since 1977. Measuring 24" x 19", the posters are lithographed on heavyweight glossy paper. The company also has a large catalogue available for $3.00, illustrating their exclusive line of stationery, memo pads, notebooks, rubber stamps, posters, stickers and so on. Dave Zimmerman wrote to me, commenting: "Novelty Press has been in existence for eight years, offering Beatle fans non-exploitative quality stationery items and assorted merchandise. Virtually all my products are designed and manufactured by myself. The uniqueness of my line of goods is self-evident. As a long time Beatle fan and collector, this is a labour of love."

The caricatures of John, Paul, George and Ringo available direct from Philip Nevitsky, can also be obtained from Beatle City and the Merseyside Tourist Office in Lime Street, Liverpool. The illustrations by Jimmy Thomson originally appeared in *Melody Maker* in 1973 and 1975. Philip bought the originals at the Sotheby's auction in 1982. Philip, who also runs the annual 'Beatles Day' in Manchester, tells me: "I collect and sell (in a small way) Beatles items. Mainly books, magazines, postcards, bubblegum cards. As a collector myself all my items for sale are in very good condition. Every page in every book or magazine is checked. Unfortunately, many people who sell collectors items of any kind are not collectors themselves and are only in it for the money and don't take care of what they are selling."

OFF THE WALL RECORDS PO Box 2248, Fullerton, California 92633.
A selection of Beatles records is available.

OZ 99 Empire Road, Winshill, Burton-on-Trent, Staffordshire DE15 OPB.
Oz deals in a selection of John and Yoko shirts with a two-colour design, hand printed on yellow or white shirts. T-shirts £3.95; sweatshirts £6.25. There is a 'War Is Over' special offer of two T-shirts for £6 or two sweatshirts for £12. When ordering, state colour and size.

OLYMPIA ENTERPRISES Box 91153, Los Angeles, California 90009.
A large illustrated catalogue of this organization's stock of Beatles memorabilia can be obtained for $1.00.

PAKRA PO Box 224, Brooklyn, New York 11210.
Pakra have a selection of Beatles T-shirts available. A 28-page Beatle catalogue is available free.

PEPPERLAND EXPRESS 11185 Lime Kiln Road, Grass Valley, California 95945.
A catalogue of this company's memorabilia is available for $2.00.

PHOTO PASS PO Box 393, Morton Grove, Illinois 60053.
Various photographs of Paul McCartney are for sale; catalogue available for $1.00

PLANET EARTH PO Box 83, Bloontstown, Florida 32424.
A catalogue of Beatles records is available for 50c. Stock includes singles with picture sleeves and Japanese box sets.

PATTI PODBOY 2953 North Narraganselt, Chicago, Illinois 60634.
Patti supplies a price list of her Beatles memorabilia on receipt of an SAE. Her stock includes clippings, buttons, videos, original sheet music, original/reissue pressbooks, original/reissue movie posters and lobbycards, promo posters, hardcover, paperback and pocketbooks, magazines, newspapers and fanzines.

FOSTER B AND HELENE POLLACK 120 Bennetts Farm Road, Ridgfield, Connecticut 06877.
Foster wrote to me with this information: "We are a full time antique and collectables dealers and we do about 30 shows a year: this includes almost all of the Beatles shows run in the US. We specialize in Beatle-related and Beatle collectables with the exception of records. We do get in 'one-of-a-kind' items from time to time which are usually of the rarer nature and have no problem in disposing of these. We travel all over the US looking for good material in addition to Beatle items." The Pollacks have literally hundreds of Beatle items, particularly button badges.

POP RECORDS 172 Kings Road, Reading, Berkshire.
A ten-page list of Beatles rarities will be sent on receipt of a large SAE. Stock includes mono albums, imports, original Parlophone, Apples, singles, EPs, picture sleeves, John Lennon, Paul McCartney, George Harrison, Ringo Starr, Wings, Apple originals, Dark Horse, Ringo-O, Beatles-related, Polydor singles and fan club flexis.

EDDIE PORTER 23 Cherryfield Heights, Liverpool L32 7PX.
Eddie has a set of 14 colour photos of Yoko and Sean when they visited Strawberry Fields, available for £5.00 inclusive of postage and packing.

JOHNNY 'Q' PO Box 65001, Los Angeles, California 90065.
Johnny 'Q' has a series of satin jackets available. One has 'The Beatles' official logo on the back, is fully lined, has stretch-knitted neck and waist bands with white piping, and expertly hand-embroidered in white on the front panel a small 'The Beatles'. 'John Lennon Rock'n'Roll You Shoulda' Been There' are the words on another, hand-embroidered in red and white. A brochure is available for £1.00 plus an SAE.

RICK RANN PO Box 877, Oak Park, Illinois 60303.
Rick provides a list of hundreds of original Beatle items for sale: picture sleeves,

books, magazines, albums, memorabilia, 45s, cards etc. The list is available on receipt of a stamp.

SUSAN REED Wish Cottage, 3 Red Delph Lane, Rainford, St Helens, Lancashire.
Susan has a poster, 23" x 16", of a portrait of John Lennon, together with his 'Imagine' lyrics, hand-scripted on blue parchment. It costs £1.20 including postage, but discounts are available for bulk orders. (for instance, £6.00 for ten).

ROBO ARTS 57 Craven Park Road, London N15.
A limited edition of 250 artist's prints on the Beatles at £7.50 each is on sale here. A brochure is available on receipt of an SAE or IRC.

ROCKAWAY RECORDS PO Box 24197, Los Angeles, California 90024.
Rare records, posters and memorabilia are listed in a catalogue available for $1.00. Among the items is 'Beatles Talk with Jerry G', a 12" in two volumes at $8.00 per volume. Postage costs are $2.00 for the US or $6.00 foreign.

ROCKGRAPHS 520 Miller Street, Hellertown, Pennsylvania.
A collection of authentic autographed items on the Beatles (group and individual). Send a stamp or IRC for full list.

ROCK RARITIES Box 471, Wrightsville Beach, North Carolina 28480.
A list of Beatles collectables is available free of charge.

ROCKY MOUNTAIN GRAPHICS Box 1617, Ruidoso, New Mexico 88345.
T-shirts featuring Lennon lithographs drawn and signed by John are available in 50/50 cotton/polyester ($8.00) or 100 per cent cotton ($12.00). Include $1.50 for post and packing and state size (S/M/L/XL) and colour (black or turquoise).

WAYNE ROGERS 145 El Ogden Road, Wilmington, North Carolina.
Wayne has a series of 5" x 7" colour photographs made from the original negatives, including shots from the Bangla Desh concert, John and Yoko in New York, John on the *Mike Douglas Show,* the group in Sgt. Pepper uniforms, scenes from Rock'n'Roll Circus, a performance at the Sahara Hotel, Las Vegas, scenes from *Help!* and from a BBC TV rehearsal. Send an SAE for details.

M RONZONE 137 Crescent Street, Elkhart, Indiana 46516.
A series of charcoal graphics of John Lennon and the Beatles suitable for framing is available. The original works measure 8½" x 11" and each print costs $2.00 plus 50c handling charge. Overseas orders are accepted with an International Money Order, together with $1.50 extra per print to cover handling charges. There are 11 graphics: Lennon '68; Harrison '70; Paul '66; Quadlennon; Lennon '69; Ringo '69; John and Yoko '73; Two Virgins; Lennon No.9; Cosmic Lennon; Beatles.

ROSTAR Box 2422, North Babylon, New York 11703.
A free list of Beatles records and memorabilia will be sent on receipt of an SAE.

JOE A RUSSO Claremont Street, Deer Park, New York, 11729.
Joe has a selection of Beatles LPs, 45s and collectors' items. A free list is available on receipt of an SAE.

SANDERAMICS PO Box 3464, Fullerton, California 92631.
A brochure describing a selection of Beatles pictures on porcelain, ceramics, china and glass is available on receipt of an SAE.

ED SCHREIBER PO Box 2704, Huntington Beach, California 92649.
Ed specializes in early Beatles memorabilia. His catalogue is available for $1.00.

SEASON OF GLASS VIDEO PRODUCTS 21-55 Seyama Kawamotomachi, Ousatogun Saitama, 369-11 Japan.
This company has a video cassette, in VHS only, simply entitled *Rare Yoko Video,* available for $69.95 or Y16.00. It is a 60-minute monochrome video of a live performance by Yoko Ono and the Plastic Ono Band in Tokyo on 11 August 1974.

The numbers on the video include 'It Happened', 'Midsummer NY', 'Angry Young Woman', 'Move On Fast', 'One Way Love' and 'Let's Have A Dream'.

SENTIMENTAL JOURNEYS INC 2801 East Oakland Park Boulevard, Suite 205, Fort Lauderdale, Florida 33306.
This travel agency organises 'In The Footsteps of the Beatles' trips.

SHINE ON! PO Box 802, Cambridge, Massachusetts 02238.
A special John Lennon T-shirt, with a silk-screened image of him taken from an original charcoal drawing covering the entire front and the words 'Lennon Lives' on the back, is available in 100 per cent white cotton. All sizes are $8.98 with $1.25 for postage and delivery takes between six and eight weeks.

BILL SIMONE 38243 Woodside Road, Willoughby, Ohio 44094.
Bill has a list of Beatles memorabilia and records available, free of charge.

D J SMITH 93 Shoreham Drive, Penketh, Warrington, Cheshire.
Smith is one of Britain's most noted Beatle collectors, having a number of unique items in the personal collection that he has been building up since the early sixties. He makes occasional offers and one of them is for 'The World's Oldest Beatles Poster'. This is an exact reproduction of the actual 1961 handbill announcing the appearance of the Beatles at Hambleton Hall in Huyton, Liverpool. It is the earliest mention of the Beatles as a group, well before they recorded 'Love Me Do' and even before Ringo joined the group. It has been made available again by the person who set the type for the original poster in 1961 and has been reproduced complete with broken type, and reprinted on similar paper to the original, in order to present a perfect replica. The poster is available for £1.50, inclusive of postage and packing in the UK. Elsewhere, postage extra.

STAN SNELLEMAN PO Box 84265, AG Den Haag, Holland.
Stan has a number of items for sale, including rare Japanese records and Lennon lithographs. A list is available.

N E SPENCER CO RECORDS & TAPES PO Box 60537, Terminal Annex, Los Angeles, California 90060.
A large selection of Beatles records from around the world is available. Send SAE for details.

STEFANO DELLO SCHIAVO CP 6053, Roma, Italy.
A list of Beatles material including all the original Italian LPs and 45s with picture sleeves is available. Stefano also has a limited set of John Lennon/Bag One catalogues from the exhibition held in Rome in October/November 1971 at $20.00 each.

STONE Box 09681, Columbus, Ohio 43209.
Copies of the John Lennon edition of the *New York Post* of 9 December 1980 can be bought for $5.00.

ERIC SWEDBERG 1635 Semain, Portland, Oregon 97214.
Eric has a selection of Beatles records, magazines, books and paraphernalia. A list is available for 50c.

BRAD TAYLOR 307 Woburn Avenue, Toronto, Ontario M5M 1LI.
Brad has a selection of memorabilia. A free list is available.

TEE PEE LTD 125 Hunnicutt Drive, Athens, California 30606
A catalogue of Tee Pee's stock is available for $1.25 each or two for $2.00 inclusive of postage.

TICKET TO RYDE LTD PO Box 3393, Lacey, Washington 98503.
One of the earliest Beatles dealers, Ticket to Ryde has been providing material of interest to Beatles collectors since 1973, and produces a quarterly catalogue of its stock.

TRFB PO Box 29523, Los Angeles, California 90029.
A free catalogue of memorabilia, records and magazines is available.

A TRIBUTE TO JOHN Box 174, Helena, Montana 59624.
This is a porcelain decanter, 15½" high, designed by artist Gary Schilst and distributed in a limited edition, each piece assigned a collector's number. $39.95 plus $3.00 post and packing charges.

TWO VIRGINS c/o K.Keyton, 49 Addison Way, Northwood, Middlesex HA6 1SS
Numerous items are available for the serious collector, including rare records, original books and magazines, fan club items, autographs and memorabilia. List of the items can be obtained from the above address on receipt of an SAE.

TRIBUTES PO Box 11062, Fort Lauderdale, Florida 33339.
A series of busts of each member of the Beatles. Each 9" tall and sculpted by Kris Smith, are for sale at Tributes. A portion of the purchase price is contributed to the Spirit Foundation. Each bust costs $49.95 plus $6.50 shipping charge ($12 for Europe and Canada).

UNION JACK 6611 North Market Street, Wilmington, North Carolina 28405.
The name says it all – this dealer specializes in imports from Britain, and has a large selection of Beatles memorabilia, including posters, buttons, key chains and Cavern mugs. A current list is available for $1.00.

UNIQUE POSTERS 37 Winchester Avenue, Weddington, Nuneaton, Warwickshire.
The company regularly issues special limited editions of Beatle posters. An example is the reproduction of a rare 1964 US tour promotion poster measuring 30" x 20", in colour, and strictly limited to 250 copies. Each poster is individually numbered, and is despatched in a strong postal tube on receipt of a cheque or postal order for £4.00 (£4.50 overseas). Another limited edition is the reproduction of an early, historic Beatles concert promotion poster, circa 1962, devised by Brian Epstein. It is 30" x 20", in colour, and strictly limited to 1,000 copies, each individually numbered. The price, inclusive of postage and packing is £3.50 in the UK and £4.00 overseas.

PHIL VERDI 152 Oak Street, Florence, Massachusetts 01060.
Phil has a list of Beatles material for sale, obtainable of receipt of two stamps or IRCs.

VERY ENGLISH AND ROLLING STONE PO Box 322, Reamstown, Pennsylvania 17567.
Rare Beatles records – coloured vinyl, promo discs and picture discs. A catalogue is available on receipt of a 20c stamp.

VIDEO SYNCROCIES PO Box 618 Freetown, Massachusetts 02717.
Rare Beatles videos available only in VHS – material from Europe and America. A full list is available on receipt of two stamps or IRCs.

MARCELLO VILLELLA Via Pirro Ligorio N. 18, 00153, Roma, Italy.
Marcello has a collection of Italian Beatles records for sale.

REGINA VOIT Lande-Graf Philipp Strasse 65, 6000 Frankfurt/M 50, West Germany
Regina has Beatles jigsaw puzzles for sale. Two different pictures, one of the Beatles, one of John Lennon alone. Each is poster size, in full colour, with 1,200 parts. $20.00 each, surface mail or $30.00 air mail.

VIDEO & RECORDS 2458 Kingston Road, Scarborough, Ontario. M1N 1VS.
A Beatles memorabilia catalogue is available for $3.00.

VINCE WALDRON 2048 North Burling, Chicago, Illinois 60614.
Vince has records for sale, including *The Beatles Complete,* Japanese pressings of all the Beatles LPs and solo LPs from around the world, encased in a specially designed wooden cabinet for $1,398; a boxed set of 12 original albums, British editions, plus the *Rarities* LP all in their original sleeves, in a hinged collector's box for $124.99, plus $3.50 postage; a boxed set of 14 albums from Japan (the same as the British set,

but pressed on the finest Japanese vinyl) for $189.99, plus $3.50 postage; a Mobile Fidelity boxed set, the original master recordings of the 12 original Beatles albums, in a deluxe collection for $324.98, plus $3.50 postage. Further details are available on receipt of an SAE.

STAN VITEK PO Box 2328, Youngstown, Ohio 44509.
Stan has a selection of dozens of Beatles interviews conducted from 1964 to 1981, plus rare Beatle recordings on cassette. Catalogue available for $1.00.

CRAIG WARREN 2141 Chapel Street, New Haven, Connecticut 06515.
Craig has a limited series of a 4" flexi-single of 'Hey Jude' from the Pocket-Disc series of 1969, at the special sale price of $300. The price includes mint disc and mint wallet-type cardboard folder. First class post and insurance is $3.00 extra.

W WELSH 4 Findon Drive, Bognor Regis, West Sussex PO22 6QJ.
A list of Beatles record and books for sale is available on receipt of an SAE.

KAREN WHEELER 2048 Derek Drive, C. Fullerton, California 92631.
Karen has full colour 5" x 8" postcards taken from original water-colours of John Lennon. Available on receipt of a cheque or money order for $2.50.

LARRY WISHERD PO Box 1323, Hagerstown, Maryland 21741.
Larry has almost 1,000 rare Beatles items for sale including 45s, EPs, LPs, promos, test pressings, radio shows, books, magazines, posters and box sets. A list is available on receipt of a stamp or two IRCs.

WYNNCO 27a Maxe, Greenville, South Carolina 29611.
Beatles records, posters, radio shows, promos, imports, concerts, memorabilia, cards, magazines, original newspaper articles and press kits are all described in a catalogue available for $1.00, refundable with the first order.

YESTERDAY LTD Box 15273, Albuquerque, New Mexico 87174.
A selection of over 24 rubber stamps of the Beatles, mounted on cherry wood, at $3.75 and $5.00 each is available. The company also provides a series of unique buttons not sold anywhere else, priced from $1.00. All items are postpaid. A full catalogue is available on receipt of $1.00.

JOHN ZASO PO Box 310, New Hyde Park, New York 11040.
John has a limited series of covers (envelopes), each commemorating an event and postmarked on the day and site of the event. They include a New York cover on John Lennon, dated New York City, 8 December 1980, for $2.75, a cover from Liverpool dated 9 December 1980, for $7.50 and a silent vigil cover from New York City for $2.50.

JAKE ZINS Box 235, Nicollet, Minnesota 56074.
Jake has a list of his Beatle books, mags, 45s, LPs, buttons, gum cards, etc for sale. Send stamp for free list.

SPECIALISTS

In addition to all these dealers and mail order services, there are a number of very specialized items exclusive to and only available from the following people or places:

Carroll James

PO Box 8686, Silver Springs, Maryland 20907

Carroll James was the first DJ to play a Beatles record on American radio. When the group arrived in Washington, James recorded an interview. Discussing it in the fanzine *Beatlefan,* he remarked: "I had questions that I had asked my listeners to send in. We got hundreds of them. I just tried to synthesise them as best I could. I asked them things like: 'Do you like coffee or tea?' John Lennon said he liked tea. I asked: 'How about tea bags?' and he said, 'I don't like them. They get stuck in me teeth.' I asked them what they had thought about doing when they grew up. Paul McCartney said he thought he might like to be a teacher, but he said it was a good thing he had become a Beatle because 'I think I would have been a bad teacher.' That was one of the few straight answers that I got out of them. George Harrison said, 'I wanna be a baggy sweeger.' I said, 'A baggy sweeger?' 'Oh, yeah' he said, 'You know, in every town there's 25 baggy sweegers and every morning they get up and go out to the airport and baggy sweeger all around.' I had them on the air for ten minutes. A lot of people had said, 'Hey, what about the interview? It would be something that collectors would really enjoy.' So I've checked the legal angles and gotten the go-ahead."

The result is the record, *The Carroll James Interview With The Beatles: February 11th 1964,* together with picture sleeve, $5.00 postpaid, autograph on request, available direct from James.

Carroll worked on the local station WWDC in Washington DC. In 1963 he received a letter from a listener, Marsha Albert, requesting some Beatles music. He had a copy of their new British single 'I Want To Hold Your Hand' flown over specially and played it on 17 December 1963. He asked listeners what they thought of it and the switchboard was jammed for hours, so he played it again within the hour, a thing he'd never done before.

James was also given tickets to the studio audience for the first *Ed Sullivan Show* and introduced the group on stage at the Washington Coliseum on 11 February 1964, their very first American concert.

Mike Mac's Black and White's

Nancy Miller Associate's St Anne House, 20 Wellesley Road, Croydon, Surrey CRO 9XB.

In the early issues of *Mersey Beat* there were some photographs credited to a Francis Michael. This was a pseudonym Mike McCartney asked me to use when I published his pictures. Even then he was reluctant to bask in the glory of the McCartney name, despite the fact that the Beatles were unknown outside Merseyside and Hamburg. He went on to find fame in his own right as Mike McGear of the Scaffold.

Mike had a natural 'eye' and his photographs were completely different from the bland publicity shots which were being published by the national music papers of the time. They had an individuality, as did the work of some other photographers whose pictures were appearing for the first time in the pages of *Mersey Beat:* Jurgen Vollmer, Astrid Kirchherr, Les Chadwick (of Peter Kaye), Dick Matthews, and others.

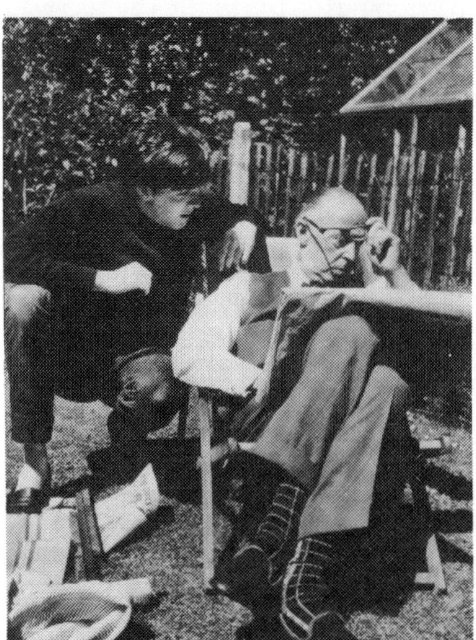

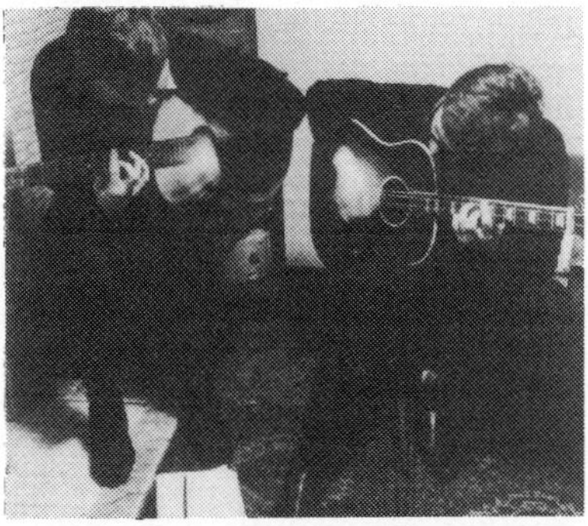

Mike's finger was never far from the camera button and he took many of the earliest shots of the Beatles which, surprisingly, were not to be widely distributed until almost twenty years had passed. In 1981, he published his book *Thank U Very Much* subtitled 'Mike McCartney's Family Album', which contained dozens of photographs he had taken in those early Mersey days. Intimate shots of 'our kid', of the Beatles with their girlfriends, socialising with fellow Mersey Beatsters such as Rory Storm, and horsing around in the days before Brian Epstein attempted to sanitise their image.

A selection of these photographs was to re-emerge in 1983 under the title *Mike Mac's Black and Whites,* published by Nancy Miller Associates, a branch of Hanson White Publishing.

There are 19 photographs available as postcards. Seven of these are also available as 14" x 11" prints and a further four as posters measuring 31" x 23½". The postcards are 20p each retail, or £1.04 per dozen; the prints 99p each or £5.12 per dozen; and the posters £1.99 each or £10.40 per dozen, all available from Beatle City.

One of the photographs is available in colour and is reputed to be the first colour picture ever taken of the Beatles. It shows George, John and Paul playing guitar in the back parlour at Paul and Mike's Aunty Jin and Uncle Harry's house in Dinas Lane, Huyton. A friend (or relative!) called Dennis, stands to the side holding a glass of a dark substance that could be Guinness. This colour shot costs £1.59 as a print (£7.80 per dozen) or £2.99 as a poster (£15.60 per dozen), and is also available from Beatle City.

Ed Rudy

PO Box 1981, New York, New York 10001

Copies of Ed's rare 1964 interview album, autographed by himself and never released in the UK or Europe, are now available directly from him by International Money Order for $17.00.

Ed was a syndicated columnist and radio journalist before the Beatles American debut. He first met Brian Epstein in New York late in 1963 through a friend, Bud Hellewell, who was promoting the non-Capitol Beatles material in the States for Epstein. Ed arranged to cover the Beatles' arrival and was at the airport on 7 February 1964, attending their famous first press conference. He also travelled with them to Washington and Miami. In an interview with Al Sussman and Bill King for *Beatlefan,* Ed described their Miami trip: "It was great fun. It was a happy time, magic time. We'd drive in my car, I had a station wagon and could get a lot of people in it, and there were reporters and Beatles and we'd tune in WYNZ. . . Sometimes they tried to run away from the press, but it was nearly impossible. There was no place they could go that someone wouldn't tell us where they were. And sometimes they let some of us go along."

Ed also says that he was the only reporter to join the Beatles on their summer 1964 tour of the US. He reported the events for 440 different American radio stations and issued a couple of albums containing interviews and background to the tours. The first of the albums was issued in June 1964, and reached No.20 in the *Billboard* charts, No.32 in *Record World* and No.55 in *Cashbox.* Mark Wallgren, in his book *The Beatles on Record* points out: "He (Rudy) then ventured into a recording studio and re-recorded himself asking all the questions which had, in fact, been asked by a wide variety of reporters. The answers given by the Beatles were spliced in. The result was an entire album of Ed Rudy 'interviewing' the Beatles.

In late 1980, Rudy decided to issue *The American Tour With Ed Rudy: News Documentary No.2.* A blurb to advertise the sale read: "This album was recorded during their American tour by the only American newsman/announcer to cover the *complete* tour, Ed Rudy. The Beatles call Ed Rudy the 'Fifth Beatle' and after listening to these exclusive recordings, you'll know why! It's fantastic!"

In their *Beatlefan* feature, Sussman and King quote Rudy explaining his claim thus: "The Beatles called me the 'Fifth Beatle'. It was good fun and I appreciated it and they did that because I was covering for a lot of stations. They knew that it would make me happy and it certainly did. That's not putting down Murray The K. Murray was the 'Fifth Beatle' as much as anyone else. The syndicators sold to the radio stations open-end portions of the Beatles introducing the 'Fifth Beatle' and on the original tape it was me, John Lennon saying 'Stay tuned for the Fifth Beatle' – and then local DJs would come on and *they* were the Fifth Beatle!"

Tony Saks
PO Box 12522, Norfolk, Virginia 23502

Tony Saks must rate as the oldest active Beatles fan. Now in his seventies, he and his wife Grace appear at numerous American conventions to display their famous Beatles Rickenbacker. He is featured in the BBC Television documentary *Beatlemania.*

Tony describes his trophy thus: "Beatle autographed guitar, the only guitar in the world that is autographed by all the Beatles (the event took place on 13 September 1964 in Baltimore)." Tony and Grace met the Beatles three times. The guitar, which was demonstrated to, and played by, the Beatles at the Savoy-Hilton Hotel on 8 February 1964, has also posed with four Miss Americas, two Miss USAs, Miss 16 of America, Jim 'Catfish' Hunter of the New York Yankees, Gene Roddenberry of *Star Trek,* Roy Rogers and many more. Apart from displaying it at conventions and allowing fans to be photographed with it, Tony offers an 8" x 10" glossy black-and-white photograph of it, which can be purchased for $3.00, plus 50c shipping charge, by writing to Beatle Guitar at the above address.

Silhouette Music
PO Box 96, Fort Hamilton Station, Brooklyn, New York 11209

This company issues special limited edition albums. An example is *The British Are Coming,* a 3-D album of which 10,000 copies were issued.

Silhouette's blurb contains this information: "Silhouette Music, for the first time ever, is proud to bring you the only Beatles three-dimensional album, *The British Are Coming,* plus a *free* pair of Beatles 3-D glasses with each album. This brilliant full colour Beatles album will be an absolute must for your Beatles collection. Follow the Fab Four in a kaleidoscopic view of their lives from 1964 to 1967. These previously unreleased interviews will bring you back to those fabulous times of Beatlemania. The photos of this fantastic full colour 3-D album are sure to blow your mind. Each album is individually numbered, to insure that you have your very own personal collectors' item.

"The price in the US is $14.49; in Canada $15.49; in Australia $19.49; and elsewhere overseas $17.49, all by cheque or money order only. There is a special offer: if you order three copies, you will receive one fourth copy free."

AUCTIONS

Where do collectors, dealers, museums, even fans, get their Beatles memorabilia? The main sources for authentic material, apart from the classified ads pages of fanzines already described, are auctions specializing in popular culture.

Sotheby's

34-35 New Bond Street, London W1A 2AA

Beatles material first went under the hammer at Sotheby's in June 1979, producing such interest that the annual Rock 'n' Roll Memorabilia auctions were launched in 1981. Although they have a general title and include material from artists ranging from Elvis Presley to Marc Bolan, the main bulk of items in these auctions concerns the Beatles.

The force behind the auctions is Hilary Kay, director of Sotheby's Collectors' Department. She originally suggested to the Musical Instrument Department at Sotheby's that a Steinway piano they had on offer was worth more than their assessment because it had once belonged to John Lennon. And she was proved right: that piano, together with another that had previously belonged to Paul, brought in far more money than anyone had dreamt they would. The Music Department had valued John's piano at £1,000 – it went for £7,500. Paul's piano, which had been considered of even less worth because of its dilapidated condition, went for £9,000!

Hilary took over the organisation of the Rock auctions from then on, also acting as auctioneer. During the past few years she has developed an astuteness for assessing the likely value of a wide range of Beatles memorabilia. Some items do, of course, go for far higher prices than expected, whilst others do not each their reserve price. Personally, I thought the Johnny 'Guitar' Byrne 'Kaiser Keller' poster, snapped up by the Hard Rock Cafe for £1,000 at the 1984 auction, was priceless. This is the original large hand-painted poster, measuring 43″ × 29″, that was displayed outside the Kaiser Keller club in Hamburg to announce the Beatles appearance there in 1960. It is the only one of its kind in the world and as such is a unique historical item. Yet an Apple poster, of which there must have been many printed and whose historical value is negligible, went for £350 at the same sale.

I've often enjoyed sitting at the auctions, observing the proceedings. There is always a fair scattering of notable Beatle fans from both sides of the Atlantic (Mark Lewisohn, Mark Lapidos, Joel Glazier, Charley Rosenay (!!!), Jim Hughes, among others), but they are generally not the major buyers. The value of Beatles memorabilia has soared since the Sotheby's auctions began, a trend which has soured many fans as they see items they would love to have bought go out of their financial reach. Yet as a result of the auctions, remarkable one-offs appear which might never have come to public notice, such as the exercise book of John's, which was submitted by Rod Murray and fetched £16,000. This is certainly a more precious item than the acoustic guitar once owned by John which sold for £15,500 at the same auction.

An element that has inevitably crept into the auctions, due to spiralling prices, is the professional dealer who is simply seeking an investment and is not interested in the intrinsic value of the items. I listened to two American dealers talking at the 1984 auction and they obviously had no interest in the Beatles or their story, but sensed that there was money to be made in buying up Beatles material, the value of which has rocketed in a very short time.

Musical instruments, photographs, posters, gold discs, telegrams, drawings, letters, Apple souvenirs and sixties memorabilia are among the regular items to be found at the Beatles auctions: in particular, drawings and paintings by Stuart

Sutcliffe, bubblegum machines, Dezo Hoffmann and Jurgen Vollmer photographs, *Yellow Submarine* celluloids, guitars previously owned by John Lennon and Christmas fan club records.

The lavishly produced catalogues will no doubt be collectable items themselves in the future. At present, they are your entrance to the auctions and can be purchased at the door on the day of auction or by post. Anyone wishing to receive future catalogues should request an order form from the Collector's Department at the above address, stating that they would like to receive future Rock 'n' Roll Memorabilia catalogues automatically. You will then be invoiced for each catalogue as it is sent. The 1984 catalogue cost £7.00. There are approximately 120 illustrations in each, a number of them in colour, and informative and illuminating descriptions of the items for sale. Here is a selection from the 1984 catalogue.

Lot 208: Letter from George Harrison to Stuart Sutcliffe, in blue ballpoint pen, concerning Harrison's journey back to Liverpool, informing Stuart of bookings for the Beatles and asking him to "come home sooner, as if we get a new bass player for the time being, it will be crumby, as he will have to learn everything"; talking about Paul McCartney, "it's no good with Paul playing bass, we've deciced, that is if he had some kind of bass + amp to play on!"; requesting Stuart to send some money to Frank Hessy because he wanted "to get an echo for Christmas £34, or £6 down, the rest when Frank catches me"; discussing his playing, "I am learning everything I can get my hands on now!" Two pages with envelope, dated 16 December 1960.

This item sold for £500.

Lot 260: Telegram from John Lennon to Bob Wooler dated '20 Ju 63', apologising for an incident between Lennon and Wooler, in original envelope. Message reads: "Really sorry Bob terribly worried to realise what I had done Stop what more can I say John Lennon." The incident referred to in the telegram was a physical fight between Bob Wooler and John Lennon resulting in Lennon being sued for injuries. The matter was settled for £200 and an apology from Lennon.

This item fetched £550. Ironic that the telegram brought Bob almost three times the amount of his original compensation!

Lot 278: Original Western Union telegram from Colonel Parker to Brian Epstein, addressed to Brian Epstein at the San Francisco Hilton from 'The Colonel', offering a welcome from Elvis Presley and himself and inviting Brian to call on him for any service 'as a friend', dated 'August 17 1964'. The text read: "Dear Mr Epstein, on behalf of Elvis and myself welcome to the USA our sincere good wishes for a successful tour and a wonderful trip to all your engagements if there is anything I can be of service with as a friend do not hesitate to call on me there isn't much I can do as I have been laid up for several weeks with a back ailment. But my efforts will be to be of some help if need be. Give my best to Chris Hutchins and if you have time give me a call when you come to town sincerely The Colonel."

The telegram was sent on the occasion of the Beatles first full American tour which commenced on 19 August and finished 20 September and was the first contact they had with Elvis Presley.

This item fetched £550.

Lot 356: The original manuscript for a book by John Lennon, unpublished, comprising 16 pages of handwritten poetry and prose in black ink highlighted with coloured inks, including nine drawings and cartoons in black and coloured inks, written in the back of a Nelson Grammar School exercise book, with additional sheet of prose in another hand in blue ink.

This lot is probably the only major unpublished manuscript of John Lennon in existence and forms an important sytlistic comparison with Lennon's first published book *In His Own Write.*

The vendor of this manuscript attended Liverpool Art School with Stuart Sutcliffe and, later, with John Lennon. Both the vendor and Sutcliffe were asked to join Lennon's new band 'The Beatles' but Sutcliffe was finally chosen since he was able to buy a bass guitar immediately (the vendor started to make one).

The Sunday People, 24 July 1960, in an article entitled 'This is the Beatnik horror' pictured the shared flat, with the vendor and Lennon relaxing at home.

In the summer of 1960 John, Stuart and the other members of the Beatles left Liverpool for Hamburg, leaving their possessions in the vendor's flat.

In 1961 the vendor saw Lennon and reminded him of the various items left at the flat. He was told to keep anything he wanted and to throw the remainder away. The vendor retained three manuscripts, the above lot and two entitled *The Daily Howl;* the remaining items, including Lennon's art school portfolio, were thrown away.

Later on a future meeting Lennon asked the vendor for the two *The Daily Howl* manuscripts if the vendor still had them. These were subsequently returned and formed the basis for Lennon's two published books *In His Own Write* and *A Spaniard In The Works*. (Photocopies of the *Sunday People* article and other photocopies of the vendor with Sutcliffe are sold with this lot).

A page from the book is reproduced in the catalogue. It says:

"A Treasury Of Art and Poetry.

"This book contains only the work of J W Lennon, with additional work by J W Lennon, and a helping hand given by J W Lennon, not forgetting J W Lennon. Who is this J W Lennon?

"Here are some remarks by a few famous newspapers.

'A good book better' – J W Lennon of the *Daily Howl.*

'This book has many good uses and should go down well' – the Sanitary Journal.

'Yes' – Fred Emny Fan Club Magazine.

'(Belch!)' – Garston Herald."

This item fetched £16,000.

The day before each auction the lots are on view at Sotheby's from 9 am to 4.30 pm. On a number of occasions Paul McCartney has arrived to view the items and has disputed the ownership of several of the lots, as a result of which Sotheby's has withdrawn them. At the 1984 sale he disputed the ownership of Lot 214 which had been submitted by Allan Williams.

The catalogue entry read: "Paul McCartney's leather trousers, of black leather, (altered and worn) with letter of authenticity, © 1960/61. The above were given, in lieu of payment for a meal, to the leader of the group Farons Flamingos who used to play at the Liverpool Cavern with the Beatles."

I'd heard of these particular trousers during a trip I made to Liverpool in the seventies. Someone told me that Faron had found the trousers (stiff and turning green) in his attic. Rumour had it that he'd passed them over to Allan Williams who had cut them into small squares of leather and was offering the pieces to fans around the world.

As the trousers are intact, either the rumour was unfounded or an awful lot of fans have useless little pieces of leather! A likely story behind the trousers is that Paul had accidentally left them behind in the Cavern dressing room, Faron had spotted them and picked them up, Paul probably couldn't remember where he'd mislaid them and Faron no doubt forgot all about them.

Sotheby's do take special care to ensure that items are submitted by their genuine owners, but inevitably ownership of some items is disputed, although this has only happened infrequently.

If you have an item which you wish to submit, contact Hilary Kay either by letter or telephone. When the item is sent by registered post, Hilary will phone the client to voice an opinion as to its value and to suggest a reserve price if the item is worth more than £100. Sotheby's do not charge for a verbal estimate; if you make an appointment to take along your memorabilia, you will receive an assessment of their value without being committed.

When an item is put forward for sale there is an insurance premium of one per cent of the price it fetches. Items above £500 are subject to ten per cent commission, those below to 15 per cent. VAT is also charged. If you bid for and successfully purchase an item, you are liable for the price you have bid, together with ten per cent commission.

The auctions are quite lively occasions, which is why British, American and Continental fans are to be found attending them each year. There is also a great deal of media attention and press and TV cameras are always on view. An added spice to the excitement has been the emergence almost every year of a particularly enthusiastic bidder who specifically wishes to purchase a large selection of items. In 1981 it was Terry Smith, Managing Director of the Liverpool radio station Radio City, who was purchasing items for Beatle City museum. In 1982 it was Kosaka Koishihara, purchasing items on behalf of the Japanese store Seibu. In 1984 it was the Hard Rock Cafe, which has premises in both London and Los Angeles and has purchased Beatles memorabilia for display.

The success of the London auctions led to the New York branch of Sotheby's launching its own Rock 'n' Roll Memorabilia sales in 1983. These have been generally dominated by John Lennon material. At the second Rock 'n' Roll Memorabilia sale in June 1984, Yoko Ono offered 117 items for sale. The auctioneer was Pamela Brown Sherer.

The January 1985 Sale

Eldon E Worrall & Co, Seel Street, Liverpool

The auction that took place on Thursday 10 January 1985 at 11am will give you some idea of the range of items which are on sale at the Eldon E Worrall auctions. The items were on view for two days prior to the actual sale and there were a total of 129 separate lots.

As the auction house is in Liverpool, a number of local people who were associated with the Beatles in one way or another put lots up for sale. No doubt there is quite a range of material still to be found on Merseyside in private collections, attics, suitcases, etc, which may well emerge if the auctions continue to generate local publicity.

Art-school model June Furlong, for instance, contributed Lots 97 to 102. June was a model at the college when I was a student there. I must have made scores of sketches of her, as did John Lennon and Stuart Sutcliffe. In fact, the painting of the nude model on display at the Beatles City exhibition is one of Stuart's paintings of June. There are many anecdotes about June in Ray Coleman's book *John Winston Lennon.* For instance, at one life-class, when the teacher was out of the room, John ran over to where June was posing and sat on her lap "groping her and necking with her." He also produced a drawing which caused the teacher some consternation – it was a sketch of her wristwatch, he'd not drawn so much as an inch of her body!

The first of June's items, Lot 97, was sheets of song music once possessed by John Lennon – 'Happy Days & Lonely Nights', 'The Window Cleaners', 'I'm Out Of My Mind', 'Love Is The Thing', 'Nobody Knows' and 'Red Sails In The Sunset'. They came complete with a letter of authentication stating provenance, as did the next five items:

98. A dark blue dress with white polka dot decoration.

99. A straw hat with pink and blue feather decoration.

100. A plain silk hat with brim.

101. A pair of pink corsets.

102. A pair of Victorian pinchbeck drop earrings.

The background to these particular Lots was that John Lennon had written a version of *Cinderella* with Rod Murray for the Liverpool College of Art in 1959. The clothes, which Lennon wore for his part as one of the two ugly sisters, were borrowed from June. The pantomime was staged in the canteen basement of the College; The other ugly sister was Geoff Mohammed, Rod Murray appeared as Dandini, June Harry as Cinderella and John Chase as Prince Charming.

Another series of sale items was provided by John Parry, an ex-employee of the Liverpool branch of Nems Enterprises. John put forward nine lots all together, including:

122. An autographed Official Beatles Fan Club card signed 'To John' by George Harrison.

123. An autographed Northern Beatles Fan Club Convention handbill for December 1963 announcing two entertainments: 1.*Juke Box Jury* with panel members the Beatles; 2. A special fan club stage performance to be televised by the BBC, *It's The Beatles.*

124. A photograph of, and autographed by, John Lennon and Paul McCartney, each playing a guitar and seated in a recording studio. 8½" x 9".

125. A Cavern Club Membership Book No.1323 1963 and an Honorary Membership Card for the Star Club, Hamburg 1964.

127. A quantity of George Harrison's hair obtained by Mr Parry and sold with an letter authenticating it.

The following is a selection of some of the other lots available at the sale:

9. Two Odeon Hammersmith tickets for the Another Beatles Christmas Show 1964, produced by Brian Epstein. A ticket for The Beatles Show 1965 at the same theatre and an unused front stall ticket for the Charity Performance Northern Premiere of *A Hard Day's Night* at the Odeon Liverpool.

10. Three Beatle postcards by Valex of Blackpool; 20 commercial photographs of the Beatles; a photograph of the 1967 reopening of the Cavern, including the Rt

Hon Harold Wilson and Ken Dodd; and a copy of *Boyfriend Extra: Date With The Beatles.*

16. *The Bealtes Collection* from Liverpool to the World, containing various postcards, bookmark etc, and a movie poster of Ringo Starr in *That'll Be The Day.*

21. Press release for *A Hard Day's Night.*

28. A rare *With The Beatles* talc tin by Margo of Mayfair. Height 7¼".

29. A scrapbook containing various cuttings relating to the Beatles, including an early photograph of Paul McCartney seated on an antique chair; a commercial photocopy of the group; and two letters from Paul McCartney, sent from 20 Forthlin Road, Allerton, Liverpool 18 with original envelopes bearing the postmarks 7 April 1963 and 27 May 1963 respectively.

40. Apple – a perspex paperweight decorated internally with a transfer and green apple. Diameter 3".

50. A porcelain plate decorated with the Beatles. Diameter 7".

55. A Canadian Pacific folder, signed on the inside by George Harrison, John Lennon, Paul McCartney and Ringo Starr.

60. An autographed photographic Lennon portrait postcard signed 'To Monica Love from John Lennon'. 3¾" x 5¼".

73. *Reveille* Beatle poster, 40" x 60", plus five other posters, various, including *Let It Be.*

77. Plaster bust of, and signed by, John Lennon.

105. An original school photograph of 1956 from The Liverpool Institute High School, showing Paul McCartney, his brother Mike, Les Chadwick who was bass player for Gerry and the Pacemakers, Don Andrew and Colin Manley of the Remo Four, Len Garry of the Quarrymen and Neil Aspinall.

106. An autographed Cavern Membership book, 1962, signed by Paul McCartney, John Lennon and George Harrison and with the dedication 'To Monica, love Paul McCartney'.

107. A hand-painted birthday card by Paul McCartney, 5" x 12½", inscribed on the outside 'The Woman of Allerton', and on the inside 'from the late Sir James Crow', 'To Dot', 'Happy Birthday', 'Highness', 'O Great Silver Bubble of the Silver Seas', 'Hand spun'.

108. A postcard bearing a message by Paul McCartney in his hand, 'To Dot of English Fame and Great renown. This one's a quick & happy. He hasn't shaved, but he looks good all time same. All my Love Paul' with kisses.

105. A metal Beatles tray decorated with portraits of the Beatles in each of the four corners.

Readers wishing either to enter material in the Beatle auctions or to purchase lots should contact the auction house at the above address for its Conditions of Sale.